D1429432

The Economics of Project Appraisal
and the Environment

NEW HORIZONS IN ENVIRONMENTAL ECONOMICS

General Editor: Wallace E. Oates, *Professor of Economics, University of Maryland*

This important new series is designed to make a significant contribution to the development of the principles and practices of environmental economics. It will include both theoretical and empirical work. International in scope, it will address issues of current and future concern in both East and West and in developed and developing countries.

The main purpose of the series is to create a forum for the publication of high-quality work and to show how economic analysis can make a contribution to understanding and resolving the environmental problems confronting the world in the late 20th century.

Innovation in Environmental Policy
Edited by T.H. Tietenberg

Environmental Economics
Policies for Environmental Management and Sustainable Development
Clem Tisdell

The Economics of Solid Waste Reduction
The Impact of User Fees
Robin R. Jenkins

Fair Principles for Sustainable Development
Essays on Environmental Policy and Developing Countries
Edited by Edward Dommen

The Economics of Project Appraisal and the Environment
Edited by John Weiss

Economics and Environmental Policy
Tom Tietenberg

The Economics of Project Appraisal and the Environment

Edited by

John Weiss

Senior Lecturer
Development and Project Planning Centre
University of Bradford

Edward Elgar

Published by
Edward Elgar Publishing Limited
Gower House
Croft Road
Aldershot
Hants GU11 3HR
England

Edward Elgar Publishing Company
Old Post Road
Brookfield
Vermont 05036
USA

British Library Cataloguing in Publication Data
Economics of Project Appraisal and the
Environment. – (New Horizons in
Environmental Economics Series)
  I. Weiss, John II. Series
  333.7

Library of Congress Cataloguing in Publication Data
The economics of project appraisal and the environment/edited by John
  Weiss.
      p. cm. — (New horizons in environment economics)
    1. Economic development projects—Evaluation. 2. Economic
development projects—Environmental aspects. I. Weiss, John.
II. Series.
HD75.9.E28 1994
338.9'0068'4—dc20
                                     93–31070
                                            CIP

ISBN 1 85278 678 7

Printed in Great Britain at the University Press, Cambridge

Contents

Contributors

Edward Barbier is Senior Lecturer, Department of Environmental Economics and Environmental Management, University of York, UK.

Katrina Brown is Senior Research Fellow at The Centre for Social and Economic Research on the Global Environment at the School of Environmental Sciences, University of East Anglia, and University College London.

Alfredo Lopes da Silva Neto is at the Department of Economics, University of Vicosa, Brazil.

Anil Markandya is Reader in Economics, University College, London.

Behrooz Morvaridi is Research Fellow at the Development and Project Planning Centre, University of Bradford.

G. Munda is at the Commission of the European Communities, Institute for Systems Engineering and Informatics, Italy.

P. Nijkamp is Professor, Faculty of Economics and Econometrics, Free University of Amsterdam, Holland.

David Pearce is Professor of Economics, University College London and Director of the Centre for Social and Economic Research on the Global Environment at University College London and the University of East Anglia.

Colin Price is Senior Lecturer at the School of Agricultural and Forest Sciences, University College of North Wales, Bangor.

P. Rietveld is at the Commission of the European Communities, Institute for Systems Engineering and Informatics, Italy.

S. N. Trivedi is Conservator of Forests, Ranchi, Bihar, India.

John Weiss is Senior Lecturer at the Development and Project Planning Centre, University of Bradford.

J. T. Winpenny is Research Fellow at the Overseas Development Institute, London.

Acknowledgements

This volume arose in part out of my editorship of the journal *Project Appraisal*, published by William Page of Beechtree Publishing, 10 Watford Close, Guildford, Surrey, GU1 2EP, UK. Chapters 2, 3, 4, and 8 were published originally by *Project Appraisal* and I am very grateful to the publishers for permission to reprint these chapters here. In addition, Chapter 6 was published originally in *Ecodecision*, The Environment and Policy Magazine, No. 1, April 1991. I am also very grateful for permission to reprint this chapter. Other chapters were written specially for this volume, and I acknowledge the effort of all the authors involved.

The manuscript was prepared by Jean Hill, with her customary skill, patience and effort, for which I am also very grateful.

John Weiss

1. Introduction: development projects and the environment

John Weiss

Today there is an increasing awareness that new development projects can have a significant impact on the environment with both national and international repercussions. Projects from different sectors producing a variety of outputs can have environmental effects. To take a few obvious examples, water supply projects can reduce waterborne disease and thus improve the human health environment; power projects may substitute a high carbon source of fuel, such as low-quality coal with cleaner energy, such as hydropower: mining projects may deposit mine-tailing in rivers damaging fish life and causing siltation; and wood logging projects may cause soil erosion and damage forest development if replanting is not undertaken. Such effects can be positive or negative, and large or small in relation to a project's basic net present value (NPV) or internal rate of return (IRR) (calculated without any adjustment for environmental effects).

With the recognition of the potential importance of environmental issues, most international aid agencies now require some form of environmental assessment for new development projects. However, as with many other aspects of applied economics, there remains a considerable gap between theoretical recommendations and what is done in practice in an operational context. The chapters in this book explore the problem of the incorporation of environmental effects in practical project appraisals. The approaches in the different chapters are from a variety of perspectives, and no standard approach is recommended. The basic premise, however, is that cost-benefit calculations are an important tool for helping in decision-taking and that as far as possible they should be modified to take account of environmental effects. This introductory chapter aims to set the scene by identifying some of the key issues and linking these with individual chapters.

Environmental Externalities

As part of the practising economists' tool kit there is a standard theorem which underlies much of the work on environmental issues. This is the tax-subsidy solution to external effects. As the introduction to one of the major texts on environmental economics put it in 1975:

The economic literature contained an apparently coherent view of the nature of the pollution problem together with a compelling set of implications for public policy. In short economists saw the problem of environmental degradation as one in which economic agents imposed external costs on society at large in the form of pollution. With no prices to provide the proper incentives for reduction of polluting activities, the inevitable result was excessive demands on the assimilative capacity of the environment. The obvious solution to the problem was to place an appropriate 'price', in this case a tax, on polluting activities so as to internalize the social costs. (Baumol and Oates 1988:1)

Although the authors go on to stress that more recent theory and practice have combined to qualify the confidence that can be placed in this apparently simple policy prescription, external effects provide a convenient starting point for considering the conventional economics response to environmental issues. The argument can be presented simply in Figure 1.1 (Pearce and Turner 1990: 84–91).

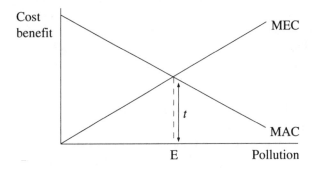

Figure 1.1   Environmental externalities

The horizontal axis shows levels of pollution and the vertical axis gives unit costs in monetary terms. All relations are shown as linear for simplicity. MEC gives marginal environmental costs, in terms of environmental damage, shown as rising with levels of pollution. MAC is the marginal abatement cost showing the unit cost of controlling the harmful effects of pollution. MAC is shown as falling as pollution grows, on the assumption there is an overhead cost in pollution abatement. Both MEC and MAC are borne by society in general and not the firm that causes pollution.

In Figure 1.1 the optimum level of pollution is at E, where the cost of avoiding pollution equals the damage that it causes (MEC = MAC). At E there will be an optimum level of tax *t* to be imposed on the original firm. Because of the optimality condition, at E, *t* equals both MEC and MAC, and in the absence of other externalities or market distortions imposition of this tax will raise unit private internal costs to the unit social cost (private cost plus the environmental externality). Obviously for positive environmental effects a subsidy will be required to equate marginal private and social benefits, but this is not shown in Figure 1.1.

The policy implications of this analysis are twofold. First, for existing producers there is a need to ensure that environmental effects are internalized so that producers can allocate resources in response to prices that reflect the social consequences of their impact on the environment. Tax-subsidy solutions are the economist's first-best solution. However, other forms of intervention are possible; these range from direct controls limiting environmentally-damaging activity to various market-solutions, for example involving the sale of permits which give the right to pollute the environment, with a view to ensuring that a given level of pollution is achieved in a least cost manner (Pearce *et al.* 1990). Second, for new projects there is a need to ensure that external effects are incorporated in any appraisal of project viability and that once a project is implemented it operates in a way that equates private and social costs and benefits.

External effects of all types have long been recognized in the cost-benefit literature, and have received particular attention in the context of developing countries (Cook and Mosley 1989). However, it is also fair to say that key texts, particularly Little and Mirrlees (1974: 336–46), tend to downplay their empirical significance for the results of appraisal.

Conceptually they can be represented simply, where for project i net present value is

$$NPV_i = PV (B - C + E)$$

where PV is present value at a discount rate r using the discount factor $1/(1 + r)^t$, for year t; B is the direct benefits from i and C is the direct costs; E is the net external effect; and B, C and E are identified for individual years and discounted to the present.

E can be either positive or negative, and for some environmental effects may occur largely at the end of a project's life as an environmental terminal value. Examples would be nuclear waste that must be disposed of when a nuclear power plant is shut down or when a forest is fully depleted of trees. In this discounted cash flow analysis the value of E in present value terms should be interpreted as a sum which when invested at a rate r will grow over time so that it will be sufficiently large to just compensate sufferers from future environmental external effects. A positive project NPV means that allowing for all costs, including environmental effects, a project can generate a return of r on its total capital investment plus an additional surplus given by the NPV. Following standard cost-benefit procedures the issue is one of whether there is sufficient income for potential compensation of losers. A mechanism to ensure that actual compensation takes place is not required. However, this may be felt to be inadequate and some of the recent literature has stressed the need to effect some form of compensation, chiefly through a compensating or shadow project.

Valuation of Environmental Effects

Conventionally, three concepts of value are identified each of which should in principle be applicable to any environmental effect. These are use, option and existence value. Taking these in turn, use value is the most straightforward. The environment has a value to all users, whether because of its contribution to production or consumption. Use value in its simplest form is what users are willing to pay to use the services of the environment.

The other two concepts of value are much less clear and do not relate to current use of the environment. Option value is based on the idea that users will be willing to pay for the option of using the environment in the future even if they do not use it currently. This arises from uncertainty and the possibility that in the future the environment may be of value, even if it is not today. Finally, there is existence value, which is what non-users are willing to pay for the preservation of the environment for its own sake based on its intrinsic worth, and unrelated to current or future use. However, where multiple environmental functions are in direct competition, it may be misleading simply to add together these three value concepts. One needs therefore a set of compatible environmental functions, which give total value.

To make these concepts more specific, farmers may place a use value on a forest due to its contribution to the productivity of land: in turn even it if does not affect their current production they may be willing to pay something extra to maintain the forest since they may benefit from its productive effects in the future; finally, non-farmers who have never seen the forest may be willing to pay something to see it preserved. The full environmental value of the forest is the sum of these three effects, so that environmental damage is in terms of this loss of value.

For illustration, Table 6.7 in Chapter 6 by Pearce in this volume on deforestation in Brazil gives a more detailed set of items under these different value headings, distinguishing between direct and indirect use values of forests and identifying several reasons for existence value.

Loss of use value associated with environmental damage can be approached from the perspectives of benefits foregone (corresponding to MEC in Figure 1.1) or from the side of cost of preventing or abating environmental damage (corresponding to MAC). Only where the optimum damage or pollution is sustained (at E in Figure 1.1) will these two measures of value be equal. The theoretical parallel is with the shadow price of a good or factor which can be derived from either the demand margin and given by willingness to pay, where supply is fixed, or from the supply margin and given by marginal cost of production, where supply is variable. Winpenny (1991) in a survey of alternatives in the valuation of environmental effects terms the benefit side approach Effect on Production and that on the cost-side Preventive Expenditure and Replacement Cost. These two cost-based approaches are acknowledged as those used in the majority of empirical case studies of environmental effects in the developing world (Winpenny 1991: 61).

Strictly the choice between these two alternatives rests on what is assumed about the likely consequences of investing in a project. If abatement expenditure will be made then a cost-based approach is appropriate. If the project itself makes the expenditure — for example a mine that disposes of its tailings in a specially-constructed pond to avoid river siltage or a logging plant that practices replanting of trees — environmental costs cease to be external and are internalized by the original project. They become part of total costs and form what is now termed a compensating project. However, where there is no guarantee that such abatement expenditure will be made, it is necessary to estimate the environmental damage the project will cause and include this as an external cost. There is an intermediate position where abatement expenditure is made but is not wholly effective. Here the environmental affect will be valued at the cost of abatement plus the residual damage (see Chapter 9 by da Silva Neto in this volume). In practice, identifying whether a cost or a benefit approach to the valuation of environmental effects is more appropriate may take second place to the problem of obtaining reasonable numerical values to attach to either. Pragmatic concerns may thus dictate the approach used.

However, whilst the idea behind use value of the environment is relatively straightforward conceptually, those behind option and particularly existence value are so esoteric that it is questionable how far they have a role in operational appraisals. In principle, direct surveys utilizing a contingent valuation approach might capture full willingness to pay for environmental services. This approach, which has been tried experimentally by the World Bank for the valuation of benefits of water supply projects (for example Briscoe *et al.* (1990) for Brazil, and Whittington *et al.* (1991) for Nigeria) involves interviews in which respondents put monetary bids on what they would pay to receive particular goods or services. However, there are serious problems in applying this approach to the environment. For example, where a market for a good like water already exists, users may be able to conceptualize its worth in monetary terms. For environmental services for which there is no market, valuation by price may not be possible in a meaningful way. Further, even if we can obtain responses in monetary terms there is the conceptual 'free-rider' problem associated with all public goods. If individuals cannot be excluded from the services of the environment why should they give accurate responses to questions on what they would pay to preserve it?

It is interesting to note that when attempts are made to quantify existence value it tends to be in a form of sensitivity analysis. For example, on the assumption that the Amazon forest is valued at USD 8 per adult in the industrialized countries this gives an existence value of USD 3.2 billion, that is 25 per cent of the Amazon's contribution to Brazilian GDP. This figure is not used in an appraisal, but to show the scope for an 'Amazon Compensating Fund' through which residents of the rich countries could pay Brazil for not exploiting the tropical rain forest (see Chapter 6 by Pearce in this volume).

Therefore if one rejects option and existence value as empty boxes for practical purposes, one is left with use value as the only operational concept of environmental value. In principle, use value can relate to both productive and non-productive (consumption) uses of the environment, although the former is likely to be both easier to estimate and more relevant for development projects. From the producer viewpoint, use value is fairly straightforward. It relates to the net loss in production due to environmental damage or the net saving in production due to the removal of environmental damage.

The production effect should be converted into a value either using a market price or, where appropriate, a shadow price for the good concerned. Where the goods involved are not sold on a market and thus have no direct price the normal procedure would be to use the price of fairly close marketed substitutes. Production effects can also relate to labour inputs. Where environmental benefits improve human health, leading to an increase in labour productivity and a reduction in resources used in medical care, these are production benefits: conversely, environmental degradation with a negative impact on health will create production costs.

In a well-functioning market, producer willingness to pay for use of the environmental should equal direct production benefits. In practice, with lack of information and other real world distortions, this equality need not hold. In other instances, as we have seen, use value may be approximated by producer willingness to pay to preserve the environment; that is by a cost-based approach. An example would be where a drainage scheme prevents waterlogging and thus has a production use value to farmers. However, if farmers in a similar area have already invested themselves by digging water ditches, this expenditure of time and materials can be a proxy for farmers' willingness to pay for the prevention of waterlogging by the original irrigation scheme.

Valuation of the use value of trees has received particular attention. Valuation of forestation is complex since the exact treatment must vary with the type of forest and trees concerned. Trees can have productive effects on crops, through for example, prevention of soil erosion and shelter from wind and storm damage. A clear relation between forestation and crop yields has been established empirically. Trees will also have a market value as timber and fuel, and from the fruit they bear. However, there can be a major variation in trees' productive effects in different types of situation, so that where it is possible to establish a direct relation between, for example, trees, soil erosion and crop yields in a particular area, it may be quite misleading to generalize this over a wider region. Anderson (1987) is one of the best known studies in this area focusing on the benefits from planting trees as shelterbelts, and defining these benefits as the net increment in crop yields valued in economic terms. Brown and Pearce in Chapter 7 in this volume give an estimate of the carbon storage value of tropical forests.

For non-productive, that is consumption, purposes use value is more difficult to capture. Difficulties with the contingent valuation procedure have been noted, although it appears there are technical solutions to the free-rider problem (Cooper 1981). Other approaches used in the context of developed economies have relied on indirect market valuations, for example taking house values in different areas as a guide to the cost of noise or air pollution and wage differentials in different jobs as a measure of the cost of different working environments. However, where markets are not well developed this approach will be of limited value.

Compensating Project

The difficulty of estimating accurately even the simpler concept of use value must be acknowledged. One way of circumventing at least part of the problem is to approach valuation from the cost side. This follows directly from the recent literature on 'sustainable development'. Pearce *et al.* (1990) define sustainable development as a policy of maintaining intact the natural capital stock of the economy, so that maintenance of natural capital (in which they include soil, ground and surface water, land and water biomass and the waste assimilative capacity of the environment) becomes a constraint on investment selection. Following the sustainability argument, where new projects have a negative effect on the natural capital stock, a compensating or shadow project (or projects) must be implemented to remove environmental damage and replace the natural capital that has been depleted. This does not mean that each individual new project has its own compensating project, but that for a group of new projects (termed a programme) there must be at least one compensating project to remove the damage caused by the group. Compensating projects, it is argued, do not have to be subject to conventional appraisal criteria (although they should be cost-effective in achieving the sustainability objective). In principle, they may have net efficiency benefits in addition to removing environmental damage. However, in the more likely case, where their only positive effects are in terms of removing environmental damage, real income in the economy will be lower as a result of these projects, as resources will have been diverted to them from productive uses. Pearce *et al.* term the net loss in income from a marginal increase in the natural capital constraint the 'sustainability premium'. Following the sustainability approach the group of new projects must be attributed with the net cost of the compensating project (or projects).

It can be argued that the compensating project concept is vague in operational terms. Different projects will have different effects and the common denominator between projects in a programme is not clear. In practice, where decisions on projects are taken sequentially, not in groups, it is difficult to envisage how a group of projects could be linked with a specific compensating project. Further, even if this is possible at the appraisal stage, there is the important operational issue of who pays for and organizes the compensating project. Finally, any application of the sustainability approach would require defining what maintenance of the natural capital stock means, in terms of explicit targets for different resources and levels of environmental damage, like gas emissions. This implies the sort of active environmental policy that is missing virtually everywhere in developing countries.

The authors appear to have predominantly agricultural projects in mind since their chief examples of compensating projects are shelterbelt planting of trees, soil conservation, afforestation and reforestation to control desertification. If the argument is narrowed to incorporate only this type of agricultural scheme, which will then no longer have to be justified on rate of return grounds, it may be more operational. However, as a blanket prescription to cover all environmental effects, it seems too loose to be very useful. On the issue of linking the cost of the schemes with environmentally negative projects, a suggestion by one of the authors from this group is that a form of environment tax (termed euphemistically a 'compensatory set-aside scheme') be imposed on the projects concerned (Turner 1991). Presumably this would be linked with the cost of the compensating projects, but the argument is not explored in detail.

Nonetheless, there are attractions in approaching the problem from the cost side, both because of the difficulties in valuing fully environmental damage and because of the desirability of preventing it ex-ante. For purposes of project appraisal an alternative approach to that of the compensating project is to make what can be termed a 'benign government' assumption. This implies that environmental regulations are always enforced and that all necessary preventive expenditures are made either by the project itself or by others. These preventive expenditures must be included as part of project cost at the time of appraisal, even if it is not clear that in practice the project itself is going to meet these costs. The assumption is that someone will be forced to incur them and that they should be attributed to the originating project. This approach differs from the compensating project solution because it does not rely on a single project to remove costs created by a set of projects and links costs specifically with the project that causes them.

In some instances this cost-based approach may require only engineering cost estimates (for example the cost of building a dam to prevent flooding), however, in others prevention may require a shift in resource use and therefore economic rather than engineering estimates.

The obvious danger is that environmental prevention costs may be overstated if each individual project has to solve its own problems, where economies of scale are significant in preventive activities. There may be cases where a single compensating project makes sense — for example to reduce gas emissions from a set of power plants it may be cost-effective to have one single compensating scheme. The cost of this shadow project can be allocated to individual plants on the basis of their respective contributions to emissions. However, at the time of appraisal of an individual plant the exact form of the compensating scheme may not be known so that costs to be attributed may only be approximate. As with the agricultural schemes referred to earlier, probably this type of situation is best treated as a special case of prevention, rather than as the norm as in the compensating project approach.

This focus on costs of prevention may have some advantages in terms of operational work. However there still remains the question of environmental benefits which will often be in terms of environmental damage avoided. One could extend the benign government assumption so that all benefits would be achieved by other means and the effect of an individual project would be only in terms of saving the costs of these other means. This is likely to be excessively optimistic and can understate environmental gains significantly where alternative ways of achieving these gains cannot be assured.

Always keeping environmental benefits as unquantifiables, that are mentioned qualitatively, may be adequate for non-marginal projects. The difficulty arises where a project has a marginal IRR but positive environmental benefits. A production-based approach to use value is the most practicable, although it is not clear how far it can be used realistically with time and date constraints. Water is one sector where there may be both more scope and need for this approach, particularly where tariffs are a very inadequate measure of benefits. Also for some land-use projects, such as tree planting or land conservation programmes, the explicit objective is to raise production through environmental improvement or avoid losses due to environmental degradation. Such projects can only be appraised if their productive effects — in terms of net incremental output — can be assessed. For example, Dixon and Sherman (1990) give interesting illustrations of the application of environmental economics to the appraisal of protected areas and parklands.

Applications in this Volume

The chapters in this volume address a variety of issues raised in the environmental literature. Chapter 2 by Barbier stresses the need for adequate data collection to allow the incorporation of environmental impact in project appraisal. This data must be sufficiently diverse to cover the multiple competing functions of the environment. Functions are broken down into marketed, tradeable and non-marketed categories. Marketed functions are those where environmental effects can be converted into physical quantities and goods that are sold on a local market and whose price in this market can be used as an approximation for economic value. Traded functions are where the environmental effects can be converted into goods which are sold internationally and whose world price gives a measure of economic value. Finally, non-marketed functions of the environment are where its effects do not correspond to goods sold in a market, so that valuation is more problematic. The limitations of surveys to determine willingness to pay, are noted, particularly in the context of developing countries.

An issue that has been debated at length is the appropriate discount rate to use for projects with major environmental effects. A common argument is that for such projects a low discount rate, well below the conventional opportunity cost of capital (typically taken as 10 per cent) should be used. This is chiefly on the grounds that environmental costs are likely to arise a considerable time into the future and will thus have a low present value if a high discount rate is used. Chapter 3 by Markandya and Pearce gives an authoritative rebuttal of this view pointing out that the appropriate procedure is to identify all genuine environmental effects and discount them at the standard efficiency or opportunity cost rate. This is partly because, if the level of investment expenditure is sensitive to the discount rate, a low rate will allow additional investment and thus extra resource depletion and environmental effects. This follows since from the 'mass balance' principle, greater natural resources are required in response to higher investment.

A counter argument which also suggests adjusting the discount rate for environmental projects is that where environmental risks are high a risk premium should be added to the discount rate. Again this is a theoretically incorrect approach, since uncertainty over the future is unlikely to grow exponentially over time which is the implication of using a single discount rate with an environmental risk premium added to the opportunity cost figure. The authors argue that risk of future environmental damage is a serious issue, but that it is best addressed by other means. To allow for potential damage to the interests of future generations from environmentally risky projects they put forward an alternative approach based on their 'sustainability criterion'. As discussed above this involves imposing the constraint of a constant natural capital stock, so that future generations will inherit the same total natural capital that is available currently. The natural capital stock constraint requires that new projects must compensate, where they reduce existing natural capital, by investing in a compensating project. The cost of the compensating project is included in the appraisal of the original project (or programme of projects) that generates the initial effect on the natural capital stock. However, project cost and benefit flows will be discounted at the unadjusted opportunity cost rate.

Forestry is a sector for which environmental issues are central, and forestry economists have long considered environmental adjustments as a central part of their methodology. Chapter 4 by Price suggests a bias in appraisals in favour of commercial logging projects, arising from the basic procedure of discounted cash flow analysis. This assumes that all project surpluses can be reinvested at the project's IRR, which may be unrealistic where the latter is high in comparison with the returns on alternative investment opportunities. Price draws on concepts from the shadow pricing literature — the premium on savings relative to consumption and different consumption weights for different income groups — to examine the returns to a hypothetical logging project. The recommendation is that a social discount rate, based on time preference for consumption, should be used in conjunction with a savings premium (termed OCIF, the opportunity cost of investment) to assess project returns. Only income that is saved is adjusted by the savings premium and all costs and benefits are discounted at the social discount rate. It is argued that this will place the logging project on a comparable basis with the assumed marginal project, representing the alternative use of funds. With this procedure commercial logging projects will look less attractive relative to alternatives that do not involve deforestation. The argument is based on a theoretically well-established case, since whenever there is a scarcity of savings, by definition the social rate of discount will be below the conventional opportunity cost rate (Marglin 1967, UNIDO 1972). This is not an argument against using discounting in the appraisal of environmental projects, but it does imply that a different concept of the discount rate be used.

Chapter 5 by Price and Trivedi also covers the forestry sector. Here the focus is on the practice of illicit felling or cutting, which is generally considered to be harmful to commercial objectives, since it decreases mean expected forest revenue and increases its variability. The argument is illustrated with forestry project data from India. Again, concepts from the shadow pricing literature are used to show that when social considerations are introduced (Squire and van der Tak 1975), illicit felling may be desirable. Illicitly cut wood is given the same market price as official fellings, whilst different consumption weights are introduced for illicit fellers (assumed to be poor) and consumers in general; government revenue is also given a higher weight than average consumption. A social time preference rate of discount (as discussed in Chapter 4) is used, which is well below the opportunity cost rate. With these adjustments the results depend upon various technical conditions. Where illicit fellings are scattered through the forest, so that complete forest cover remains, they will be desirable because of their positive distributional effect. However, where trees are removed illicitly from a concentrated area, so that replanting is required, illicit felling is undesirable even with shadow pricing. Where illicit felling is scattered, but the removal of trees leads to loss of volume increment, the outcome is ambiguous and varies with the parameters involved. The conclusion is that what matters is both how illicit felling takes place and its distributional effect.

As we have noted, valuation of environmental effects is an area of considerable complexity. Chapter 6 by Pearce sets out the principles involved in relation to the case of the Brazilian Amazonia forest. The recent history of deforestation there is surveyed, before the economic approach to valuation of a tropical forest is set out. Total economic value is composed of use values, further decomposed into direct and indirect value, option value and existence value. Direct use value should, in principle, be fairly easy to measure, although there will be some forest products, such as medicinal plants, for which it may be extremely difficult to obtain a market price. Indirect use values correspond to the ecologist's concept of ecological functions and include nutrient cycling, watershed protection, air pollution reduction and micro-climatic effects. The chapter concentrates on two elements of total economic value, the 'carbon store' function which is part of indirect use value, and existence value.

On the first, tropical forests are major stores of carbon, so that use of forest land is an important factor in global warming, although the environmental effects will vary with how timber is removed and how the deforested land is managed subsequently. In planning for forestry use a tropical forest should be credited with the value of global warming damage avoided, if the forest is conserved. Conversely, if the forest is used for commercial purpose the commercial projects should be debited with the global warming damage caused. In the case of existence value some approximate estimates are put forward, as noted above, showing that even modest per capita values for adults in developed countries could finance a major conservation fund for Amazonia. However, if developed countries are to persuade developing countries to forego projects in the interests of global environmental conservation there is a need to establish international mechanisms for affecting such transfers.

Few serious attempts have been made to quantify directly the carbon store value of forests. Chapter 7 by Brown and Pearce follows directly from Chapter 6 and attempts to place a monetary value on the carbon storage function of the Amazon forests. The approach involves surveying alternative estimates of global damage costs per tonne of carbon (a figure of US$ 10 per tonne is taken as the shadow price of carbon) and deriving a range of reasonable estimates for changes in carbon storage due to different land-use patterns. The largest loss of carbon from both biomass and soils occurs with a shift from tropical forest to permanent agriculture, with a move to shifting agriculture having a lower loss of carbon. Losses, and therefore environmental damage costs, also vary with the type of forest (classified as either open, closed primary and closed secondary forest). The important result of Chapter 7 is that the estimate range of damage costs of deforestation per hectare are well above the market price of land in the Amazon. If the latter is used as a proxy for economic benefits from farming or other activities the implication is that the environmental cost of deforestation exceeds these benefits substantially thus justifying forest conservation. Inevitably, there is uncertainty in these calculations, and these estimates may be questioned by others, but this is an important result that substantially reinforces the case for an active environmental policy for the region.

As noted earlier, environmental effects can be approached from the perspective of damage incurred or cost of abatement. Pollution emissions, for example, may damage health, materials and buildings, and in the longer term have climatic effects, however, it is difficult to establish clear causal relations between level of emissions and these negative consequences. An operational approach that is suggested in Chapter 8 by Winpenny is to use as a measure of value the cost (strictly marginal rather than average) of reducing emissions. If there is an overall country ceiling or target for emissions then a project that reduces emissions saves others from investing to make this reduction: conversely, a project that raises emissions requires others to invest to lower emission levels.

It is suggested that a 'savings curve' relating the cost of abating a unit of gas emission to the volume of abatement be estimated and that different alternative forms of abatement be represented as points on the curve. For developed economies, for example, the respective costs of reducing carbon-dioxide emissions have been compared, with fuel efficiency measures in industry and power-station rehabilitation appearing the least-cost form of abatement. If a particular project reduces emissions, one can assume that it saves the cost of the most cost-effective (that is, marginal) form of abatement, and conversely creates this cost where increases in emissions are involved. These costs or savings can be included in the appraisal of the original project, as a form of shadow project. Since the costs or savings involved are from marginal national sources, only by chance will they coincide with the costs if the original project itself made the necessary expenditure to reduce emissions. However, this cost-based approach is only valid where the ceiling is enforced. If it is not, one is back in the situation of having to estimate environmental damage from emissions.

Another approach to environmental valuation is illustrated in Chapter 9 by da Silva Neto. This chapter gives a detailed appraisal of the Carajás iron-ore mine in Brazil, which has received considerable international publicity. The project has a direct economic effect in terms of iron-ore production, chiefly for export, as well as some relatively minor effects within the region. Its direct environmental effects are controlled by a compensating project, financed as part of the original mine project. This compensating scheme is precisely in the spirit of the recommendations of Pearce *et al.* (1990) and was insisted upon by the World Bank. It is directed at a range of effects, including removal of polluted water in the Amazon basin, prevention of soil erosion around the railway line and a resettlement scheme for native tribes.

As the compensating project is included in the direct costs of the mine, its direct environmental effects are both compensated and internalized. The complication is that there are also indirect environmental effects. With the availability of iron-ore, small-scale pig-iron producers set up in the region. Once in operation they started to degrade the environment by cutting trees to obtain charcoal, which they use as a cheap fuel. This cost is linked with the mine project, in that in its absence the pig-iron producers would not operate in the region. The most effective way of avoiding this situation is to ban the further cutting of trees for this purpose and to force pig-iron producers to use coke, which must be imported, as an alternative to charcoal.

In the economic appraisal of the Carajás mine this indirect environmental effect is valued at the import cost of the coke necessary to give the fuel equivalent of the charcoal involved. This assumes that forest depletion will not be continued and that either the pig-iron producers or the government, if it subsidizes coke imports, will meet the extra costs of switching to coke as a fuel. This illustrates, what we term above the benign government assumption, since at existing relative prices pig-iron producers would not voluntarily shift to coke and government intervention is required to enforce this solution. As it happens the final NPV and IRR of the project are not very sensitive to the inclusion of this effect although under one set of assumptions regarding environmental cost the project IRR falls below the test discount rate of 10 per cent.

Environmental issues normally have been approached by economists in conventional benefit and cost terms. However, there is a very substantial literature setting out an alternative multi-criteria approach (Nijkamp 1980). This assesses projects by different criteria, of which environmental impact will be one. These various impacts can be in quantitative or qualitative terms. However, provided quantitative information can be transformed into a cardinal form it can be assessed in a quantitative way. The basis objective is to derive a measure of project worth that quantifies the net effect of a project in terms of the relevant criteria, which requires an explicit or implicit set of weights for the various criteria.

Particular problems arise from the existence of uncertainty and the fact that different individuals, classes, or groups will be involved in the final decision on a project, necessitating some form of compromise. These issues are addressed in Chapter 10 by Munda, Nijkamp and Rietveld. To allow for uncertainty, a fuzzy clustering technique is developed to identify possible alliances among groups with different interests. The methodology, which is mathematically rigorous, is illustrated by means of a land-use planning problem from the Netherlands. The case involved is of a cement plant that extracts the raw material marl on an open-cast basis, with serious environmental consequences. Seven possible alternative policies are considered and while four are shown to be always superior to the other three, it is possible to identify the one of the four which minimizes conflict between the different groups affected by the decision on the cement plant. This approach is of potential interest as an alternative to conventional benefit-cost calculations, particularly where conflict minimization is a key issue.

Chapter 11 by Morvaridi questions the relevance of cost-benefit values in actually helping resolve issues raised by the sustainable development literature. Dam projects are used as examples of how projects can affect communities in profound ways that often cannot be incorporated in precise monetary calculations. The implication, which is perhaps a reasonable conclusion to this introductory chapter, is that project calculation must be seen as part of a wider environmental strategy, which project level decisions can support. However, one cannot expect such a strategy to emerge from deliberations over individual projects.

References

Anderson, D. (1987), *The Economics of Afforestation: a case-study in Africa,* Baltimore: John Hopkins.

Baumol, W.J. and Oates, W.E. (1988), *The Theory of Environmental Policy*, 2nd ed., Cambridge: Cambridge University Press.

Briscoe, J., Furtado de Castro, P., Griffin, C., North, J. and Olsen, O. (1990), 'Towards Equitable and Sustainable Rural Water Supplies: A Contingent Valuation Study in Brazil', *The World Bank Economic Review*, **4**, (2), 115–34.

Cook, P. and Mosley, P. (1989), 'On the Valuation of External Effects in Project Appraisal', *Project Appraisal*, **4**, (3).

Cooper, C. (1981), *Economic Evaluation and the Environment*, London: Hodder and Stoughton.

Dixon, J.A. and Sherman, P.B. (1990), *Economics of Protected Areas*, London: Earthscan.

Little, I.M.D. and Mirrlees, J.A. (1974), *Project Appraisal and Planning for Developing Countries*, London: Heinemann.

Marglin, S. (1967), *Public Investment Criteria,* London: Allen and Unwin.

Nijkamp, P. (1980), *Environmental Policy Analysis,* New York: Wiley.

Pearce, D.W., Barbier, E.B. and Markandya, A. (1990), *Sustainable Development: Economics and the Environment in the Third World*, London: Edward Elgar.

Pearce, D.W. and Turner, K. (1990), *The Economics of Natural Resources and the Environment*, Hemel Hempstead: Harvester.

Squire, L. and Van der Tak, H. (1975), *Economic Analysis of Projects*, Baltimore: Johns Hopkins.

Turner, K. (1991), 'Environmentally Sensitive Aid', in D. Pearce (ed.), *Blueprint Two: Greening the World Economy*, London: Earthscan.

UNIDO (1972), *Guidelines for Project Evaluation*, New York: UN.

Whittington, D., Lauria, D.T. and Mu, X. (1991), 'Study of Water Vending and Willingness to Pay for Water in Onitsha, Nigeria', *World Development*, **19**, (2/3), 179–98.

Winpenny, J.T. (1991), *Values for the Environment*, London: ODA HMSO.

2. Economic valuation of environmental impacts: data and methodology requirements with the example of Indonesia

Edward Barbier

The growing recognition that environmental considerations must be incorporated into development strategies is starting to have some influence on policy making and planning in developing countries. This has led to the recent interest in the economic valuation of environmental impacts, which has already started to influence project-appraisal techniques and other areas of policy analysis.

For example, as pointed out by the authors of the classic UNIDO Guidelines, the main rationale for conducting social cost-benefit analysis is 'to subject project choice to a consistent set of general objectives of national policy' (UNIDO 1972). As perceptions of national policy objectives in developing countries have changed, for instance emphasizing the need for scarce foreign exchange and equitable income distribution, project appraisal and planning have been expanded to reflect the new objectives (Little and Mirrlees 1974; Squire and van der Tak 1975). Consequently, the recent emphasis on the role of environmental quality and the long-run productivity of natural resource systems in sustaining economic development has led to further extensions of social cost-benefit analysis to include environmental impacts (Dixon *et al.* 1986; Dixon and Hufschmidt 1986; Hufschmidt *et al.* 1983). That is, in contrast to traditional project evaluation which considers only the direct project benefits and costs, `the expanded approach includes the external and environmental improvement benefits from environmental protection), as well as the costs of external and/or environmental damages and of environmental control measures (Dixon and Hufschmidt 1986: 7). The basic methodology is first to identify and measure the environmental effects, and then, secondly, to translate them into monetary terms for inclusion in the formal project analysis.

However, extending cost-benefit analysis to incorporate the environmental impacts of projects encounters a number of problems. First, physical estimation of environmental effects is often difficult. Second, as most environmental resources are non-marketed common-property 'goods', economic valuation of their services is not straightforward. Third, little consensus exists regarding methods for monetary valuation of 'intangible' environmental goods, such as the need to preserve unknown species and 'natural beauty'. Finally, since this expanded approach inevitably raises issues of intertemporal choice, the interest rate chosen to discount the future may determine whether environmental degradation is 'optimal'. It is often stressed that the appropriate discount rate should emerge from the project appraisal process (UNIDO 1972). In practice, imperfect capital markets, inconsistent data on the productivity of capital, and large variances in domestic borrowing for investment makes it difficult to establish an economic accounting rate of interest for developing countries (Phillips 1986). Introducing environmental considerations further complicates the picture. As Markandya and Pearce in Chapter 3 of this volume observe, natural resources are more likely to be overexploited at high discount rates than at low ones whereas low discount rates discriminate against projects with an environmental dimension that have a long gestation period. Given the additional problems posed by environmental risk and intertemporal impacts, these authors conclude that it is generally preferable to adjust the project costs and benefit values and adopt additional sustainability criteria as constraints on these values than to adjust the discount rate.

All these considerations point to the need for proper economic valuation of the environmental impacts of development, which in turn requires developing an effective environmental and resource data base for economic indicators of sustainability. This chapter therefore focuses on the establishment of a feasible set of environmental and natural resource data consistent with this objective. Some of the relevant environmental and resource data may already exist in developing countries, but not collected or aggregated in a form proper for economic valuation of environmental impacts. More data collection may be required to assist policy and planning choices concerning sustainable resource use; however, there are limits as to the desirability of increased collection, monitoring and evaluation of environmental impacts if the costs of the extra information received exceed the benefits to policymakers in terms of a more informed choice. Although such a data base is expected to be particularly useful in project appraisal, this chapter assumes that proper economic valuation of environmental impacts is also important for a variety of policy approaches that range from 'state of the environment' indicators to proper resource accounting methods to natural resource management policy analysis. Obviously, the data and methodological requirements for establishing a set of environmental indicators would be significantly different from that for a system of resource accounts, for project appraisals, for simulation models or for policy analysis. Nevertheless, as the least common denominator for all these approaches is some form of economic valuation of the environment, they share certain fundamental data needs. These include adequate biophysical and resource stock assessment, proper accounting and valuation of environmental functions, sufficient data flexibility to reflect changes in key resource systems and zones (for example, watersheds, and coastal areas), and high-quality standards. These basic data and methodological requirements are examined in this chapter, using examples from Indonesia where appropriate.

Economic Valuation of Environmental Degradation

The evaluation of environmental impacts must take into account the multi-functionality of resources, the irreversibility of environmental degradation and the need for data on these impacts to fulfil many purposes.

A key feature of any natural resource is its multifunctionality; that is, each resource serves more than one function — water resources can be used for municipal and industrial supplies, irrigation, waste disposal, and so forth. Proper economic valuation of environmental impacts on a whole range of resource functions is therefore crucial to understanding and analysing the trade-offs among the various functions of the environment, trade-offs between development and one or more of the environmental functions, and any spatial and intertemporal dimensions of these possible trade-offs. It is also important for emphasizing the value of the environment as an intermediate good (for instance as the resource base for production) as opposed to its value solely as a final good (for example as a source of amenity value to be preserved). Such a valuation procedure therefore implies:

(a) Understanding the functions of the natural resource base/stock and basic ecological functions in a given economic-environmental system, and how these functions interact with each other.
(b) Proper valuation of each of these functions, to the extent that economic and ecological data allow, at least to derive some broad orders of magnitudes of value for these functions.
(c) Using these valuations to indicate and determine the trade-offs that may emerge from natural resource degradation over time.

Proper evaluation of environmental impacts in this manner is essential for a wide range of issues central to the analysis of natural resource management. These include:

(a) Understanding the implications of environmental degradation for crucial resource systems and ecosystem functions (for example, watersheds, drylands, maintenance of soil fertility and cohesion, coastal zones, and waste assimilation).

(b) Understanding the implications of irreversible choices with regards to the potential loss of environmental functions.

(c) Incorporating analysis of environmental impacts in project appraisals, as well as in sectoral programmes and activities.

(d) Developing a national system of resource/environmental accounts.

(e) Incorporating analysis of environmental impacts into the economic planning process through convincing policymakers of the need to integrate sustainable natural resource management into this process, and facilitating the design of appropriate policies, incentive structures and investment strategies for environmentally sustainable development.

Thus the data requirements for the analysis of natural resource impacts must initially focus on the appropriate data set for proper economic valuation of environmental assets, their multifunctional services, and the impacts of environmental degradation and subsequent loss of these services over time.

Multifunctionality of Data

However, in order to determine the appropriate environmental and resource data requirements, the specific functions of the data set need to be clarified. Economic valuation of environmental impacts in developing countries could perform many functions, such as early warning systems of environmental degradation and impending natural (or man-made) disasters; state of the environment indicators; policy analysis and design; long-term forecasting; model-building; resource accounting; and so forth. As each function has its own data demands, the priority in determining the appropriate environmental and resource data base to be compiled must be to decide what functions the data are to serve. For example, the degree and coverage of data required for developing state of the environments indicators is much less than that for policy analysis, forecasting, resource accounting and model building. Without clarifying these functions of the data base, it is difficult to indicate precisely its requirements; nevertheless, the following indicates the general guidelines that any such data base needs to fulfil.

Data and Methodological Requirements

An appropriate data base for analysing environmental impacts must satisfy a number of general requirements. The first is an accurate estimation of physical resource stocks and assimilative capacities, including rates of depletion and additions, and the composition of important resource systems (such as watersheds and coastal systems). Appraising the functions, or services, of these natural resources and resource systems is also important, and would include assessments of waste assimilative capacity, pollution stocks and discharge rates; productive functions; protective functions; and socio-cultural relevance. Methods of valuing these various functions — taking into account domestic and even international price trends where appropriate, existence of rent, social versus private values, and valuation procedures for non-marketed services — need to be developed.

Finally, the data base needs to be flexible; data are routinely collected through administrative/political units (for instance, provinces, districts, sub-districts, and villages), yet the nature of environmental degradation problems often require data based on geographical/biophysical boundaries (for example, soil erosion of upper watersheds, and mangrove destruction in coastal zones).

Resource Stock Assessment

The starting point for compiling an environmental and resource data base is of course regularly assembling accurate information on the biophysical characteristics and changes in the natural resource base. One possible method of classification is to distinguish between non-renewable resources, non-renewable/renewable resources, renewable resources, waste assimilative capacities and important resource systems (see Table 2.1). In general, what is required is accurate information on the size, depletions and additions to this resource base.

For all resources, the challenge is to determine the total reserves or area initially and then to account accurately for changes in these stocks over time. Determining the net depletion of most exhaustible resources is fairly straightforward and is routinely performed as part of commercial operations; what is required is information on extraction rates, new discoveries and extensions of existing reserves, as well as estimates of losses from inefficient operations and wastage.

Land area is a special category of non-renewable resource. Unless new frontiers or annexations are possible, land area is essentially a finite, non-reproducible asset. Although land is not exactly extracted, land capability and its utilization does change over time — sometimes with significant scarcity impacts. Thus it is important to classify and keep track of changes in land utilization and types of land, for example the conversion of forest land to agriculture, urban encroachment on arable land, and increases in irrigated land through public works schemes.

The extra dimension that needs accounting for with renewable resources and certain mixed renewable/non-renewable resources is biological growth rates and natural recharge (recovery) rates. In addition, improper exploitation or management of these resources may severely impair biological productivity or natural recharge/recovery rates, which is often termed resource degradation.

Physical damage from fire, man-made disasters and encroachments and even deliberate destruction should also be noted. In the case of soils, natural restoration of soil fertility occurs over a long period of time; consequently, measures

Table 2.1   Biophysical and resource stock assessment

Resource base	Physical assessment		
	Stock data	Depletions	Additions
Non-renewables (e.g., metals, minerals, land, fossil fuels)	Total reserves Classes	Extraction rates Losses	New discoveries Extensions Revisions
Renewables (e.g., aquatic and terrestrial biomass, water)	Total reserves Classes	Extraction Degradation Damage	Growth Recharge New discoveries Extensions Revisions
Semi-renewables (e.g., soils, genetic diversity)	Total reserves Classes	Extraction/losses Degradation Damage	Growth/recharge New discoveries Extensions Revisions
Assimilative capacities (e.g., water, air, land quality)	Pollutant stocks Classes/toxicity	Pollution discharge Point/non-point sources	Recharge Dispersion
Resource systems (e.g., coastal zones, drylands, watersheds)	Total area Classes	Extraction/losses Degradation Damage	Growth/ extensions

of soil losses and sedimentation from wind and water erosion, landslides and other geologically 'natural' sources are essential. Whereas individual species of flora and fauna may be renewable, genetically diverse ecosystems and habitats may not be. Thus assessment and classification of biologically diverse regions and resource systems, as well as individual species known and thought to exist, are vital tasks.

It may be worthwhile to collect biophysical data specific to certain resource systems or 'eco zones', such as coastal systems, watersheds/river basins and dryland areas. If so, collecting information on the resources particular to these zones and assessing it as an integrated whole would be appropriate.

Accounting for Multiple Functions

As noted above, economic evaluation of environmental impacts requires taking into account that resources often have multiple, competing functions. Assessing these various functions is therefore at least, if not more, important as analysing the physical changes in the resource base. Ideally, sufficient information should be gathered on these multiple functions in order to assess the impacts of development on:

(a)   trade-offs among the various functions of the environment;
(b)   trade-offs between development and one or more of the environmental functions;
(c)   development in one geographical area that affects environmental functions in another area; and
(d)   development in one period of time that affects environmental functions in another period of time.

A useful way of classifying these functions may be to distinguish among major production, minor production, environmental protection and system maintenance and socio-cultural support functions. Table 2.2 indicates some of these functions for certain major renewable resources in Indonesia. Note that the relationship among these functions is not necessarily competitive. For example, clear or even selectively cutting a forest for timber production may affect its provision of minor forest products (such as resins, honey, and rattan) and some of its environmental protection functions, but exploitation of minor forest products may not necessarily reduce the environmental protection afforded by forests and may actually benefit indigenous forest dwellers.

The importance of collecting sufficient data to analyse these trade-offs is illustrated by the case of coastal zone exploitation in Indonesia. The recent policy strategy is to expand fish and shrimp production through increasing coastal and tambak (shrimp ponds) fishing in these zones. However, as noted in Ackermann *et al.* (1987) policies for sustainable management of tambak, offshore and estuarine fisheries face crucial trade-offs in coastal land use:

(a)   Mangrove versus offshore fisheries — Indonesia's mangrove forest systems serve as a habitat for breeding species important for offshore fisheries. At the same time, mangrove forests are exploited in 12–20-year harvest cycles for woodchip production, which has significant export potential. These competing uses occur mainly along the south coast of Java and in the Outer Islands.
(b)   Mangrove versus tambak — In coastal areas off Java, namely in South Sulawesi, Sumatra and South Kalimantan, mangrove forest systems are also

Table 2.2   The multiple functions of Indonesia's renewable resource system

| Resource | Functions | | | |
	Major production	Minor production	Environmental protection	Socio-cultural support
Soil	Staple crops Export crops Livestock	Minor crops Bricks/tiles Minerals	Landslip prevention Flood prevention Water holding	
Freshwater	Irrigation Power Domestic Industrial Transport	Fish ponds	Saline intrusion prevention Water assimilation	
Forests/Trees	Timber Fuelwood Ecosystem values	Minor forest products	Soil/water conservation Windbreaks Microclimate	Minority forest communities
Coastal zones	Fish/shrimps Rice Ports/industry	Mangroves	Waste assimilation	Fishing communities
Bio-diversity	Drugs/pharmaceuticals Tourism Genetic information	New crops	Pest/disease control	Hunter/gatherers Education Science

Source: Adapted from Ackermann *et al.* (1987).

being threatened by tambak expansion. This, in turn, is reducing the natural shrimp breeding grounds in mangrove swamps and coastal areas. In addition, the destruction of mangrove forests for tambak also increases the risk of shore erosion, which in turn threatens the tambaks themselves.

(c) Tambak versus rice cultivation — On Java, rice cultivation and tambak are competing for scarce coastal lands. In addition, water reaching tambak from rice systems up the river basin needs to be regular in flow to control salinity and to be relatively free from agrochemicals and fertilizers.

Valuation of Multiple Functions

In determining the trade-offs among the multiple functions of the environment it is essential to have proper valuation of these functions, in so far as the economic and biophysical data allow, at least to derive some broad orders of magnitudes of value. Ideally, the data should be sufficient to give an indication of the costs borne by society of losses in environmental functions. These costs would include:

(a) user costs — the direct private costs to the user of a resource for a particular function;
(b) intertemporal user costs — the benefits foregone by those who might use the resource in the future for the same function. Unless a user owns all future rights to the resource, these costs will be borne by others, including possibly future generations;
(c) social costs — the inefficiency and external costs imposed on non-users, both now and in the future, from any loss of other functions due to exploitation of the resource (Dewees 1987).

Methods for valuing environmental functions in developing countries have been considerably improved in recent years (see, for example, Dixon *et al.* 1986; Dixon and Hufschmidt 1986 and Hufschmidt *et al.* 1983). Although it may not be feasible to implement all of these techniques, any valuation approach will require basic data on the values to be assigned to various environmental functions. To determine the data needed, it may be useful to distinguish among tradeable, marketed and non-marketed functions of the environment.

In general, where environmental functions are marketed, such as the majority of major and minor production functions in Table 2.2, their prices should serve as the basis for estimating their value — assuming that market prices closely reflect social values. Thus amassing price and cost series data for these functions would be a first priority. This should include estimates on exploration and extraction costs (for exhaustible resources); harvesting costs (for renewables); producer margins (the proportion of market price actually received by resource users); tax/subsidy margins (the proportion of market price appropriated/subsidized by government); and economic rent (users' revenues less costs). Together, this data can provide a base for properly valuing these functions as well as providing indicators of their increasing scarcity. Note that market prices of environmental functions may not always be a reasonable approximation of their social value. For example, in Indonesia, in the late 1980s users of irrigation water were paying only 13 per cent of the full costs of supply; consequently, user charges would not be an accurate measure of the value of irrigation. In such cases where observed prices and costs deviate significantly from social values, shadow pricing should be employed.

If the marketed functions of the environment are also tradeable (such as, export crops, timber, fish and shrimps) then international prices should be used to indicate their value. Thus the loss to society of these functions would be represented as the loss in foreign exchange earnings to the economy. In addition, it is increasingly useful to have sufficient data (for example, on export/import taxes and transport costs) to calculate the effective rates of protection afforded to these functions by government policy, which in turn have a significant impact on patterns of resource use. For example, high effective protection rates for sawn timber and plywood were an important element in the rapid expansion of the timber processing industry in Indonesia, which has had a profound influence on the rate of timber extraction (Gillis 1987). Similarly, high rates of protection for fruits and vegetables explain their increasingly widespread cultivation in the uplands of Java, with varying impacts on soil erosion (World Bank 1987).

The non-marketed functions of the environment (such as environmental protection and socio-cultural support functions) are, of course, the most difficult to value. As suggested by Dewees (1987), there are three basic approaches:

(a) Valuing non-marketed functions through the value of associated market goods.
(b) Valuing non-marketed functions through 'willingness to-pay' surveys; i.e., surveys and experiments in which individuals reveal either the amount that they would pay to secure the benefits or the amount they would demand to give up the benefits.
(c) Valuing non-marketed functions through the cost of social programmes and other investments that would be necessary to 'restore' the functions or substitute for the loss of them.

The appropriateness of any one of these approaches will depend on the nature of the environmental function to be valued. It may also depend on the inherent limitations of the approach in a developing country context. For example, willingness-to-pay surveys are thought to have limited applications in Indonesia, mainly in urban areas where there are large samples of income-earning households with high literacy rates. On the other hand, more than one approach may be employed to provide estimates of the value of an environmental function. For example, the value of the environmental protection function of forests, trees and other vegetative cover in providing soil/water conservation and windbreaks in upper watersheds may be approximated by both estimates of the costs of soil erosion in terms of agricultural output losses (plus any off-site costs where estimatable) and the costs of reforestation programmes in upper watersheds. Thus a recent study of the on-site agricultural productivity costs of soil erosion on

Java suggests an annual loss of US$324 million (Arens and McGrath 1987) — plus an additional US$25 to US$91 million in off-site sedimentation costs, whereas total regreening expenditures in Javan watersheds for one year, 1982–83, were US$23.35 million (World Bank 1987).

These figures would therefore suggest an upper and lower bound on the value of upper watershed protection afforded by forest and other vegetative cover. Other important methods of valuation include travel cost method, property value studies, simulation modelling and contingent valuation.

Flexibility of Data

A final criterion for data on environmental functions is flexibility. Data are currently collected and aggregated by administrative/political unit; that is from village to sub-district to district to provincial and finally to regional and national level. Many environmental and resource problems, however, require information based on geographical/ecological boundaries (for example, soil erosion in upper watersheds, mangrove destruction in coastal zones, pollution discharges in major river basins). Thus the data collected by administrative/political units need to be sufficiently flexible and detailed to allow it to be easily reaggregated along geographical/ecological lines. Standard methods for translating data in this manner need to be developed to avoid widely differing results and to make such procedures a routine part of data collection.

Another check on the flexibility of data is usefulness for monitoring and evaluation. The same information collected to provide indicators of environmental impacts should have a dual function as indicators of sustainability for any subsequent activity or programme in response to these impacts. Similarly, it is inefficient and misleading to have one set of indicators for environmental impacts and another for sustainability. For example, studies examining the extent of industrial pollution in waterways may choose to look at certain measures of pollution stocks and discharge rates. Studies to monitor and evaluate any clean-up efforts should therefore agree to use the same indicators. Thus, to be consistent, data collected for economic valuation of environmental impacts should also be used for monitoring and evaluation efforts, and the indicators should be carefully chosen to ensure fulfilment of this dual function.

Policy Requirements

So far, the chapter has emphasized mainly the role of economic valuation of environmental impacts in project appraisal. As stressed throughout, however, this may be only one of many possible functions of an environmental and resource data base for developing countries. For example, there is increasing interest in ensuring that the appropriate quality of the data base is consistent with the policy requirements for overall effective natural resource management in developing countries. This in turn necessarily imposes limits on data accuracy and precision.

Barbier (1987) identified two overriding needs for natural resource management policies to be effective in Indonesia, which in turn can be generalized for all developing countries. There is a need for substantive and extensive analysis on the natural resource implications of various macroeconomic, trade and sectoral policies. Firstly, given the increasing population pressure and economic demands on developing countries' natural resource base, problems arising from environmental and natural resource degradation will continue to act as a constraint on the successful implementation of economic development policies. Alternative policy options that explicitly take these resource constraints into account, therefore, need to be formulated and analysed.

Secondly because macroeconomic, trade and sectoral policies influence and constrain what is possible to accomplish at the programme or project level, it is essential for successful investment activity that analyses are conducted of the natural resource management implications of these policies.

In addition, at the micro level, there is a need for more analysis of the economic costs of environmental impacts. Micro-level analysis of natural resource allocation decisions at the village or farmer level is needed in order to design appropriate policies and investment programmes for natural resource management. Such micro-level analysis is also important for monitoring the impacts of policy decisions and investment programmes at the village and household levels, not just in agriculture, but for all investment projects/programmes. Although some of this information is sometimes available from research stations, and independent project and provincial studies, it needs to be coordinated and reviewed consistently at the national level for national policy and investment decisions.

These policy requirements for effective natural resource management should form the broad guidelines for the type of environmental and resource data base needed in developing countries. Attempting to assess and value the functions of the environment will not be a useful endeavour unless it can contribute to these policy requirements. The quality of the data collected must therefore be regularly reviewed to ensure that it is consistent with these policy objectives.

In addition, the above needs for effective natural resource management policy suggest the broad institutional arrangements for this data base. On the one hand, to be useful for policy analysis, data on environmental and resource impacts must be coordinated and reviewed at the national level, which implies some centralized location of a national data base. On the other hand, the need for more micro-level and project evaluation of the economic costs of environmental impacts also implies the routine collection and analysis at the local and sectoral level of data on these impacts. Thus the existence of local data bases, perhaps at the provincial or even district level, linked and coordinated with a more centralized national data base centre seems the most appropriate institutional arrangement.

Limits on Data Accuracy

The importance of both the accuracy and precision of data at the laboratory level has been stressed by Aertgeerts (1987), where 'accuracy can be expressed quantitatively through calculations of the absolute and relative errors, and is a measure for the difference between an analytically obtained datum or means of data and the true value. Precision relates to the spread of individual data around the mean and can be quantified by means of the standard deviation of the measurement.'[1]

The accuracy and precision of data are therefore considered to be essential for successful laboratory and field analysis. As a result, it may be thought desirable to achieve the same degree of accuracy and precision in the data bases needed for natural resource management policy decisions.

However, for policymaking purposes, there are limits to the accuracy and precision of the data actually required. The general rule is that more information should only be obtained on a particular environmental problem if the benefits to decision-making exceed the costs of collecting the extra data. Additional information, or 'refinements' in existing information, that does not assist policymakers in arriving at a decision should not be collected. In many instances, broad 'orders of magnitudes' of the economic consequences of environmental impacts may be sufficient to reach a policy decision — any additional information collected to improve the accuracy and precision of the data base for policymaking purposes would give rise to unnecessary costs.

This is not to imply that precision, accuracy and general data quality control are not important, especially at the laboratory, experimental testing station or collecting level. As pointed out by Aertgeerts (1987), the costs of any analytical quality control programme at this level should be compared against the expenditure the laboratory, and ultimately society, would incur in the production of data of lesser quality. Moreover, errors in data quality will be magnified as the data are compiled and aggregated for use in larger data bases. In fact, if proper quality control measures are implemented at the laboratory and collecting levels, then the data base should be sufficiently accurate and precise for policymaking purposes.

Conclusions

This chapter has broadly outlined the data and methodology requirements for economic valuation of environmental impacts in developing countries. Although these requirements appear formidable, the growing demand for such valuation techniques at all levels of the planning and policymaking process will surely lead to rapid improvements in existing (or in many cases non-existent) environmental and resource data bases in developing countries.

Currently, the most progress seems to be made in incorporating economic valuation techniques for the environment in project appraisal analysis. This chapter has stressed, however, that this may not necessarily be the only purpose that these valuation techniques should serve; on the other hand, if the environmental and resource data base is also directed to a different purpose, say, for improving the effectiveness of natural resource management policies or devising a system of natural resource accounts, this has implications for the data and methodology required.

Finally, to be truly useful for economic policymaking and planning, any environmental and resource data base for a developing country must go beyond being just a set of environmental indicators. It must also tackle the more difficult task of valuing the various economic and social functions of the environment. This is nevertheless a most interesting challenge for those interested in improving project appraisal and policy analysis of resource and environmental problems in developing countries.

Note

1. These definitions of 'accuracy' and 'precision' are respectively analogous to the definitions of 'unbiased' and 'efficient' estimators in econometrics.

References

Ackermann, R., Barbier, E.B., Conway, G.R., and Pearce, D.W. (1987), 'Environment and Sustainable Economic Development in Indonesia. An Overview Report', draft report, December, Washington, DC: World Bank.

Aertgeerts, R. (1987), 'Data Quality and Robustness Study', *Environmental Sector Review of Indonesia Phase II*, working paper, UNDP/Ministry of State for Environment and Population, Jakarta, Indonesia.

Arens, P. and McGrath, W.B. (1987), *The Costs of Soil Erosion on Java — A Natural Resource Accounting Approach*, Washington, DC: World Resources Institute.

Barbier, E.B. (1987), 'Natural Resources Policy and Economic Framework', in J. Tarrant *et al.*, *Natural Resources and Environmental Management Review*, Jakarta, Indonesia: USAID.

Dewees, D.N. (1987), 'Towards Conceptual Frameworks for Economic Evaluation of Natural Resources and the Environment for Sustainable Development', *Environmental Sector Review of Indonesia Phase II*, working paper, UNDP/Ministry of State for Environment and Population, Jakarta, Indonesia.

Dixon, J.A. and Hufschmidt, M. (eds) (1986), *Economic Valuation Techniques for the Environment*, Baltimore: Johns Hopkins University Press.

Dixon, J.A., Carpenter, R.A., Fallon, L.A., Sherman P.B. and Manopimoke, S. (1986), *Economic Analysis of the Environmental Impacts of Development Projects*, Manila: Asian Development Bank.

Gillis, M. (1987), 'Indonesia: Public Policies, Resource Management and the Tropical Forest', draft paper, Washington, DC: World Bank.

Hufschmidt, M.M., James, D.E., Meister, A.D., Bower, B.T. and Dixon, J.A. (1983), *Environment, Natural Systems and Development: An Economic Valuation Guide*, Baltimore: Johns Hopkins University Press.

Little, I.M.D. and Mirrlees, J.A. (1974), *Project Appraisal and Planning for Developing Countries*, London: Heinemann.

Phillips, D.A. (1986), 'Pitfalls in Estimating Social Discount Rates: A Case Study', *Project Appraisal*, **1**, 15–20.

Squire, L. and van der Tak, H.G. (1975), *Economic Analysis of Projects*, Baltimore: Johns Hopkins University Press.

UNIDO (1972), *Guidelines for Project Evaluation*, New York: United Nations.

World Bank, (1987), 'Indonesia — Java Watersheds: Java Uplands and Watershed Management', draft report, Washington, DC: World Bank.

3. Natural environments and the social rate of discount

Anil Markandya and David Pearce

The choice of a discount rate to incorporate into social cost-benefit analysis has long been a topic of extensive debate among economists. Seminal works include Ramsey (1928), Marglin (1963a, 1963b), Arrow (1966), Sen (1967), Baumol (1968), Olson and Bailey (1981), and Stiglitz (1982).

In recent years, environmental and scarce natural resource concerns have prompted a further set of considerations for the choice of discount rate. In particular, positive discounting appears to discriminate against future generations if projects can be chosen so as to bias benefits in favour of current periods and place social costs in future periods. Examples might include ozone layer depletion through the uses of chlorofluorocarbons (CFCs), global climatic warming from carbon-dioxide emissions associated with fossil fuel burning, nuclear power generation with associated waste disposal problems, and toxic chemical accumulation in ecosystems.

The issues have been addressed by economists (such as Page 1977, 1983 and the collection of essays in Lind 1982) and philosophers (such as Barry 1977, Parfit 1983 and Goodin 1982, 1986).

In this chapter we summarize the 'environmental' objections to the conventional rules for determining social discount rates; rules which are themselves disputed. We evaluate the objectives with particular reference to two propositions:

1. that environmental considerations dictate zero discount rates, that is, no discounting at all;
2. that environmental considerations dictate a reduction in positive discount rates, but not to zero.

We argue that, provided other adjustments are made to cost-benefit criteria to reflect environmental concerns, conventional 'weighted average' rules for selecting discount rates are adequate. The literature has, in our view, placed too heavy a burden on the discount rate in terms of the functions it is meant to serve.

The preferred course is to introduce 'sustainability criteria' into cost-benefit analysis and we hint at the nature of such criteria without developing them here. If sustainability criteria cannot for one reason or another, be introduced, then we accept that discount rates must be adjusted because of environmental factors, and we suggest how.

Environmental Critique

One important feature of the literature on environment, natural resources and development is its requestioning of the fundamental arguments for discounting. This re-analysis arises partly because of the alleged 'discrimination' of conventional discount rate selection processes against the 'interests' of the environment, and partly because concern for natural environments is often (but not always) associated with an ethical stance on intergenerational justice.

As an example of the former, high discount rates tend to encourage early, rather than later, depletion of exhaustible natural resources. As an example of the latter, it is widely argued that, say, investment in nuclear power shifts forward in time the costs associated with that energy source, notably waste management and decommissioning.

The use of positive discount rates, and particularly rates in the region of 10 per cent — a fairly typical practical rate — plays down future benefits that may be foregone, as well as future costs that may be incurred, to the detriment of future generations.

In fact, there is no unique relationship between high discount rates and environmental deterioration as is often supposed. Thus, high rates may well shift cost burdens forward to later generations, but if the discount rate is allowed to determine the level of investment they will also slow down the general pace of development through the depressing effect on investment.

Since natural resources are required for investment, a relationship established in the environmental economics literature through the mass balance principle (Ayres and Kneese 1969), the demand for natural resources is generally less with high discount rates than with low ones. High rates will also discourage environmentally-benign land uses — such as watershed development — as opposed to an existing wilderness use.

Exactly how the choice of discount rate impacts on the overall profile of natural resource and environment use is thus ambiguous. This point is important since it reduces considerably the force of arguments to the effect that conventionally determined discount rates should be adjusted to accommodate environmental considerations.

Nonetheless, concern for the environmental dimension of development policy has led to a questioning of the basic rationale for discounting. We outline below some of the points that have been raised. Note that what is being argued generally is that, if we cannot substantiate the case for positive discounting, the presumption must be that a zero discount rate is, initially anyway, the more appropriate choice.

Consumption Rate of Interest

It is convenient to analyse some of the arguments in terms of the components of the 'social time preference rate' (or 'consumption rate of interest') which is defined as:

$$i = ng + p$$

where n = the elasticity of the marginal utility of consumption function; g = the expected rate of growth in per capita real consumption; and p = the pure time preference rate reflecting impatience.Let us consider first the pure time preference rate p.

Individuals are impatient and prefer the present to the future. This shows up in a positive value of the pure time preference rate, p. Society is no more than the sum of individuals and hence society prefers the present to the future. This temporal preference translates into a positive discount rate.

As a fact of human nature nobody appears to deny this. The philosophical tenets of cost-benefit analysis suggest that the dominant underlying value judgement is that people's preferences should count. If people prefer the present over the future, for whatever reasons, then pure time preference indicates that discount rates are positive. Some say that positive time preference arises from uncertainty about being alive to receive future benefits.

The objections to permitting pure time preference to influence social discount rates are as follows. First, individual time preference is not necessarily consistent with individual lifetime welfare maximization (Strotz 1956). This is a variant of the more general view that time discounting, because of impatience, is generally irrational (Jevons 1871, Bohm-Bawerk 1884, Ramsey 1928, Pigou 1932).

Second, what individuals want carries no necessary implications for public policy. This amounts, of course, to a rejection of the underlying value judgement of cost-benefit comparisons.

Third, the underlying value judgement is improperly expressed. A society that elevates want-satisfaction to high status should recognize that it is the satisfaction of wants as they arise that matters. But this means that tomorrow's satisfaction matters, not today's assessment of tomorrow's satisfaction (Goodin 1986).

Fourth, if the 'risk of death argument' is used, it is illegitimate to derive implications for potentially immortal societies from risks faced by mortal individuals.

(However, the implications of risk of death for the existence of positive discount rates are disputed (Olson and Bailey 1981).)

What view is taken on the normative relevance of pure time preference depends on the acceptability of one or more of these objections. We would argue that to overturn the basic value judgement underlying conventional cost-benefit analysis requires good reason — the rationale for paternalism should be a strong one.

If the context is one of the development of poorer countries, one has to weigh carefully the contrasting forces of meeting basic needs and diverting resources to achieve their long-term development potential. The former might favour accepting pure time preference, the latter might not. Philosophically, the argument that the value judgement needs re-expressing in line with the third observation above is impressive. In practical terms, however, the immediacy of wants in many developing countries where environmental problems are serious might favour the retention of the usual formulation of the basic judgement.

Diminishing Marginal Utility of Consumption

Critics of positive consumption rates of interest also question the ng component, suggesting either that it is irrelevant because n is not an observable or measurable entity, or that it could take any value, including a negative one, since g could be greater or less than zero. Objections to assuming $ng > 0$ are as follows.

First, many economists dispute whether there is any meaningful way of measuring n. This is a complex debate which we do not review here. Empirical estimates of n do exist (Stern 1977). Others dispute the possibility of empirically measuring the entity (Pearce 1964). Further objections arise because the measure implies interpersonal comparisons of utility if a person is regarded as being a different entity in different time periods. On this issue it seems fair to say, however, that the problem of interpersonal comparisons is a much exaggerated heritage of inter-war welfare economics.

Second, and especially relevant for developing country appraisals, there can be no guarantee that g will be positive. Table 3.1 shows how a social time preference rate of discount would be calculated for sub-Saharan African economies as a group, from data for the 1973–83 period.

Two important points arise. First, growth in real consumption per capita was negative over this period for both the low- and middle-income countries. Taking a typical estimate of the elasticity of the marginal utility of consumption schedules of −1, a pure time preference rate (p) of 1 per cent yields a social discount rate which is negative for the low-income countries and only marginally positive for the middle-income countries.

The second point arises from the objection to the realism of such low rates: surely a value for p of only 1 per cent is unrealistic? Such an objection arises from either the casual observation that individuals do not engage in, for instance, sustainable farming practices (practices which conserve soil quality, irrigation water and rainfall) and hence have high implied personal time preference rates, or inspection of prevailing interest rates, particularly in rural areas.

Table 3.1   Illustrative social time preference rates for sub-Saharan countries

	$g\%$	$n = -1, p = 1\%$	$n = -1, p = 5\%$
Low-income countries	−1.9	−0.9	+3.1
Middle-income countries	−0.1	+0.9	+4.9

Note: Social time preference rate, i, is given as per cent.

Source: Authors' estimates based on 1973–83 data in World Bank (1984).

The final column shows the effect of raising the pure rate to 5 per cent. Note that even at this rate we are not close to the kinds of discount rates widely used for project appraisal in developing countries. To get to rates of 10 to 15 per cent, which are typical of international donor agency appraisals, we require that p increase to 12 to 17 per cent in the low-income case and 10 to 15 per cent in the middle-income case.

Assuming that it is legitimate to include pure time preference rates at all, are such rates realistic? Many would argue that they are because the mere presence of poverty itself induces high discount rates as concern is focused on food security over the next year or even few months rather than the long term. Proponents of the mortality-based time preferences rates would argue that risk of mortality is also higher the poorer is the country, so that p will be high on these arguments.

There is, however, a problem with inferring high time preference rates from the observation of poverty, particularly in the context of environmental problems. High discount rates are a cause of much environmental degradation as individuals opt for short-term measures designed to satisfy immediate wants, at the expense of sustainable practices. But, in turn, poor prospects arising from environmental degradation actually assist in generating the poverty that 'causes' high discount rates.

The apparently high values of p are not independent of environmental conditions. To use those rates to evaluate environmentally-oriented investments (such as soil conservation measures, afforestation, water harvesting) is to commit a basic error of analysis.

What can we conclude on diminishing marginal utility? Its suitability as a source of discounting appears to be reasonably unambiguous only in contexts where we can reliably expect positive sustainable changes in real consumption per capita. In poor countries where environmental damage is often high, those conditions may well not pertain.

The apparent rescue for the utility-discounting argument arises from inferring high pure time preference rates in those contexts, perhaps citing the argument that only high rates will explain some of the environmental degradation. But the discount rate in such circumstances is not independent of the conditions in question, so that one cannot infer the 'desirability' of such degradation from the inferred discount rates, nor the relative undesirability of conservation investment.

If high personal time preference rates are allowed to influence the value of i, the implication may therefore be that the discount rate unjustly reflects constrained activity, a situation where individuals are unable to act in a normal economic and environmental framework. This raises questions about the validity of such rates, perhaps abandoning the search for a social time preference rate altogether, or modifying the choice of rate to reflect the constraints on behaviour.

The problem then is that there are no clear rules for choosing a discount rate. Essentially, g and p in the social time preference rate formula are not independent: the lower the expected values of g the higher p will be. At the very least, then, advocacy of the use of social time preference rates requires some downward adjustment of p in contexts where the environment-poverty linkage is strong.

Risk and Uncertainty

Since Bentham (1789), it has been argued that a benefit or cost is valued less the more uncertain is its occurrence. Since uncertainty is usually expected to increase with time from the present, this declining value becomes a function of time and hence is formally expressible as a discount rate for risk and uncertainty.

The types of uncertainty that are generally regarded as being of relevance (although they are very often confused) are:

(a) uncertainty about the presence of the individual at some future date (the 'risk of death' argument);
(b) uncertainty about the preferences of the individual even when his or her existence can be regarded as certain;
(c) uncertainty about the availability of the benefit or the existence of the cost.

The objections to using uncertainty to justify positive discount rates are several. First, uncertainty arising from not being sure that the individual will be present to receive a distant benefit — the 'risk of death' argument — ignores the argument presented earlier about the 'immortality' of society in contrast to the mortality of the individual. Nonetheless, a number of attempts have been made to measure time preference rates using survival probabilities (Eckstein 1961, Kula 1984, 1985, 1986).

Second, uncertainty about preferences is clearly relevant if we are talking about certain goods and perhaps even aspects of environmental conservation (as the 'environmentalism' of the 1970s and 1980s demonstrates), but hardly seems relevant if we are considering projects or policies whose output is food, shelter, water and energy. If anything, we can be more sure of future preferences for these goods, not less (Barry 1977).This suggests that preference uncertainty is relevant to developed but not developing countries in the context of discount rate selection. However, even where preference uncertainty is relevant, powerful arguments exist for treating it through revaluation of benefits and costs, the relevant concept being option value (Bishop 1982).

Third, uncertainty about the presence or scale of benefits and costs may be unrelated to time, and certainly appears unlikely to be related in such a way that the scale of risk obeys an exponential function as is implied in the use of a single rate in the discount factor: e^{-rt}, or $1/(1 + r)^t$, where r is the discount rate.

What is being argued is not that uncertainty and risk are irrelevant to the decision-guiding rule, but that their presence should not be handled by adjustments to the discount rate. For such adjustments imply a particular behaviour for the risk premium which it is hard to justify. This argument is in fact widely accepted by economists (Dasgupta and Pearce 1972, Stiglitz 1986), although it appears to underlie the 2 per cent 'premium' attached to the officially recommended 5 per cent test discount rate in the United Kingdom in the presence of 'benefit optimism' (UK Treasury 1979, 1980).

If uncertainty does not take on a form consistent with exponential increase, the suggestion is that risk and uncertainty are better handled by other means, via adjustments to cost and benefit streams, leaving the underlying discount rate unadjusted for risk. This argument seems to us to be correct despite the fact that adding a premium to the discount rate for risk is widely recommended (Brown 1983, Prince 1985).

Opportunity Cost of Capital

The position taken by many economists is that the proper social rate of discount is the rate of return on the marginal project displaced by the investment in question. Investments may well displace a mix of investment and consumption, leading to weighted or 'synthetic' rates of discount reflecting the relative value of consumption and investment (Marglin 1963a, 1963b, Squire and van der Tak 1975).

The environmental literature has made some limited attempts to discredit discounting due to opportunity cost arguments (Parfit 1983, Goodin 1986). This literature is, however, confusing since most of the objections arise because the implication of opportunity cost discounting is that some rate greater than zero emerges and this is then held to be inconsistent with a concept of intergenerational justice. This aspect of the debate is considered later on. There do, however, appear to be two criticisms which are generally, but not wholly, independent of this wider concern.

The first arises because the discount factor arising from a constant discount rate takes on a specific exponential form. This is because discounting is simply the reciprocal of compound interest. In turn, compound interest implies that if we invest £100 today it will compound forward at a particular rate, provided we keep not just the original £100 invested but also reinvest the profits.

Now suppose the profits are consumed rather than reinvested. The critics suggest that this means that those consumption flows have no opportunity cost. What, they say, is the relevance of a discount rate based on assumed reinvested profits, if in fact the profits, are not reinvested but consumed? Thus:

> When such benefits are received later, this involves no opportunity costs. If I take my annual vacation in August rather than June, what opportunity cost do I thus incur?

and, considering an airport that destroys beautiful countryside:

> If we do not build the airport, such benefits would be enjoyed in each future year. At any discount rate, the benefits in later years count for much less than the benefits next year. How can an appeal to opportunity costs justify this? The benefits received next year — our enjoyment of this natural beauty — cannot be profitably reinvested. (Parfit 1983)

If the argument is correct, it provides a reason for not using a particular rate — the opportunity cost rate — for discounting streams of consumption flows as opposed to streams of profits which are always reinvested. But, in that context, it would not provide a reason for rejecting discounting altogether, since consumption flows should be discounted at a social time preference rate.

That is, the critics have not seen that a future holiday is worth less than a current holiday if we admit any of the arguments for a social time preference rate. As it happens, the particular critics in question would not admit to believing the arguments for a time preference rate either, so their position would be consistent.

The second argument relates to intertemporal compensation. Consider an investment which has an expected environmental damage of £X in some future time period t. Should this £X be discounted to a present value? The argument for doing so on opportunity cost grounds is presumably something like the following. If we debit the investment with a social cost now of $£X/(1 + r)^t$, then that sum can be invested at *r* per cent now and it will grow to be £*X* in year *t* and can then be used to compensate the future sufferers of the environmental damage.

Parfit (1983) debates that this argument has confused two issues. The first is whether the future damage matters less than current damage of a similar scale. The second is whether we can devise schemes to compensate for future damage.

The answer to the first question, he argues, is that it does not matter less than current damage, or if it does, it matters less only because we are able to compensate the future as shown. If we are not able to make the compensation, the argument for being less concerned, and hence the argument for discounting, become irrelevant.

Part of the problem here is that actual and potential compensation are being confused. As typically interpreted, cost-benefit rules require only that we could, hypothetically, compensate losers, not that we actually do. In this case, the resource cost to the current generation of hypothetically compensating a future generation is, quite correctly, the discounted value of the compensation. Really what Parfit is objecting to, we suggest, is the absence of built-in actual compensation mechanisms in cost-benefit appraisals. We have considerable sympathy with that view, but it is not relevant to the issue of how to choose a discount rate.

These particular arguments against opportunity cost related discounting are not, in our view, persuasive. It seems fair to say, however, that they are not regarded by their advocates as the most forceful that can be advanced against discount rates *per se*. Those rest with arguments about intergenerational justice, and these are addressed later.

Conclusions on Environmental Critiques

The environmental debate has undoubtedly contributed to intellectual soul-searching on the rationale for discounting. But, in our view, it has not been successful in demonstrating a case for rejecting discounting as such. It does raise issues of concern with respect to the uses of rates of interest which reflect pure time preference, but it does not provide a case for rejecting pure time preference completely.

It also raises further concerns about the compatibility of time preference based discounting and opportunity cost discounting especially in the context of developing countries. For, as we have seen, utility-of-consumption arguments may well suggest very low discount rates (ignoring pure time preference), whereas opportunity cost arguments might suggest very much higher ones.

We further observed that traditional arguments for adding risk premia on discount rates are fallacious: risk and uncertainty are properly handled in investment appraisal through adjustments to costs and benefits streams, not the discount rate. Lastly, we found environmental critiques of opportunity cost rates wanting.

We now consider the wider intergenerational aspects and argue that the environmental critique that discount rates are in some sense 'too high', reflects real concerns, but these concerns are better dealt with by not adjusting discount rates, but through other means that we describe.

Much of the modern discussion on how to integrate environmental factors into investment appraisal has tried to do so by making adjustments to discount rates, of which the two main kinds are:

(a) adding a premium to discount rates to reflect risk and uncertainty about environmental consequences of investments;
(b) lowering discount rates to reflect the interests of future generations.

We argue that neither of these constitutes a reason for adjusting the discount rate. But because we will be arguing that these very relevant and important factors do need to be taken into account in the appraisal of investments and in general policy, it is necessary to understand why the arguments for making adjustments to the discount rate are not persuasive.

Environmental Risk

Earlier, we argued that it is not advisable to adjust discount rates to reflect environmental risk. Essentially this was because such an adjustment assumes risk to behave in a manner that is very unlikely to be realistic.

For instance, consider an investment which has a high environmental cost in the final years of the project, perhaps arising because of the need to dismantle equipment which contains toxic materials. Now assume that we are uncertain about the size of this cost. The uncertainty ought to make the investment less attractive compared to a situation in which we knew the dismantling costs with certainty. If we raise the discount rate this will certainly be the effect. However, while the direction of adjustment is correct, we have no foundation for believing that the present value of the dismantling cost has been accurately represented by the adjustment to the discount rate.

In theory, it is possible, under special circumstances, to obtain a discount rate which reflects risk. In practice, we argue that adjusting discount rates for risk is not an efficient procedure because it imposes a time-profile for risk onto the project which has no particular justification, and because it requires information on certainty equivalence that is more effectively used directly in the valuation of the project.

It is well known that the problem of accommodating risk can be overcome by using certainty equivalence procedures. A simple example will suffice here.

Table 3.2 gives a cost-benefit profile for a hypothetical project. The second column shows the expected net benefits. These are the average values arising from assessing the chances of the benefit occurring. For example, if the net benefit in year two is a 50 per cent chance of £200 and a 50 per cent chance of nothing, the expected value is £100 [(0.5 x 200) + (0.5 x 0)].

Table 3.2   Risk adjustment and discounting

Year	Expected net benefit	Risk adjustment	Certainty equivalent	Discount factor	Adjusted flows
1	−100.0	1.0	−100.0	1.0	−100.0
2	+100.0	0.9	+90.0	0.95	+85.5
3	+100.0	0.8	+80.0	0.91	+72.8
4	+100.0	0.75	+75.0	0.86	+64.5
5	−80.0	1.20	−96.0	0.82	−78.7
Total					+44.1

The third column contains the adjustment for risk (sometimes confusingly termed the risk discount factor). What this adjustment shows is the way in which attitudes to risk modify the expected values. Thus in year 2 the expected net benefit is 100. This might be compared to a return of 90, that is expected with complete certainty. That is, we would be indifferent between the gamble of the 100 and an absolutely certain return of 90. This adjustment converts the expected net benefits to their certainty equivalents. For example, the expected value of £100 in year two is risky. We are likely to prefer a smaller but certain sum of money to this risky £100. This smaller sum is shown as £90 in column 4 and hence 0.9 is the risk adjustment. Notice that in this example the risk adjustment has nothing to do with time. This should be sufficient to differentiate adjustments for risk from adjustments for time discounting. This is shown in column 5 using a hypothetical 5 per cent discount rate.

Irreversibility

One special environmental consideration that might, prima facie, imply the adjustment of the discount rate is that of irreversibility. The issue, as the term implies, is that the costs associated with a large number of decisions are irreversible.

A valley that is flooded for a hydroelectric dam cannot be restored to its original state. Ancient buildings that are pulled down for a road development may be reproducible if dismantled and moved, but invariably are lost forever. Radioactive waste, once produced, cannot be destroyed: it must be stored somewhere, and no storage option is without risk. That risk is then present for at least hundreds of years and maybe more.

Clearly, any policy of not developing a valley, of not building a road, and of not building nuclear power stations involves a foregone benefit. The damage avoided by not taking a development decision has to be weighed against the benefits that the development would have conferred. But the 'no development' decision at least leaves the option to develop at a later stage, whereas the development decision leaves no option to reverse irreversible damage.

One approach which goes some way towards building these problems into a benefit-cost methodology has been developed by Krutilla and Fisher (1975) and conveniently extended and formalized by Porter (1982).

The net benefits, of an irreversible development can be written:

$$\text{Net benefits} = B(D) - C(D) - B(P)$$

where $B(D)$ are the benefits of development, $C(D)$ are the development costs, and $B(P)$ are the net benefits of preservation, all items being expressed in present value terms.

Some would argue that the discount rate itself should be set very low for projects with long-term environmental benefits or costs. In this case it would have the effect of making $B(P)$ large because they are foregone for ever, whereas the net benefits of development will be dissipated once the life of the dam is finished — perhaps 50 years after its construction.

Indeed, this difference in the time duration of development and preservation is critical to the discount rate adjustment argument. Yet in the Krutilla–Fisher approach, the discount rate is conventional in that it is set equal to some measure of the marginal productivity of capital.

The way in which the Krutilla–Fisher approach deals with irreversibility is to leave the underlying discount rate unmodified, but to apply a growth factor to preservation benefits and a decay factor to development benefits. Thus, if initial year preservation benefits are P_0, then in year t they will be $P_0.e^{ct}$ where c is the rate of growth of preservation benefits in real terms.

The idea here is that areas of wilderness, natural habitat and so on are becoming more and more scarce so that their price relative to other goods will rise. The argument on development benefits, a considerably weaker one than the preservation thesis, is that certain types of development are likely to become technologically outmoded as new technologies displace them. A decay factor is thus applied such that $D_t = D_0.e^{-dt}$, where D is preservation benefits and d is the decay factor.

Effectively, the cost-benefit rule is modified to produce two effective discount rates, $r - c$ for preservation benefits, and $r + d$ for development benefits. It will be evident that development benefits are more heavily discounted under this rule, while preservation benefits are inflated, biasing the decision rule more towards the preservation option.

The Krutilla–Fisher approach can thus be interpreted as a discount rate adjustment procedure arising from environmental considerations. But such an interpretation breaks faith with the original intent which is to avoid adjusting discount rates and adjust the benefit and cost streams instead, rather in the same way that certainty-equivalence approaches can be translated into risk-adjustments to discount rates. This approach to handling irreversibility does not therefore qualify as a procedure or justification for adjusting discount rates for environmental reasons.

Future Generations

The higher the rate of discount the greater will be the discrimination against future generations. First, projects with social costs that occur well into the future and net social benefits that occur in the near term will be likely to pass the standard cost-benefit test the higher the discount rate is. Thus future generations may bear a disproportionate share of the costs of the project.

Second, projects with social benefits well into the future are less likely to be favoured by the cost-benefit rule if discount rates are high. Thus future generations are denied a higher share of project benefits. Third, the higher the discount rate the lower will be the overall level of investment, depending on the availability of capital, and hence the lower the capital stock inherited by future generations.

The expectation must be, then, that future generations will suffer from rates of discount determined in the market-place since such rates are based on current generation preferences and/or capital productivity, which is not associated with the general existence of future markets.

It might be thought, however, that existing preferences do take account of future generations' interests. The way in which this might occur is through overlapping utility functions such that my welfare (utility) today includes as one of the factors determining it the welfare of my children and perhaps my grandchildren. Thus, if i is the current generation, j the next generation and k the third generation, we may have:

$$Ui = Ui(Ci, Uj, Uk)$$

where U is utility and C is consumption.

In this way, we could argue that the future generations' problem is automatically taken account of in current preferences. Notice that what is being evaluated in this process is the current generation's judgement about what the future generation will think is important.

It is not therefore a discount rate reflecting some broader principle of the rights of future generations. The essential distinction is between generation i judging what generation j wants (the overlapping utility function argument) and generation i engaging in resource investment so as to leave generation j with the maximum scope for choosing what it wants.

The issue is whether such an argument can be used to substantiate the idea that current, market-determined rates reflect future generations' interests. The basic reason for supposing that the argument does not hold is that market rates are determined by the behaviour of many individuals behaving in their own interest. If future generations enter into the calculus, they do so in contexts where the individual behaves in his or her public role.

The idea is that we all make decisions in two contexts — private decisions reflecting our own interests, and public decisions in which we act with responsibility for our fellow beings and for future generations. Market discount rates reflect the private context. This is what Sen (1982) calls the dual role rationale for social discount rates being below the market rates because of the future generations' issue.

It is also similar to the assurance argument, namely that people will behave differently if they can be assured that their own action will be accompanied by similar actions by others. Thus, we might each be willing to make transfers to future generations, but only if we are individually assured that others will do the same. If we cannot be so assured, our transfers will be less. The assured discount rate arising from collective action is lower than the unassured discount rate.

There are other arguments that are used to justify the idea that market rates will be too high in the context of future generations' interests. The first is what Sen (1982) calls the super-responsibility argument. Market discount rates arise from the behaviour of individuals, but the state is a separate entity with the responsibility of guarding collective welfare and the welfare of future generations as well. Thus, the rate of discount relevant to state investments will not be the same as the market discount rate and, since high rates discriminate against future generations, we would expect the state discount rate to be lower than the market discount rate.

The final argument used to justify the inequality of the market and social rate of discount is the isolation paradox (Sen 1961, 1967). This is often confused with the assurance problem referred to above, but the isolation paradox says that individuals will not make transfers even if assurance exists.

Collective Decision-making

Any positive social rate of discount will discriminate against future generations' interests. This suggests that the social discount rate is to be determined in the context of collective decision-making rather than some aggregation of individuals' decisions.

This might mean looking at individuals' public role behaviour, leaving the choice of discount rate to the state, or trying to select a discount rate based on a collective savings contract. None of these options offers a theory of how to determine a discount rate in quantitative terms. What they do suggest is that market rates will not be proper guides to discount rates once future generations' interests are incorporated into the social decision rule.

The view taken here is that these arguments can be used to justify rejecting the market rate of interest as a social discount rate if it is thought that the burden of accounting for future generations' interests should fall on the discount rate. However, we consider this an unnecessarily complex and almost certainly untenable procedure. It is better to define the rights of future generations and use these to circumscribe the overall cost-benefit rule, leaving the choice of discount rate to fairly conventional current-generation oriented considerations.

We suggest that it is better to adjust other aspects of the investment appraisal to account for future generations' interests. A telling reason for this is that lowering rates will encourage more investment overall, and this will increase the demand for resources and environmental services. A lowering of rates across the board could thus have counter-productive results if the aim is to accommodate environmental concerns.

One alternative, of course, is to lower discount rates for environmental projects, but not for other projects. In practice this is likely to be impossible to do because of the problems of deciding which is an environmental project and which is not. Is any rural development investment, for example, an environmental project? Since most projects will have an environmental dimension — they will all impact positively or negatively on the environment — the analyst would have to have some idea of the scale of the environmental dimension before deciding which discount rate to choose. Then he would need a cut-off point in order to decide which projects qualify for the lower rate and which for the higher one. Altogether, the procedure has large arbitrary features.

We suggest, then, that, while there are attractive features in the future generations' argument, they may either backfire in the sense of not accommodating the concerns that motivate a reduced discount rate, or they will result in largely impractical procedures.

A Sustainability Criterion

The general thrust of the argument of this chapter is

1. that the environmental critique of discounting at all is not persuasive,
2. that arguments for adjusting discount rates do contain persuasive elements, but

3.   adjusting the discount rate is a clumsy way of handling these legitimate concerns.

Now we pursue the final observation by suggesting a way in which the telling problem of intergenerational justice might be approached. We shall assume that the future has at least some claim on the present simply because it has an interest in the present. This interest, arising from the fact that what we do now affects the future, regardless of the fact that we do not know who future people will be, confers rights on future generations (Feinberg 1980, Goodin 1986). For our purposes, we accept that a case for intergenerational justice exists, and that the process of discounting appears to discriminate against it.

How might these future rights be protected in practice? Certain minimum requirements emerge with respect to any investment appraisal. Above all, it is essential that any investment appraisal should check on the resource and environmental consequences of the investment. This much has been recommended as standard procedure, for example by OECD (1986).

A second requirement is that efforts should be made to measure environmental damage at least in physical terms, but preferably in monetary terms (Pearce and Markandya 1988).

The procedures identified above are, of course, essential whether environmental considerations are located in the current or the future period. The interests of the future require something more, however, and this is captured in the idea of sustainable development.

Without investigating the concept deeply (see the discussion in Pearce *et al.* 1990), the basic idea is simple in the context of natural resources (excluding exhaustibles) and environments: the use made of these inputs to the development process should be sustainable through time. Unless there are good reasons to the contrary, the time horizon in question is an infinite one. The problem is how to attach meaning to this general concept. If we now apply the ideas to resources, sustainability might mean that a given stock of resources — trees, soil quality, water and so on — should not decline. The way in which it can be preserved is by harvesting only the sustainable yield of that resource. In turn, the sustainable yield may vary with the stock size and, more importantly, with the management regime.

For example, forest yields obviously vary with the size of the forest, and are noticeably higher in managed forests than in virgin forest. This all suggests that one should have some idea of the optimum stock of the resource to begin with. This is notoriously difficult to determine, even in reasonably well-defined conditions.

In a great many less developed countries, however, the complexity is reduced because stocks are known to be well below any optimum. A reasonably simple indicator of this can be found by comparing resource demands with measures of carrying capacity. It follows, then, that for these economies, no project should reduce the stock of the resource unless there is some compensating increase elsewhere.

The sequence of argument then is as follows:

1. the sustainable use of resources and environments serves two interests:
2. current generations over their lifetimes, and future generations since they inherit no smaller a stock than their predecessors;
3. sustainable use requires harvesting, or using, only the sustainable yield of the resource;
4. ideally, the relevant sustainable yield is the one at the optimal stock, but there are obvious problems in measuring the optimal stock;
5. in practical terms, then, resource-using projects should use only the sustainable yield, or should include as a cost in the project the regeneration of any stock that is otherwise permanently removed.

Obviously, these requirements may turn out to be quite formidable for some projects since it is likely to be the cost of regeneration that will be relevant. Some projects may cease to be profitable and others may well have their apparent rate of return reduced. Really what is happening is that the project is being debited with the true cost of resource depletion. If it cannot meet that cost then it is not a project that is consistent with the sustainability requirement.

The implications for the discount rate are interesting. What this approach suggests is that we do not need to adjust the discount rate for the interests of future generations. They are met by the sustainable use constraint and hence the changed cost profile for the project. The discount rate that is used can then be the opportunity cost of capital, adjusted, if necessary, for any consumption displacement effects. Moreover, it is in keeping with the arguments made earlier that adjusting the discount rate for future generations' interests is both clumsy and inefficient.

There are clearly major problems with the sustainability requirement as interpreted above. It makes sense in the context of many rural development projects, where the impact on local environments and resources should be capable of estimation. What if the investment is, say, a rural road? Then it remains important to obtain some idea of what the road will do to settlement patterns, such that new settlers make demands on local resources. Probably more important, the road may well make resource demands from urban areas easier to satisfy. An example would be the transport of charcoal — as new roads are built so the area of resources that can supply urban areas is expanded. The road has, then, to be debited with the costs of regeneration of the stock that comes under demand (provided, of course, that the stock is not judged to be excessive).

For many urban projects the sustainability requirement may well not apply, but it will, for example, if the project has a significant demand for water such that existing water quality is impaired or other resource-using activities are affected. The problem is then that the sustainability requirement could, if applied to each and every investment, amount to actual compensating investments for every externality arising from the project. This could readily become stultifying and inoperable.

The way round this problem is to ensure that in any portfolio of investments there are compensating investments in resource regeneration. This would mean a procedure something like the following:

1. engage in the normal investment activity, but with careful checks for environmental repercussions as discussed;
2. where resource demands are significant, estimate the cost of regenerating the resource loss and include the regeneration project in the overall investment portfolio;
3. where resource demands are small or too difficult to accommodate by in-project compensation, check the resource demands of the whole portfolio of investments and adjust the portfolio so that it includes specifically resource-generating investments. In this way, it is the whole portfolio of investments that bears the cost of the sustainability requirement, by having the marginal project removed and replaced with the environment improvement project.

Strictly, the environmental compensation project will not require assessment by standard cost-benefit procedures: it is designed to honour the sustainability constraint and is itself not to be evaluated by the conventional criteria. Nonetheless, such an appraisal should be carried out to check the price of the sustainability requirement. For example, if the compensating investment turns out to be one with a negative rate of return, this will indicate the sum of the sustainability costs omitted from the other projects.

Exhaustible Resources

The discussion has implicitly assumed that it is possible to regenerate the resources that are used up. This is acceptable for trees, soil quality, water in most cases (but not all — such as groundwater losses) and generally for renewable resources. But it is patently untrue for exhaustible resources — minerals and energy. What is to be done in this case?

Page (1977, 1983) has suggested mechanisms involving severance taxes which equalize the availability of the resource in terms of constant real prices (see also Pearce 1987). But, even if such suggestions were practicable, they stray beyond the context of investment appraisal.

The alternatives appear to be extending the compensating investment concept to include investments in renewable resources to compensate for exhaustible resources losses, or simply ignoring the exhaustible resource problem, perhaps on the grounds that technological change might enable the yield (in terms of services or welfare) of exhaustible resources to rise through time.

There are other problems with the sustainability requirement as interpreted. It may appear too narrow in focus since it makes only natural resources subject to the sustainability requirement. But sustainable development is open to much wider interpretation. As resources are reduced in size now, their yield in the future may be higher because of technological change. Substitution possibilities may emerge along with technological change.

This all suggests that sustainability might be redefined in terms of a requirement that the use of resources today should not reduce real incomes in the future, allowing resources to be used up now and converted to real capital which is available for the benefit of the future. Indeed, this would be the more traditional interpretation of sustainable development.

One problem with this is that it opens the way to regarding almost any resource-using activity as sustainable. To become helpful as a definition it requires some method of ensuring that such conversion and substitution can and will take place.

The concept of the environmentally-compensating investment is thus a practical one and reflects the wider concerns of sustainability or permanent liveability. It needs to be stressed that such pressure is not a blind 'replace a tree for every tree removed' requirement. This would make much investment inoperable in practical terms, even if it could be regarded as having a rationale. Rather it is an attempt to accommodate the interest of future generations in a practical way by debiting projects or programmes with the costs of resource losses. At the very least it forces an environmental/resource assessment of investment activity.

References

Arrow, K. (1966), 'Discounting and Public Investment Criteria', in A.V. Kneese and S. Smith (eds), *Water Research* Baltimore: Johns Hopkins University Press.

Ayres, R.U. and Kneese, A.V. (1969), 'Production Consumption and Externality', *American Economic Review*, **59**, 268–84.

Barry, B. (1977), 'Justice between generations', in P. Hacker and J. Raz (eds), *Law, Morality and Society*, Oxford: Clarendon Press.

Baumol, W.J. (1968), 'On the Social Rate of Discount', *American Economic Review*, **57**, December, 788–802.

Bentham, J. (1789), *An Introduction to the Principles of Morals and Legislation*, London: Athlone Press.

Bishop, R. (1982), 'Option Value: an Exposition and Extension', *Land Economics*, 58, 1–15.

Bohm-Bawerk, E.v. (1884), *The Positive Theory of Capital*, New York: Stedard.

Brown, S. (1983), 'A Note on Environmental Risk and the Rate of Discount', *Journal of Environmental Economics and Management*, 10, 282–6.

Dasgupta, A.K. and Pearce, D.W. (1972), *Cost-Benefit Analysis: Theory and Practice*, London: Macmillan.

Eckstein, O. (1961), 'A Survey of the Theory of Public Expenditure', in J. Buchanan (ed.), *Public Finances: Needs, Sources and Utilisation*, New Jersey: Princeton University Press.

Feinberg, J. (1980), *Rights, Justice and the Bounds of Liberty*, New Jersey: Princeton University Press.

Goodin, R. (1982), 'Discounting Discounting', *Journal of Public Policy*, 2, 53–72.

Goodin, R. (1986), *Protecting the Vulnerable*, Chicago: University of Chicago Press.

Jevons, W.S. (1871), *The Theory of Political Economy*, London: Macmillan.

Krutilla, J. and Fisher, A.C. (1975), *The Economics of Natural Environments*, Washington, DC: Resources for the Future.

Kula, E. (1984), 'Derivation of Social Time Preference Rates for the United States and Canada', *Quarterly Journal of Economics*, 99, (4), 873–82.

Kula, E. (1985), 'An Empirical Investigation on the Social Time Preference Rate for the United Kingdom', *Environment and Planning*, series A, vol. 17.

Kula, E. (1986), 'The Analysis of Social Interest Rate in Trinidad and Tobago', University of Ulster, Department of Economics, mimeo.

Lind, R. (ed.) (1982), *Discounting for Time and Risk in Energy Policy*, Baltimore: Resources for the Future Inc and Johns Hopkins University Press.

Marglin, S. (1963a), 'The Opportunity Costs of Public Investment', *Quarterly Journal of Economics*, 77, May, 274–89.

Marglin, S. (1963b), 'The Social Rate of Discount and the Optimal Rate of Investment', *Quarterly Journal of Economics*, 77, February, 95–111.

OECD (1986), *OECD and the Environment*, Paris: OECD.

Olson, M. and Bailey, M. (1981), 'Positive Time Preference', *Journal of Political Economy*, 89, 1–25.

Page, T. (1977), *Conservation and Economic Efficiency*, Baltimore: Johns Hopkins University Press.

Page, T. (1983), 'Intergenerational Justice as Opportunity', in D. MacLean and P. Brown (eds), *Energy and the Future*, Ottowa: Rowman and Littlefield.

Parfit, D. (1983), 'Energy Policy and the Further Future: the Social Discount Rate', in D.S. MacLean and P. Brown (eds), *Energy and the Future*, Ottowa: Rowman and Littlefield.

Pearce, D.W. (1987), 'Foundations of an Ecological Economics', *Ecological Modelling*, 38, 9–18.

Pearce, D.W. and Markandya, A. (1988), *The Benefits of Environmental Policy*, Paris: OECD.

Pearce, D.W., Barbier, E.B. and Markandya, A. (1990), *Sustainable Development: Economics and the Environment in the Third World*, Aldershot: Edward Elgar.

Pearce, F. (1964), *A Contribution to Demand Theory*, Oxford: Clarendon Press.

Pigou, A.C. (1932), *The Economics of Welfare*, London: Macmillan.

Porter, P. (1982), 'The New Approach to Wilderness Preservation through Benefit-Cost Analysis', *Journal of Environmental Economics and Management*, **9**, 59–80.

Prince, R. (1985), 'A Note on Environmental Risk and the Rate of Discount: comment', *Journal of Environmental Economics and Management*, **12**, 179–80.

Ramsey, F.P. (1928), 'A Mathematical Theory of Saving', *Economic Journal*, 38, 543–59.

Sen, A. (1961), 'On Optimising the Rate of Saving', *Economic Journal,* **71**.

Sen, A. (1967), 'Isolation, Assurance, and the Social Rate of Discount', *Quarterly Journal of Economics*, **LXXXI**, 112–24.

Sen, A. (1982), 'Approaches to the Choice of Discount Rate for Social Cost-Benefit Analysis', in R. Lind (ed.), *Discounting for Time and Risk in Energy Policy*, Baltimore: Johns Hopkins University Press.

Squire, L. and van der Tak, H. (1975), *Economic Analysis of Projects*, Baltimore: Johns Hopkins Press.

Stern, N. (1977), 'The Marginal Valuation of Income', in M.J. Artis and A.R. Nobay (eds), *Studies in Modern Economic Analysis,* Oxford: Blackwell.

Stiglitz, J. (1982), 'The Rate of Discount for Benefit-Cost Analysis and the Theory of the Second Best', in R. Lind (ed.), *Discounting for Time and Risk in Energy Policy*, Baltimore: Johns Hopkins University Press.

Stiglitz, J. (1986), *Economics of the Public Sector*, New York: Norton.

Strotz, R. (1956), 'Myopia and Inconsistency in Dynamic Utility Maximization', *Review of Economic Studies*, **23**, (3), 165–80.

UK Treasury (1979), *The Test Discount Rate and the Required Rate of Return on Investment,* London: HM Treasury.

UK Treasury (1980), *Investment Appraisal and Discounting Techniques and the Use of the Test Discount Rate in the Public Sector*, London: HM Treasury.

World Bank (1984), *World Development Report*, Washington, DC: World Bank.

4. Deforestation and economic criteria

Colin Price

The future of tropical forests has become a widely-discussed issue. The popular concerns have been with economic externalities, such as effects on river run-off, depletion of gene resources, loss of the livelihoods and cultures of forest-living peoples, and the implications for climatic change. Failure to include such externalities in evaluations by logging companies, by national forest services and even by multilateral funding agencies is clearly a potential cause of wrong decisions. But another less-widely debated cause may be equally significant: the application to deforestation projects of economic criteria which do not realistically reflect the relative values of the resulting costs and benefits. This chapter examines the application of such criteria to an illustrative logging project. It shows that formal economic criteria for project appraisal frequently reproduce the dubious assumptions of over-optimistic development policies. It argues that, when more realistic criteria are applied, the economic case for logging projects tends to diminish.

Forests, Development and Projects

At first sight the case against deforestation seems unequivocal, given the range of costs incurred and benefits lost. In some countries, the current rate of loss of forest cover would lead to forest extinction, perhaps irreversible, by early in the next century. The Ivory Coast has 5.9 per cent deforestation per year, Paraguay 4.6 per cent , Nepal 3.9 per cent (Repetto and Gillis, 1988).

There are, however, immediate and countervailing benefits, such as the supply of fuelwood and building materials and, crucially in the development debate, earning of foreign exchange. The late Jack Westoby focused on these potential benefits in a paper optimistically entitled 'The Role of Forest Industries in the Attack on Economic Underdevelopment' (Westoby 1962). By liquidating part of their forest capital, developing countries could make hard currency available to build up their infrastructure and industry, to the much-discussed point of take-off into self-sustaining growth.

Twenty-five years later, a collection of Westoby's papers was published (Westoby 1987). It records his progressive disillusionment with governments' ability and willingness to turn this potentially valuable process into reality. Even when the profits of logging were left in the country of origin by the logging companies, they were too-frequently frittered away on prestige projects without development content, or diverted to additional consumption by the relatively well-off. Even the minimal investment required to replace the lost tree cover all-too-often was not forthcoming, as foresters found to their great cost (Nadkarni 1989).

As the forest resource disappears, several countries are nearing the end of the development 'runway' it could have provided, without the aircraft of self-sustaining economic development seeming any closer to becoming airborne. The point is that, unless they are reflected in what is happening at the project level, even the most plausible, attractive and high-sounding development policies are at best a meaningless sham, and at worst a dangerous lie. Experience of real-world politics is indeed one force that has driven economists over the past 25 years to seek methods for predicting and evaluating the real effects of projects (Marglin 1967; UNIDO 1972; Little and Mirrlees 1974; Squire and van der Tak 1975; Bruce 1976; Hansen 1978; Irvin 1978; Weiss 1980; Overseas Development Administration 1988).

Rates of Return

The simplified project presented in Table 4.1 is representative of tropical forest logging projects. It serves to illustrate how different criteria affect the way a project is appraised by economists. The national government is assumed to be in direct control of the costs included here, and the revenues. Alternatively, the cash flow may be considered as the domestic contribution to an operation largely carried out by a transnational logging company.

Table 4.1   Cash flow profile of illustrative forest exploitation project

Item	Year	Annual cash flow equivalent($)
Investment in infrastructure	1	−1 000 000
Revenues from logging	2–7	400 000
Labour cost (200 workers)	2–7	−100 000
Income increase (200 workers)	2–7	40 000
Sale of land for ranching	7	1 000 000
Lost subsistence (100 forest-dwellers)	7–∞	−15 000

Note: For simplicity, all cash flows are allocated to the middle of the appropriate year when making discounting calculations.

Despite criticisms (Feldstein and Flemming 1964; Price and Nair 1984), the internal rate of return (IRR) remains a popular criterion for judging forest investments (Gane 1969; Busby 1985). It represents apparently the rate at which a project generates funds for investment in further development. The financial IRR of this hypothetical project is 30 per cent, modest by the norms of logging projects, yet probably an attractive investment proposition.

This initial figure is deficient in two ways however. First, it takes no account of the subsistence benefits lost in perpetuity, or any of the other externalities mentioned earlier. These can be included by evaluating them in dollar terms. Environmentalists, anthropologists and others can debate the calibre of existing methods of quantification, given the uncertainty about many of the impacts of logging in the short and especially the long term. Thus the tables use hypothetical figures for this component ($15 000 per year in perpetuity).

Second, the workers' wage cost ($100 000) is purely financial. It can be replaced by a value which is perhaps more relevant to the broader perspective: the opportunity cost of employing them in that project ($60 000, say). The IRR now increases to 33.6 per cent. But there is the classic problem of the IRR to contend with: there may be more than one IRR for a given project (as there may be more than one solution to the equation net present value (NPV) equals zero). Thus there is also a very low IRR, of 0.7 per cent.

Since this low IRR would certainly indicate an economically unacceptable project, a means is needed of distinguishing the correct IRR, or at least the 'most representative' one. The normal reference point is the rate of return at which cash revenues may be reinvested (Schallau and Wirth 1980). The justification of the IRR as a measure of efficiency relies upon the possibility of reinvesting in more projects of the same type.

The high IRR is largely based on rapid short-term financial returns. Once logged, the land can be sold for, say, ranching; at least, let that be the financial assumption. In our illustration, this sale of land suffices to replace the initial investment by a new area of forest. In addition, the annual cash surplus from logging of $300 000 allows rapid expansion (at 30 per cent per annum compound) of the logging programme. This assumes there are no physical or other limits to the area potentially available for logging during the period of evaluation. The loss of subsistence products, or equivalent externalities, pose a problem, because they continue indefinitely. Indeed, these costs mount steadily as the deforested area expands.

For the purposes of cost-benefit analysis, such losses are monetized as the sum which, if available to the losers, would compensate them for the losses. The validity of methods to assess the appropriate sum is the subject of extensive debate not entered into here. With the illustrative figures adopted in Table 4.1, reinvestment of revenues which allows the area being exploited to increase by just over 5 per cent every six years is sufficient to pay compensation for such accumulated losses in perpetuity. Funds to achieve such a modest expansion require only small inroads into the financial surplus arising from the logging.

Thus the lower of the two IRRs (0.7 per cent) clearly understates the potential of the project to create a perpetually expanding basis for general economic development. One question is, however, to what extent is this potential, in practice, realized or even realizable? The rolling programme of logging, the modest expansion needed to compensate for an ever-growing volume of lost subsistence, and new investment in separate logging projects, all put pressure on a limited, and non-self-regenerating, resource. The expansion of any logging project must ultimately be curtailed (at the latest, when the last tree goes). Regardless of when that is, the accumulation of lost subsistence values will continue thereafter, while the accumulation of logging revenues ceases once logging ceases. A policy of total reinvestment, with 30 per cent expansion every year, would rapidly reach the physical limits of any country's forest resource.

The physical limits of natural forests make it necessary, eventually, to refer to the earning of other projects within the economy. For that is where the revenues of forest exploitation are ultimately invested, in so far as they stay within the country. If such projects offer a rate of return in excess of 0.7 per cent , then reinvested revenues will suffice to pay compensation to forest-dwellers in perpetuity. On the other hand, if the rate of return exceeds 33.6 per cent , alternative projects offer a better potential return than forest exploitation. Between these rather broad limits of discount rate, logging has a positive NPV, and therefore apparently constitutes a desirable investment.

However, the assumptions remain implicit that forest exploitation does in fact compete with investment, and compound reinvestment, elsewhere in the economy, and that forest revenues will be wholly reinvested. This is precisely the point being questioned in this chapter. To begin with, not all the economic benefits of exploitation accrue to the government. Increased income to workers is mostly consumed. Profits to transnational logging companies may be repatriated with only light tax deductions (Repetto and Gillis 1988). Secondly, the pressure of more immediate demands on public funds usually limits governments' scope to reinvest revenues, supposing they should even desire to do so. The will and the ability of governments to reinvest is in fact doubtful in many economic contexts (Price 1973).

Once the compound rate of return on reinvestment fails to reflect the true rate of growth of invested funds, the social discount rate can no longer be equated with that rate of return. The function of discounting is now to give appropriate weights to revenues, costs and benefits accruing at different points in time. The opportunity cost of investment funds is represented, not by a rate of interest, but by the discounted value of benefits generated by investment in the economy generally, or in a 'typical marginal project' which represents the characteristics of marginal investment (Marglin 1967; Feldstein 1964; Squire and van der Tak 1975; Harou 1985).

A widely-reproduced formula for the opportunity cost of investment funds (OCIF) is

$$OCIF = (q - sq)/(i - sq)$$

where q is the financial rate of return on investment, s is the proportion of investment revenues which is reinvested in the economy; and i is the social discount rate.

Where social opportunity cost is to be calculated, a rate of return, b, of non-market benefits-less-costs should be (but often is not) added to the numerator, so that

$$OCIF = \frac{(q - sq)}{(i - sq)} + b$$

The consumed portion of financial revenues $(I - s)$ is assumed for convenience to be distributed to consumers having the mean income level. The OCIF is expressed as a value relative to that of immediate consumption by such consumers.

Value of Parameters

Among the factors determining OCIF, two of them (q and s) are in principle measurable from national economic data. The social discount rate, i, is more controversial. In social cost-benefit analysis it is generally estimated as

$$i = ng + p$$

where n is the absolute value of the elasticity of marginal utility of income, g is the rate of growth of GNP per head, and p is the pure rate of time preference (see also Chapter 3 by Markandya and Pearce in this volume).

There is some dispute about whether econometric estimates of n are valid and reliable (Kula 1987). It is doubtful whether mean growth rates of income yield a representative measure of diminishing marginal utility of income for a whole nation (Price and Nair 1985). Also, not everyone accepts pure time preference as a valid component of a social discount rate (Price 1989a, 1989b, 1993). Even if a precise value of i cannot be defined, however, some estimate of it must be made for social cost-benefit analysis, since q is usually not an appropriate social discount rate when reinvestment is less than total.

For purposes of illustration, the following reasonable values are adopted:

q = 12 per cent

s = 10 per cent

b = 9.6 per cent (attributed to employment-generation benefits, commensurate with those of forest investment)

i = 6 per cent (attributed to 3 per cent per year growth in gross national income per head, and elasticity of marginal utility of income of −2. Pure time preference is excluded from the social discount rate.)

On this basis, the opportunity cost of investment funds is $4.25 per dollar invested. Such figures are generally applied to the value of all uncommitted government funds, for it is argued 'a rational government should see to it that the value of its expenditure at the margin is equal in all lines' (Little and Mirrlees 1974: 35). The validity of this viewpoint will be reviewed later.

Within the perspective of social cost-benefit analysis, benefits to individuals are weighted according to the individuals' income (Squire and van der Tak 1975). The weights used in the following calculations are derived from these assumptions:

- an income increase from $300 to $500 for the logging workers,
- a subsistence income decrease from $300 to $150 for the forest-dwellers, and
- a mean income of $600 per head for the population generally.

In these calculations, the changes of income are non-marginal for workers and forest-dwellers and marginal for the population generally. The formulae used to calculate consumption weights reflect this.

The overall cost-benefit analysis of exploitation is summarized in Table 4.2.

Despite the perpetually lost subsistence, the project shows an attractive net social worth, when all the specified costs and benefits are discounted at the social discount rate. The objection may be raised that not all groups in society participate in the growth of gross national income on which the social discount rate is based (Price and Nair 1985; Price 1989c: 316). In particular, the subsistence population displaced by exploitation may have a static or declining income. Even supposing that this population achieves a growth rate in real income per head of 1 per cent per year following displacement, a low discount rate of only 2 per cent would be appropriate. The total value of lost subsistence discounted at this rate is $5 380 843, and the net social worth of the project is marginally negative (−$50 689).

There is in fact an element of circularity in an analysis which discounts long-term loss of income on the basis that income will grow in the long term.

This circularity is inherent in much of the debate about natural resource use (Price 1984).

Table 4.2   Social cost-benefit analysis

Item	Year	Annual cash flow equivalent($)	Weight	Discounted value($)
Infrastructure	1	−1 000 000	4.25	−4 127 965
Logging	2–7	400 000	4.25	8 119 410
Labour cost	2–7	−100 000	4.25	−2 029 852
Income increase	2–7	40 000	2.4	458 508
Sale of land	7	1 000 000	4.25	2 910 053
Lost subsistence	7–∞	−15 000	8	−1 451 603
Total				3 878 551

Note: For simplicity, all cash flows are allocated to the middle of the appropriate year when making discounting calculations.

Reality of Reinvestment

Let us suppose, however, that the forest-living population, following initial displacement, shares in the growth of national income, and that 6 per cent is therefore the appropriate rate of discount for all items. There is, nonetheless, a remarkable inconsistency of treatment between net revenue to the logging project, and to the typical marginal project on which the calculation of the opportunity cost of investment funds is based. The inconsistency appears, moreover, to be enshrined in many standard works on project appraisal.

For example, UNIDO (1972) and Little and Mirrlees (1974) both discuss possible differences between the opportunity cost of investment funds (OCIF), the weight to project net revenues and uncommitted social income. The following quotation, however, reveals their final viewpoint.

> It should be noted that we have substituted s (the price of uncommitted social income) for the UNIDO Pinv which is the price of investment in terms of consumption. This however is justified on our present assumption that the whole of the surplus thrown up by a public project is uncommitted social income for us: while for UNIDO, to call it investment requires the assumption, also made, that the government uses new uncommitted social income entirely for investment. (Little and Mirrlees, 1974: 359).

In Squire and van der Tak (1975: 68) we find 'it might be possible to assess the value of public investment relative to private sector consumption, the resulting value would also be the correct value of v (the value of public income)'.

Irvin (1978) says 'hence average consumption must be translated into the LMST (Little and Mirrlees–Squire and van der Tak) numeraire by means of a social accounting ratio, v, or "value of public income". The parameter v is the LMST equivalent of the UNIDO "premium on investment".'

The view adopted by Weiss (1980) can be deduced from the following equivalences:

- 'all investment… is treated as equivalent to the numeraire'
- the numeraire is 'units of private consumption in domestic prices in the hands of consumers at the "base level of consumption".'
- the 'base level of consumption' derives from 'the idea that governments will feel that a rupee going to a private individual at a certain standard of living, or level of consumption, will have the same social value as an extra rupee of income going to the government itself' (Weiss 1980: 5).

Thus the value of investment is equal to consumption at the base level, which is equal to the value of income to the government.

A similar deduction can be made from Overseas Development Administration (1988):

- 'a significant amount of the project surplus is often captured by the government…, and this proportion of the surplus is valued at the numeraire rate'
- 'the numeraire should be uncommitted government income…'
- 'v is the value of uncommitted government income…'
- '$v=q - sq/(i-sq)$', (equals the value of investment) (Overseas Development Administration 1988: 58).

In practice, therefore, government net revenues are pervasively given equal value with government investment funds. As both the Little and Mirrlees and (since 1980) UNIDO schools of thought use a numeraire which also has this value, all government funds appear with an apparently uncontroversial unit weighting.

In determining the OCIF, it is normally assumed that reinvestible revenue from the typical marginal project accrues annually, at the rate q. Of this q, a proportion (90 per cent in our case) is immediately consumed. Only the remaining 10 per cent is reinvested. By contrast, the annual revenue of logging (or in general, the project being appraised) is commonly assumed to be reinvested in its entirety.

In fact the implausibly optimistic postulate of take-off into self-sustaining growth — that all profits of exploitation are ploughed into investment in the general economy — is meticulously reproduced in the supposedly more sensitive and realistic project appraisal methodology!

Given this extraordinarily asymmetric assumption about reinvestment, any particular project under appraisal tends to be favoured by comparison with the typical marginal project. The whole appraisal methodology becomes 'project friendly' whenever projects generate reinvestible revenues. The asymmetry is similar to the tendency to identify employment and environmental benefits lavishly in the project under appraisal, and not at all in the 'typical marginal project' (Price and Nair, 1984). Thus any agency capable of identifying projects, and powerful enough to draw them to government attention, will find the task of justifying the project much easier.

The appendix to this chapter shows how the agency responsible for the typical marginal project might appraise it, the logging project now providing the OCIF. On this basis, the typical marginal project appears a better use of funds than the logging project.

Using such project-friendly techniques, more worthwhile projects may be identified than can be funded. Little and Mirrlees (1974) suggest that selection should then be achieved by raising the discount rate until the remaining profitable projects can all be funded. But this is tantamount to adopting projects in rank order of IRR, with the problems discussed above. Moreover, the performance of projects with long-term costs may even be enhanced by raising the discount rate.

To achieve consistency between the logging project and the typical marginal project, we should assume that the net revenues of logging, as of the typical marginal project, are divided 90 per cent to immediate consumption (with a weighting of unity) and 10 per cent to reinvestment (with a weighting of 4.25). The combined weight to such revenues would be

$$0.9 \times 1 + 0.1 \times 4.25 = 1.325$$

Applying this weight to financial costs and revenues during the period of profit gives the results summarized in Table 4.3.

There are two reasons for the unacceptable performance of logging under this set of weights:

1. investment costs now have a higher weight than logging revenues; and
2. non-monetary lost subsistence has gained in importance relative to the rein-vestible (but in practice largely consumed) logging revenues.

The analysis has still not treated the typical marginal project and forest exploitation equally. The usual implicit assumption for the typical marginal project is that it will continue in perpetuity, being either maintained from a depreciation fund, or replaced by a similar typical marginal project from a sinking fund at the end of its life. The exploitation project, on the other hand, expires after (in our example) seven years.

Table 4.3   Social cost-benefit analysis — low reinvestment

Item	Year	Annual cash flow equivalent($)	Weight	Discounted value($)
Infrastructure	1	−1 000 000	4.25	−4 127 965
Exploitation	2–7	400 000	1.325	2 531 346
Labour cost	2–7	−100 000	1.325	−632 836
Income increase	2–7	40 000	2.4	458 508
Sale of land	7	1 000 000	1.325	907 252
Lost subsistence	7–∞	−15 000	8	−1 451 603
Total				−2 315 298

Note: For simplicity, all cash flows are allocated to the middle of the appropriate year when making discounting calculations.

This anomaly may be corrected by dedicating sufficient of the final year's revenue entirely to reinvestment in typical marginal projects. The sale of land conveniently provides sufficient revenue for the purpose. Weighting this item at 4.25 rather than 1.325 brings the project nearer to social profitability (NPV = −$312 497), without actually making it desirable.

Table 4.4   Social cost-benefit analysis — low reinvestment rolling programme

Item	Year	Annual cash flow equivalent($)	Weight	Discounted value($)
Infrastructure	1	−1 000 000	4.25	−4 127 965
Exploitation	2–25	400 000	1.325	6 460 690
Labour cost	2–25	−100 000	1.325	−1 615 173
Income increase	2–25	40 000	2.4	1 170 238
Sale of land	25	1 000 000	4.25	1 019 520
Lost subsistence	7–∞	−15 000	8	−1 451 603
Lost subsistence	13–∞	−15 000	8	−1 023 323
Lost subsistence	19–∞	−15 000	8	−721 403
Lost subsistence	25–∞	−15 000	8	−508 561
Total				−797 580

Note: For simplicity, all cash flows are allocated to the middle of the appropriate year when making discounting calculations.

Alternatively, the $1 000 000 from sale of land may be entered into a rolling programme of exploitation. Table 4.4 shows the results from continuing this through four cycles, then ploughing the revenue from the last land sale back into typical marginal projects.

The overall result, as might be expected, is simply to augment the scale of loss resulting from one cycle. If exploitation continued longer, the loss would be greater still.

Distributional Effect

The foregoing discussion centres on the uses to which project revenues are put. Whom the revenues accrue to is also relevant. The assumption has been that government uses revenues to enhance the consumption of consumers at the mean consumption level. However, a greater utility would arise from consumption being distributed throughout the population so as to increase everyone's income by the same percentage. This follows from the shape of the marginal utility of consumption function. The higher marginal utility of consumption of people $X below the mean consumption level more than offsets the lower marginal utility of consumption of those $X above the mean consumption level.

This higher consumption weight applies to:

- that part of the value of typical marginal projects due to generally increased consumption;
- the component of net revenue from a specific project (90 per cent) disbursed as generally increased consumption.

However, the value of investment which is attributed to income gains by specified project beneficiaries is unaffected. Proportionally, then, OCIF increases less than the weight on revenues does.

Applying one such plausible distribution produced an NPV of $510 762 for the four-cycle forest exploitation project. The change to a positive value is attributable to:

1. increased importance of government revenues in relation to the (negative) consumption changes specific to the project; and
2. reduction of the ratio between OCIF and the weight on revenues.

Conversely, a policy of using net revenues to increase the consumption of individuals at twice the mean national consumption level increased the project loss to $2 648 933.

These two variants show that one cannot afford to be casual in assumptions about distribution of benefits from either the typical marginal project or from the project under review.

One might also examine the implications of the precept that rational governments distribute revenues only to consumers at the base level of consumption (here, $291), at which consumption has the same weight as investment. This widely-endorsed theoretical expedient unfortunately has bizarre consequences. The 90 per cent of revenues devoted to consumption now have weight 4.25, and the OCIF rises to

$$(4.25 \times 0.9 \times 0.12 + 0.096) / (0.06 - 0.012) = 11.56.$$

The base level of consumption must be revised down again, so that the weight on it rises to 11.56. But this again increases the OCIF endlessly, and exponentially. The simple truth is that an unconstrained government cannot rationally allocate funds to increased consumption for a particular income group, rather than investment for the benefit of that income group, if the rate of return on investment exceeds the discount rate for that group. But, in practice, governments are either constrained, irrational, or both.

It has, however, been suggested (Little and Mirrlees 1974; Choksi, quoted in Bruce 1976), that in due course q and i will tend to equality. This in itself reduces the opportunity cost of investment funds, which over a certain period will fall further, to unity. For example, if the period is 25 years, Choksi's formula gives OCIF 2.159.

The fall in value of investment funds relative to consumption justifies a higher discount on such funds than the 6 per cent social discount rate (in this case 9.31 per cent is the appropriate rate). The weight on net revenues is also adjusted downwards to reflect the reduced weight on the investment portion. The consumption portion of net revenues should be discounted at 6 per cent , and the investment portion at 9.31 per cent.

When the new weights and discount rates are applied to the four-cycle logging project, the NPV is –$478 180. The reduced ratio of OCIF to the weight on net revenues in itself would make the loss on exploitation only $32 955. However, the increased discount on investment funds has partly offset this.

Choksi's refinement adds an interesting new dimension to the proliferating possibilities of sensitivity analysis. However, there seems to be little evidence for asserting that developing countries will reach an optimal level of investment in the foreseeable future.

Conclusion

Deforestation of the tropics, largely for the benefit of rich nations and at the expense of the poor, is by no means new. It is a sad commentary on worldly ways that concern in developed countries has emerged only with awareness of impending material shortages and possible global disaster.

Economists in developed countries have played their part as apologists for the forest destruction, at first in terms of profit-maximization, later in terms of development theories, and later still in terms of social cost-benefit analysis. Only very lately has a realization begun to dawn that reinvestment potential is a good basis neither for discounting environmental and social costs heavily, nor for placing an attractive premium on all revenues.

Still, late is better than never. The best reparation economists can make for their earlier advocacy of destructive policies is to adopt criteria of project appraisal which reflect the realities of exploitation and reinvestment. Such criteria are not always self-evident.

On the one hand, reflecting the high opportunity cost of capital in a high discount rate gives strong emphasis to rapid returns, but little weight to long-term environmental and social costs. Discount rates based on (often optimistic) estimates of the return on reinvestment therefore favour speedy deforestation over typical marginal projects while devaluing investment in long-term forestry. This has been so in quantitative project evaluations, as much as in sweeping policy pronouncements.

On the other hand, lower discount rates give more, but not necessarily sufficient emphasis to long-term costs. This effect may, however, be more than compensated by the increased weight which low discount rates would give to the revenues of deforestation, if they were to be reinvested.

But if the opportunity cost of capital is expressed as a premium on investment funds, and if only a portion of net revenues is deemed to be reinvested, a high opportunity cost of capital militates against deforestation. This more realistic view, combined with fuller appraisal of the external costs of deforestation, would certainly indicate a dramatic drop in the rate of destructive exploitation.

Appendix

In the following appraisal of a 'typical marginal project', the opportunity cost of investment funds is based on the value they would have attained, had they been devoted to the forest exploitation project outlined in Table 4.2. Sale of land in year 7 of this project is used to fund a continuing exploitation programme.

The present value of the net benefit stream from investing $1 000 000 in this alternative has three components:

1. net financial returns of $300 000 per year ($q = 30$ per cent), with distributed benefits weighted at 1;
2. consumption benefits to the labour force of $40 000 per year, weighted at 2.4 ($b = 9.6$ per cent);

3. lost subsistence benefits which accrue in a discontinuous manner: an extra stream of $15 000 per year, weighted at 8 (= –$120 000), is added after every six years following project initiation.

Using the formula quoted above and the same values of s and i as before, the OCIF per $ from (1) and (2) is

$$\$(0.30 - (0.1 \times 0.30) + 0.096) \div (0.06 - (0.1 \times 0.30)) = \$12.200$$

The delayed and discontinuous nature of (3) requires a more complex formulation:

$$\frac{[\text{Annual loss}]}{\begin{bmatrix} \text{Discount rate} \\ \text{adjusted for growth} \\ \text{of investment stream} \end{bmatrix}} \times \begin{bmatrix} \text{Multiplier for} \\ \text{discontinuous} \\ \text{increase in lost} \\ \text{subsistence} \end{bmatrix} \times \begin{bmatrix} \text{Discount factor} \\ \text{for delay until} \\ \text{opportunity costs} \\ \text{are initiated} \end{bmatrix}$$

$$\frac{-\$120\,000}{0.06 - 0.03} \times \frac{1.06^6}{1.06^6 - 1} \times \frac{1}{1.06^5} = -\$10\,131\,000$$

or a cost of $10.131 per $ invested.

Thus the weight on investment funds is 12.200 – 10.131 = 2.069. Table A.1 also uses this weight for net revenues, just as Table 4.2 uses 4.25 as the weight for investment funds and net revenues.

Table A1   Social cost-benefit analysis of 'typical marginal project'

Item	Year	Annual cash flow equivalent($)	Weight	Discounted value($)
Investment	0	1 000 000	2.069	–2 069 000
Income increase	1–∞	40 000	2.4	1 600 000
Financial profit	1–∞	120 000	2.069	4 138 000
Total				3 669 000

Note: For simplicity, all cash flows are allocated to the middle of the appropriate year when making discounting calculations.

References

Bruce, C. (1976), 'Social Cost Benefit Analysis', *World Bank Staff Working Paper*, 239, Washington, DC: World Bank.

Busby, R.J.N. (1985), *A Guide to Financial Analysis of Tree Growing*, Rome: FAO.

Feldstein, M.S. (1964), 'Net Social Benefit Calculation and the Public Investment Decision', *Oxford Economic Papers,* **16**, 114–31.

Feldstein, M.S. and Flemming, J.S. (1964), 'The Problem of Time-Stream Evaluation: Present Value versus Internal Rate of Return Rules', *Bulletin of the Oxford University Institute of Economics and Statistics,* **26**, 79–85.

Gane, M.(1969), 'Priorities in Planning', Commonwealth Forestry Institute Paper 43.

Hansen, J.R. (1978), *Guide to Practical Project Appraisal,* New York: United Nations.

Harou, P.A. (1985), 'On a Social Discount Rate for Forestry', *Canadian Journal of Forest Research,* **15**, 927–34.

Irvin, G. (1978), *Modern Cost-Benefit Methods,* London: Macmillan.

Kula, E. (1987), 'Social Interest Rate for Public Sector Project Appraisal in the UK, the US and Canada', *Project Appraisal,* **2**, (3), September, 169–74.

Little, I.M.D. and Mirrlees, J.A. (1974), *Project Appraisal and Planning for Developing Countries,* London: Heinemann.

Marglin, S.A. (1967), *Public Investment Criteria,* London: Allen and Unwin.

Nadkarni, M.V. (1989), *The Political Economy of Forest Use and Management,* New Delhi: Sage.

Overseas Development Administration (1988), *Appraisal of Projects in Developing Countries,* 3rd ed., London: HMSO.

Price, C. (1973), 'To the Future: with Indifference or Concern?', *Journal of Agricultural Economics,* **24**, 393–8.

Price, C. (1984), 'Project Appraisal and Planning for Overdeveloped Countries', *Environmental Management,* **8**, 221–42.

Price, C. (1989a), 'Equity, Consistency, Efficiency and New Rules for Discounting', *Project Appraisal,* **4**, (2), June, 58–64.

Price, C. (1989b), 'Social Discounting: a Game Played with Meaningless Marks on Paper', in M.C. Whitby and D.J. Dawson (eds), *Land Use for Agriculture, Forestry and Rural Development,* Proceedings of the 20th Symposium of the European Association of Agricultural Economists, Department of Agricultural Economics and Food Marketing, University of Newcastle upon Tyne.

Price, C. (1989c), *The Theory and Application of Forest Economics,* Oxford: Basil Blackwell.

Price, C. (1993), *Time, Discounting and Value,* Oxford: Basil Blackwell.

Price, C. and Nair, C.T.S. (1984), 'Cost-Benefit Analysis and the Consideration of Forestry Alternatives', *Journal of World Forest Resource Management,* **2**, 81–104.

Price, C. and Nair, C.T.S. (1985), 'Social Discounting and the Distribution of Project Benefits', *Journal of Development Studies,* **21**, 525–32.

Repetto, R. and Gillis, M. (1988), *Public Policies and the Misuse of Forest Resources,* Cambridge: Cambridge University Press.

Schallau, C.H. and Wirth, M.E. (1980), 'Reinvestment Rate and the Analysis of Forestry Enterprises', *Journal of Forestry,* **78**, 740–42.

Squire, L. and van der Tak, H. (1975), *Economic Appraisal of Projects,* Baltimore: Johns Hopkins University Press.

UNIDO (1972), *Guidelines for Project Evaluation,* New York: United Nations.

Weiss, J. (1980), *Practical Appraisal of Industrial Projects,* New York: United Nations.

Westoby, J.C. (1962), 'The Role of Forest Industries in the Attack on Economic Underdevelopment', *Unasylva,* **16**, 168–201.

Westoby, J.C. (1987), *The Purpose of Forests,* Oxford: Basil Blackwell.

5. Plantation appraisal under the threat of illicit felling

Colin Price and S.N. Trivedi

It is a sad but inevitable fact that projects do not always go to plan. It is an even sadder — though less inevitable — fact that project evaluators and managers are often tempted to present projects as though their success is assured, and to appraise them on that basis.

This is nowhere clearer than in the case of forestry, where an intimidating battery of climatic, biological, anthropogenic, economic and political agents threatens the survival of plantations throughout their life. Foresters are trained to treat plantation management as an orderly sequence of planned and sustainable operations, each falling in due time, with predictable inputs and predictable yields. Even when they encounter the different reality, there may be professional pressures to maintain the myth of the planned plantation. Forest economists (and the textbooks they peruse) generally follow the same tradition, applying discounting techniques to a known profile of cash (or cost and benefit) flows. Predictable plantation projects are more likely to be funded; and they are easier to evaluate.

Among the problems besetting managers of tropical plantation projects is the illicit removal of trees during the course of the planned rotation. Such fellings could have adverse effects, both by reducing the sustainable yield of existing plantations, and, possibly, by causing site deterioration with more permanent detriment to the productivity of the site. However, the seriousness ascribed to losses depends on three factors:

1. the way in which losses are physically concentrated in the plantation, and the subsequent pattern of plantation growth;
2. the boundary within which project costs and benefits are evaluated;
3. the criteria used to judge an investment whose financial, economic and social value is threatened by this attrition.

This chapter examines the effect of these factors on *Eucalyptus* plantations in Bihar State, India. It considers both overall viability of such plantation projects, and the rotation deemed to give the best returns, under a range of criteria.

Three models of the distribution and effect of illicit felling are presented, and the effect of each on project viability is shown.

Illicit Felling in Context

Two major causes of illicit felling in the tropics are rural poverty and the need-availability gap for fuelwood and other basic wood products. The former means that people cannot afford to obtain their wood requirements through regular markets. The latter works in a vicious downward spiral: the shortage of wood causes forest areas to be overexploited; that leads to declining productivity and, sometimes, to complete deforestation; that in turn reduces the sustainable out-turn of wood products; and that increases the pressure for unsustainable overexploitation of the remaining forest areas.

One development strategy in the face of this problem is to increase the area of high-productivity plantations — often exotics, among which the genus *Eucalyptus* is the most widely planted. But these plantations, too, are subject to illicit felling, especially where tribal populations have been displaced from their traditional lands to make way for such plantations.

Response to such a perceived threat is perhaps predictable. Forest administrations in India and worldwide have traditionally been revenue orientated. Selling a coupe with high out-turn per hectare, at a high price per cubic metre, is considered a matter of pride among forest managers: illicit felling is seen as a threat to perceived professional competence. Thus forest departments treat incidents of illicit felling, by and large, as an administrative rather than an economic problem. Usually, enquiries are set up to fix the responsibility, if any, of the staff, and offence reports are drawn against the culprits. However, the basis of all these actions is the reported cases, which are few and far between in comparison with the number of actual occurrences. So wide and intense are the incidents of illicit felling that drawing reports against offenders and penalizing some officers in a few reported cases, coupled with weak forest laws and general sympathy for impoverished offenders, becomes an administrative exercise in futility, as far as its impact on deterring future incidents is concerned.

In the meantime, working plans continue to be written without reference to the causes and impacts of this apparently inevitable phenomenon. This official 'turning of a blind eye' has led to lack of formal investigation into the actual effects of illicit felling on forests. In some areas an anecdotal figure of '10 per cent loss per year' is estimated, but without specification of how the loss is distributed. It is, however, possible to model the mechanisms of loss from the forest, and this is done below.

The basic models of forest growth are those presented by Sharma (1978), which show expected volume for *Eucalyptus* of various productivity, planted at various densities. Three possible kinds of illicit felling are considered.

Model 1:   Illicit felling entails removal of all trees from a concentrated area. The plantation is wiped out, and no further wood production takes place unless and until the area is replanted.

Model 2:   Illicit fellings are scattered through the forest. Volume is removed, but more-or-less complete forest cover remains, and the total volume increment is unaffected.

Model 3:   Illicit fellings are scattered, but the removal of trees leads to a loss of volume increment commensurate with the reduced stocking.

Further details of these models are given in Trivedi (1987) and Trivedi and Price (1988).

Financial Models of Threat Appraisal

The datum against which the economic effects of illicit felling are to be judged is the performance of unaffected plantations. Table 5.1 shows predicted cash flows for the most productive *Eucalyptus* — quality class I — in the absence of illicit felling. Tables 5.2 to 5.4 also refer to quality class I publications. Net present value (NPV) for one crop rotation and net present value for an infinite series of plantings and replantings (NPVinf) are given for rotation lengths from 1 to 15 years. A discount rate of 10 per cent is used. All but the shortest rotations are profitable. The value of land for plantations in perpetuity is indicated by NPVinf. This is maximized by adopting a rotation of 14 years.

For a given physical kind of illicit felling, the threat of loss may reduce the value ascribed to plantations for two reasons.

1.   The mean expected revenue to the forest department is reduced.
2.   The variability of that revenue is increased — receipts and profits become less predictable.

Variability of revenues should, however, only be considered a problem for risk-averse organizations. Governments usually have a large and diversified portfolio of investments of which individual plantations form a minute part, and it is argued that they should not be risk averse (Arrow and Lind 1970): projects should be evaluated according to their mean expected discounted cash flow. Nonetheless, for individual managers a single plantation may form a large part of their responsibility, and a certain revenue may be preferred to an unpredictable one of the same mean expected value.

Both factors may be quantified by adding a premium to the discount rate. If 10 per cent of plantations are lost each year, then the mean expected value of a given revenue is reduced at 10 per cent compound per year: this is no more

*Table 5.1   Discounted cash flow for various rotations — no illicit felling;
cash flows in rupees.*

Operation	Time	Cash flow	NPV	NPVinf
Establish crop	0	–3 976		
Weed and repair	1	–496		
(Final felling)	1	31	–4 399	–48 388
Repair fence	2	–96		
(Final felling)	2	1 674	–3 123	–17 993
(Final felling)	3	7 053	–792	3 186
(Final felling)	4	15 425	6 029	19 019
(Final felling)	5	24 709	11 457	30 223
(Final felling)	6	37 202	16 493	37 869
(Final felling)	7	49 482	20 886	42 900
(Final felling)	8	62 297	24 555	46 028
(Final felling)	9	75 486	27 507	47 763
(Final felling)	10	88 948	29 787	48 476
(Final felling)	11	104 126	31 989	49 251
(Final felling)	12	123 057	34 703	50 932
(Final felling)	13	142 594	36 798	51 804
(Final felling)	14	162 637	38 321	*52 019
(Final felling)	15	183 106	*39 328	51 706

Notes:
1.   For simplicity, cash flow are assigned to points in time, not distributed over time.
2.   General management costs, which are independent of age or rotation length, are omitted.
3.   * indicates the optimal rotation period under the two criteria.

than a matter of arithmetic. It is also claimed that the variability element explains the rates of return at which investors are willing to adopt risky projects, particularly through the capital asset pricing model (Sharpe 1964; Lintner 1965). Table 5.2 shows the effect of adding a risk premium to a basic 10 per cent discount rate. Column 2 interprets the 10 per cent annual loss as a simple addition to the discount rate. In reality, however, discount factors interact multiplicatively. A 10 per cent discount for illicit felling together with a 10 per cent normal discount gives a joint discount rate of $(1 + 10\%) \times (1 + 10\%) - 1 = 21\%$. This rate is used for column 3. Thirdly, column 4 considers somewhat more analytically the meaning of '10 per cent loss'. Logically, it implies a remainder of 90 per cent. Thus the discount factor should be $90\% / (1 + 10\%) = 0.81818$ which yields a discount rate of $1 / 0.81818 - 1 = 22.22\%$.

Table 5.2   Risk premia and more apt models of threat; cash flows rupees

Rotation	NPVinf @ 20%	NPVinf @ 21%	NPVinf @ 22.22%	Explicit model 1	Replant on loss
6	12 032	10 742	9 592	15 415	19 181
7	12 974	*11 507	*10 204	*15 813	*20 406
8	*13 072	11 491	10 092	15 115	20 180
9	12 619	10 972	9 522	13 815	19 041

Notes:
1. For simplicity, cash flow are assigned to points in time, not distributed over time.
2. General management costs, which are independent of age or rotation length, are omitted.
3. * indicates the optimal rotation period.

These apparently trivial differences in interpretation of risk premium cause substantial differences in NPVinf, and even lead to a slight shortening of the optimal rotation. All rotations are much shorter than for crops without illicit felling: as expected, the higher discount rate gives emphasis to short-term revenues. In the explicit model 1, the advantage of early felling lies in harvesting forest areas before they are illicitly destroyed.

The discount rate premium approach to risk is widely discussed (Bromwich 1976). But it is also widely condemned. Firstly, it embodies an assumption, not generally valid, that the level of risk remains constant through the lifetime of a project (see Chapter 3 in this volume). The assumption is particularly inappropriate for biological systems like forests whose vulnerability to various threats may alter dramatically through their life-cycle. In models 1 to 3, however, for the sake of simplicity, a constant level of attrition through the life-cycle is assumed.

Secondly, risk is unlikely to be cumulative from one investment cycle to the next (Price 1993). Thus an annual threat of 10 per cent loss compounds to a survival probability to the end of a 15-year rotation of $(100 - 10 \text{ per cent})^{15} = 24$ per cent. When the crop is harvested (illicitly or otherwise) the slate is wiped clean. The replacement crop has the same 24 per cent probability of surviving to age 15 as its predecessor. And yet incorporating a 10 per cent risk factor in the discount rate has the effect of reducing survival probability endlessly through time: the replacement crop is given a survival probability of only $(100 - 10\%)^{30} = 6\%$.

In the explicit model 1 the value of one 15-year rotation is determined from the revenue, Rs 183 106, at that age, multiplied by the probability, 24 per cent, of surviving to that age, multiplied by the discount factor, 0.23939, for 15 years at the normal 10 per cent discount rate, giving a present value of Rs 43 834. Explicit model 1 in fact gives the same result, for any single rotation, as the equivalent single rotation using a 22.22 per cent risk-adjusted discount rate. The difference between the approaches only becomes apparent when one applies the multiplier for an infinite series of rotations

$$[1 + (\text{discount rate})]^{(\text{rotation})} / \{[1 + (\text{discount rate})]^{(\text{rotation})} - 1\}$$

This is much smaller for the risk premium approach, reflecting its undervaluation of second and subsequent rotations. The magnitude of the resulting difference is shown in Table 5.2.

But explicit model 1 is itself deficient in its assumptions about the second and subsequent rotations, because the infinite series multiplier is based on the planned optimal rotation. In reality, the rotation is likely (with 76 per cent probability for a 15-year rotation) to end before the planned time. While this in itself is undesirable, there is some compensation in that successor rotations can be initiated earlier. The overall effect can be determined as follows.

Let M be the mean expected value of an infinite series of rotations of T years. Whenever felling, planned or illicit, occurs, another series of rotations is initiated. This also has value M at the time of initiation, but the value has to be discounted to the beginning of the first rotation. Considering failure and reinitiation at yearly intervals,

$$
M = \begin{bmatrix} \text{probability} \\ \text{of achieving} \\ \text{planned rotation} \end{bmatrix} \times \left\{ \begin{bmatrix} \text{discounted} \\ \text{revenue from} \\ \text{planned rotation} \end{bmatrix} + \begin{bmatrix} \text{discounted } M \\ \text{from planned} \\ \text{successor crops} \end{bmatrix} \right\} -
$$

$$
\begin{bmatrix} \text{planting} \\ \text{cost} \end{bmatrix} + \sum_{t-1}^{t-T} \begin{bmatrix} \text{probability of} \\ \text{illicit felling} \\ \text{in year } t \end{bmatrix} \times \begin{bmatrix} M \text{ for} \\ \text{replacement} \\ \text{crops} \end{bmatrix} \times \begin{bmatrix} \text{discount} \\ \text{factor for} \\ t \text{ years} \end{bmatrix}
$$

Rearrangement gives a bulky but straightforward formula for M. This approach to evaluating uncertain rotation periods is discussed more fully elsewhere (Price 1989: chapter 17). A QUATTRO-PRO spreadsheet for accelerating the rather tedious calculations is available from Colin Price.

As the last column in Table 5.2 shows, the resulting adjustment in NPV, compared with explicit model 1 which considers only replacement after the planned rotation, is considerable.

In all the following model 1 calculations, it is assumed that crops will be replanted in the year following illicit removal, and NPVinf is calculated according to the formula above.

The internal rates of return (IRRs) — the highest rates of discount at which the plantation does not make a loss — are 43 per cent in the absence of illicit felling, and 28 per cent for model 1. Both occur on a six-year rotation.

Under none of the evaluative systems above are the less productive plantations (designated as quality classes II and III) profitable.

Alternative Models of Attrition

The financial effect of illicit felling may be much less serious if removals are scattered through the forest, rather than occurring as concentrated deforestations. Table 5.3 shows the effect on NPV of each of the explicit models.

Table 5.3   Different physical models of illicit felling; cash flows in rupees

Rotation	Net present values			
	No illicit	Model 1	Model 2	Model 3
6	37 869	19 181	36 695	21 971
7	42 900	*20 406	40 882	*23 283
8	46 028	20 180	44 865	23 150
9	47 763	19 041	49 342	22 125
10	48 476	17 355	52 004	21 996
11	49 251	15 744	53 214	21 357
12	50 932	14 566	*53 288	20 201
13	51 804	13 067	52 493	18 721
14	*52 019	11 388	51 050	17 057
15	51 706	9 632	49 136	15 312

Notes:
1.   For simplicity, cash flow are assigned to points in time, not distributed over time.
2.   General management costs, which are independent of age or rotation length, are omitted.
3.   * indicates the optimal rotation period.

In model 2, for which forest increment is not reduced by illicit felling, NPVs of all rotations are greater than in model 1. Since the disadvantages of crop loss are less, there is less incentive for the forest department to undertake pre-emptive felling, and the optimal rotation is much longer. (Felling at the model 1 optimum would reduce NPV by 25 per cent.)

What is more surprising is that the maximum NPV in model 2 exceeds that with no illicit felling. This is explained by the thinning effect. With scattered removal of trees, volume increment is concentrated onto a smaller number of trees, each of which subsequently grows faster. Since a much better price per cubic metre is paid for large trees, total revenue per hectare may be greater for a plantation with low total volume but high individual tree volume.

Of course, it is technically feasible for the forest department itself to carry out the thinning and achieve benefits in final felling revenue. However, lack of resources, or administrative factors, may prevent this happening. Hagerdon and Wong (1986) report a parallel case from the United States, where illicit felling was institutionalized: the local population paid a nominal fee for the right to remove marked stems; the forest department achieved improved tree growth at no cost to itself.

Despite the thinning effect, model 3 does not give dramatically higher NPVs than model 1. The beneficial effect on tree size is largely offset by the reduced increment associated with a smaller number of trees per hectare.

Lower quality classes of plantation also show improved performance. Quality class II is profitable under models 2 and 3, with IRRs of 14.5 per cent and 11.3 per cent respectively (both on a 15-year rotation). This compares with 13.5 per cent (14 years) with no illicit felling, and only 2.1 per cent (15 years) under model 1. Quality class III remains unprofitable.

Social Forestry by Default

During the last 20 years, social forestry, in contradistinction to industrial forestry, has come into vogue. 'Making trees serve people' (Westoby 1975) has become a popular slogan, entailing plantation and small woodlot formation specifically for local use. Within this philosophy, illicit felling is just another term for 'harvesting non-market products', an activity which has received much attention in the recent literature.

Table 5.4   Models 1 and 3 under financial and economic appraisal; cash flows in rupees

Rotation	Model 1		Model 3	
	Financial	Economic	Financial	Economic
6	19 181	28 824	21 972	29 750
7	*20 046	32 599	*23 283	33 498
8	20 180	34 834	23 150	35 717
9	19 041	36 020	22 125	36 897
10	17 355	36 499	21 996	38 877
11	15 744	36 924	21 357	40 288
12	14 566	37 704	20 201	41 088
13	13 067	38 050	18 721	41 436
14	11 388	*38 084	17 057	*41 457
15	9 632	37 901	15 312	41 248

Notes:
1. For simplicity, cash flow are assigned to points in time, not distributed over time.
2. General management costs, which are independent of age or rotation length, are omitted.
3. * indicates the optimal rotation period.

Including such non-market benefits is, in theory, a routine part of economic appraisal. Table 5.4 shows the result of doing so. Illicit fellings are regarded as having an equivalent cash value to legitimate fellings of trees of the same size. For both models and all rotations there is, as expected, an increase in NPV. Since longer rotations entail a greater proportion of wood being harvested illicitly, the increase in NPV through including illicit felling value is greater (proportionately and absolutely) for longer rotations. This leads to dramatic lengthening of optimal rotations under the economic criterion: if illicit fellings are given value parity with forest department fellings, there is no pressure to fell early simply to annex revenue to the department.

For quality classes II and III, all rotations remain unprofitable under economic appraisal in model 1. However, model 2 gives better results (see Table 5.5).

Table 5.5 *Lower quality classes under various models: 15-year rotation in all cases; cash flows in rupees*

| | Quality Class II | | Quality Class III | |
Rotation	Financial	Economic	Financial	Economic
No illicit	3 459	3 459	−2 980	−2 990
Model 1	−3 914	−2 503	−8 387	−7 612
Model 2	4 798	12 408	−1 921	194
Model 3	1 122	6 860	−4 753	−3 927

Notes:
1. For simplicity, cash flow are assigned to points in time, not distributed over time.
2. General management costs, which are independent of age or rotation length, are omitted.

In quality class II, model 2 greatly outperforms no illicit felling, and quality class III achieves, for the first time, a small profit.

Financial, Economic and Social Cost-benefit Analysis

Of course, different perspectives on cost-benefit analysis entail different ways of pricing, as well as different definitions of what is to count as cost and benefit. Table 5.6 compiles results from three approaches (for details, see Trivedi 1987).

In the financial cost-benefit analysis, as before, the prices and relevant cash flows are only those facing the project agency — the forest department — and the discount rate is the rate of interest (after adjustment for inflation).

In the economic cost-benefit analysis the shadow prices represent gains and losses of products and resources to the national economy, in this case of India, irrespective of who makes cash transactions, or whether such transactions are made at all. Thus not only are illicit fellings included as benefits, but also labour is priced at its opportunity cost, which during periods of labour surplus is considered to be zero. The 10 per cent financial rate of discount is replaced by a 14.52 per cent estimated marginal productivity of capital (see Phillips (1986) and Adhikari (1987) for discussion of methods to estimate this in practice).

Table 5.6 *Optimal rotations for quality class I plantations, under financial, economic and social prices (model 3); cash flows in rupees*

Rotation	Financial NPVinf	Economic NPVinf	Social NPVinf
6	21 971	20 584	503 847
7	*23 283	22 117	635 284
8	23 150	22 809	725 294
9	22 125	22 941	785 808
10	21 996	23 557	867 369
11	21 357	23 871	932 958
12	20 201	*23 878	980 229
13	18 721	23 678	1 012 858
14	17 057	23 349	1 033 837
15	15 312	22 943	*1 045 588

Notes:
1. For simplicity, cash flow are assigned to points in time, not distributed over time.
2. General management costs, which are independent of age or rotation length, are omitted.
3. * indicates the optimal rotation period.

The social cost-benefit analysis follows the general philosophy detailed by Little and Mirrlees (1974), Squire and van der Tak (1975), Weiss (1980), ODA (1988) and Price (1989); values relate to the Indian case. The numeraire (the unit in which values are measured) is consumption by individuals having mean income. The discount rate is taken to be the consumption rate of interest, generally expressed as $CRI = ng + p$ where n is the absolute of elasticity of marginal utility of consumption, g is the growth rate in real consumption per head, and p the pure time preference rate. The estimation for n was 2.07, using the method discussed by Fellner (1967), g was estimated at 0.95 per cent. No pure time preference was included, for reasons elaborated in Price (1993). The result is a discount rate of 1.97 per cent.

Consumption weights are inversely related to consumption level, and are also based on the above-estimated value of n, giving weights of 2.705 for the lower half of the income distribution profile (assumed to include the illicit fellers) and 1.618 for the population generally.

The weight on government investment funds was calculated using a complex formula given by Bruce (1976), the assumptions being:

- the real rate of return on investment is 14.52 per cent (as for economic cost benefit analysis);
- 22 per cent of revenues from investment are reinvested;
- the discount rate is 1.97 per cent (as above);
- the consumption benefits of investment accrue to the population generally, with a weight of 1.618.

The resultant weight on government investment funds was 11.894. However, a weight of only 3.878 was assigned to government revenues, on the grounds that only a proportion of them (22 per cent) would be reinvested (see Price, Chapter 4 in this volume, for a discussion of this issue).

The shadow wage rate was determined on the basis of transfers between government and workers, the weights being those given above.

Economic analysis uses a higher discount rate than financial analysis, and would be expected to produce a shorter optimal rotation. However, this factor is outweighed by the advantages of lengthening the rotation, once benefits to the illicit fellers are included.

The high values in the social analysis are attributable to:

(a) the high weights applied to department revenues and benefits to illicit fellers;
(b) the low discount rate, which enhances the value of first and (particularly) subsequent rotations.

Even with model 3 (increment reduced by illicit felling) illicit felling may increase NPV. For example, in quality class II, illicit felling is beneficial if departmental revenues are only partially reinvested (weight 3.878), but it reduces NPV if departmental revenues are wholly reinvested (weight 11.894) or if illicit removals are made by individuals spread across the income distribution profile (weight 1.618).

In all circumstances, model 2 illicit felling produced a superior result to no illicit felling.

For completeness it can be recorded that, under social cost-benefit analysis, quality class II plantations give net benefit for all models of illicit felling. For quality class III plantations, however, only model 2 gives net benefit. In the other models the high weight on initial investment funds more-than-balances the high values attributed to illicit fellings.

The overall picture is that economic and social cost-benefit analysis both evaluate plantations subject to illicit felling more favourably than financial appraisal does. Both suggest, at least under models 2 and 3 of illicit felling, that lower quality classes may pass project adoption tests, and both imply lengthened crop rotations.

Conclusion

The sentiments expressed above may seem to suggest that illicit felling, far from being a major problem, might be a blessing in disguise. This conclusion might legitimately be drawn, if it could always be assumed that felling would occur according to model 2. The case for tolerating, or even encouraging illicit felling could then be made whenever departmental resources do not suffice to make timely thinnings. Even when such resources are available, it may be better to permit illicit felling, if higher weight is given to consumption by the impoverished than to departmental revenue. Plantation projects thus would act as an instrument of redistributive policy, which may be particularly appropriate for peoples in a subsistence economy. (Whether monocultures of exotic species provide the desirable product mix for such peoples is another question.)

In practice, models 1 and 3 may be more realistic. Model 1 always gives undesirable results. Illicit removal of timber occurs before the optimal time, whether this is judged in physical, economic or social terms. Moreover, there may be a substantial time lag between illicit felling and departmental replanting of the site. In extreme cases the site may be abandoned, either because of site deterioration or because departmental officials become disheartened by repeated failure. This results in (possibly permanent) loss of sustainable production.

Model 3 is more equivocal. On the one hand, the thinning effect is beneficial to price per cubic metre. On the other, serious loss of sustained biomass production occurs, the more so as the rotation proceeds. If biomass production is the critical factor, as when fuelwood is the dominant need, model 3 always gives lower sustainable production than a plantation free of illicit felling. The problem is particularly serious if the loss of overall productivity increases pressure on remaining resources. For example, cow-dung may be used as an alternative fuel, diverting it from use as a fertilizer, with implications for the sustainability of agriculture; other forest areas, possibly on more fragile soils, may be pressed into production; or more intensive exploitation of the same plantation may take place, with further reduction of increment.

The purpose of this chapter is not to suggest which model is most appropriate, since this must be a matter of local judgement. Instead, we aim to demonstrate that it matters rather critically, to physical productivity as to economic profitability, how illicit felling takes place: there is a pressing need for systematic investigation of the physical nature of the phenomenon.

Then, and only then, can forest managers and project appraisers respond appropriately. In particular, it is vital that the response of forest managers to illicit felling is not a panic one, motivated by a desire to maximize departmental revenues by premature felling. This leads to even lower volume out-turn than model 1, which in turn vitiates the role of plantations in relieving regional shortages.

As for project appraisers, they need to inform themselves of the local circumstances of illicit felling, to obtain realistic estimates of its effects, and to incorporate the results, even at the cost of more effort, into their analyses. Only then can project design and funding respond appropriately to the phenomenon.

References

Adhikari, R. (1987), 'Estimation of Economic Discount Rate for Practical Project Appraisal: the Case of Nepal', *Project Appraisal,* **2**, 113–22.

Arrow, K.J. and Lind, R.C. (1970), 'Uncertainty and the Evaluation of Public Investment Decisions', *American Economic Review,* **60**, 364–78.

Bromwich, M. (1976), *The Economics of Capital Budgeting,* Harmondsworth: Penguin.

Bruce, C. (1976), 'Social Cost-Benefit Analysis', *World Bank Staff Working Paper,* 239, Washington, DC: World Bank.

Fellner, W. (1967), 'Operational Utility: the Theoretical Background and Measurement', in W. Fellner (ed.), *Ten Economic Studies in the Tradition of Irving Fisher,* New York: Wiley.

Hagerdon, C.W. and Wong, C.P. (1986), 'Thinning in Exchange for Firewood', *Journal of Forestry,* **84**, (7), 44–6.

Lintner, J. (1965), 'The Valuation of Risk Assets and the Selection of Risky Investments in Stock Portfolios and Capital Budgets', *Review of Economics and Statistics,* 47, 13–37.

Little, I.M.D. and Mirrlees, J.A. (1974), *Project Appraisal and Planning for Developing Countries,* London: Heinemann.

ODA (1988), *Appraisal of Projects in Developing Countries,* London: HMSO.

Phillips, D.A. (1986), 'Pitfalls in Estimating Social Discount Rates: a Case Study', *Project Appraisal,* **1**, 15–20.

Price, C. (1989), *The Theory and Application of Forest Economics,* Oxford: Blackwell.

Price, C. (1993), *Time. Discounting and Value,* Oxford: Blackwell.

Sharma, R.P. (1978), 'Yield Tables for *Eucalyptus* Hybrid (Plantation) for Various Levels of Stocking', Indian Forester, **104**, 387–97.

Sharpe, W.F. (1964), 'Capital Asset Prices: a Theory of Market Equilibrium', *Journal of Finance,* **19**, 425–42.

Squire, L. and van der Tak, H. (1975), *Economic Appraisal of Projects,* Baltimore: Johns Hopkins University Press.

Trivedi, S.N. (1987), *Utility-based Social Shadow Pricing and its Comparison with Other Evaluation Techniques: a Cost-Benefit Study of Fuelwood Plantations in Bihar. India,* unpublished PhD thesis, University College of North Wales.

Trivedi, S.N. and Price, C. (1988), 'The Incidence of Illicit Felling in Afforestation Project Appraisal: Some Models Illustrated for Eucalyptus Plantations in India', *Journal of World Forest Resource Management,* **3**, 129–40.

Weiss, J.(1980), *Practical Appraisal of Industrial Projects,* UNIDO, New York: United Nations.

Westoby, J. (1975), 'Making Trees Serve People', *Commonwealth Forestry Review,* **54**, 206–15.

6. Deforesting the Amazon: towards an economic solution

David Pearce

Probably the most popular explanation for deforestation and other examples of environmental degradation is that they are caused by a combination of population pressure and poverty. Population growth and pressures for commercialization of crops, we are told, force poor farmers to cultivate marginal areas and eliminate fallow periods in traditional crop rotations. The result is the 'colonization' of forests and ultimately, their removal.[1] There is undoubted truth in this story, but it is far from being a correct generalization. Many forces are at work in bringing about environmental degradation. An enlightening perspective can be gained by pursuing a somewhat different line of inquiry based on environmental economics.

Environmental economics stresses the links between economic incentives and environmental loss.[2] The basic guideline is that where environmental destruction is taking place, it is useful to look at the way the economy is managed. This guideline reflects a more general view that economy and environment are inextricably interlinked. Whatever is done in the economy has an impact on the environment, for better or for worse. If there is a change in the economy, the very fact that economic activity necessarily uses up materials and energy means that change will also occur in the environment. The economic change could range from building a road to altering a central bank interest rate; both actions would have an environmental impact.

If this view is right, then the same approach can be inverted: we can manage the economy in such a way as to minimize any environmental impact. Doing so is possible through links between economic activity and environmental impact. An extra $1 of gross national product (GNP) does not have to produce the same emissions of carbon dioxide, say, as the previous $1 of GNP. Technology has the capacity to alter the coefficient between GNP and CO_2 releases.

Much environmental degradation in the developing world can be traced to economic mismanagement. Better economic policy will frequently foster better environmental quality. In arguing for the importance of the economic dimension, we must not lose sight of the underlying problems caused by excessive population growth and poverty. But popular explanations of environmental degradation that are based solely on the poverty-population nexus point toward impossibly grand solutions. If poverty causes environmental loss, then only the removal of poverty can be expected to solve environmental problems. If population growth is the culprit, then only massive changes to population policy will solve the problem. Either way, while both objectives are self-evidently laudable,[3] they divert attention away from more immediately effective policy in the sphere of economic management.

This chapter examines how the economic approach can be applied to deforestation problems in one area of the world, the Amazon region of Brazil. It studies rates of forest loss, the factors that cause it, the economic value of the forest, and the ways in which deforestation may be contained through economic policy.

Deforestation of the Amazon

Figure 6.1 shows a map of the Amazon region of Brazil. 'Legal Amazonia' is an area of some 5 million km^2 and is larger than 'classic Amazonia' (or the 'North Region').

Figure 6.1   The Brazilian Amazon

Source: Adapted from Goodman and Hall (1990).

Legal Amazonia includes the states of Mato Grosso, Acre, Amapá, Amazonas, Pará, Rondônia, Roraima and large parts of Goiás and Maranhão. Classic Amazonia is made up of Acre, Amapá, Amazonas, Pará, Rondônia and Roraima. When referring to the Amazon region, care must be taken to ensure that the two definitions are not confused. The rain forest coincides approximately with the classic region, but deforestation is extensive in the Maranhão, Mato Grosso and Goiás, i.e., the areas outside the rain forest. Table 6.1 shows one set of estimates of deforestation in terms of percentages of the area of legal Amazonia. Note that the forested area of legal Amazonia is not 5 million km^2, but it is customary to express deforestation as a fraction of the total area of legal Amazonia whether it was ever forested or not.

Deforestation estimates are disputed however. The data in Table 6.1 suggest that something like 400 000 km^2 have been deforested (that is 8 per cent of 4.9 million km^2). Table 6.1 is constructed from official estimates of Brazil's National Space Research Institute (INPE), based on the interpretation of LANDSAT imagery. The estimates are significantly lower than some suggesting that total deforestation may be as high as 600 000 km (Mahar 1989). There are some reasons for supposing that the lower estimates are closer to the truth. Table 6.1 clearly indicates a marked increase in the rate of deforestation in the 1980s, but suggests that this rate has slowed markedly in the last few years. Preliminary estimates for 1990 suggest a clearance rate of perhaps 20 000 km^2 compared to the following annual average rates implicit in Table 6.1:

1975–78	16 200 km^2
1978–80	24 000 km^2
1980–88	59 227 km^2

Myers (1989) suggests that deforestation was some 50 000 km^2 in 1987 and 48 000 km^2 in 1988, with a speculative estimate of 50 000 km^2 for 1989. INPE estimates suggest rates of deforestation as follows:

1987	80 000 km^2
1988	48 000 km^2
1989	24 000 km^2

As we shall see, the suggested decline from an abnormal peak in 1987 is consistent with events in Brazil.

Table 6.1 Rates of deforestation in the Brazilian legal Amazonia

State or territory	Area (000km²)	% of area classified as clear				
		1975	1978	1980	1988	1989
Acre	153.7	0.8	1.6	3.0	4.7	5.7
Amapá	140.3	0.1	0.1	0.1	0.4	0.6
Amazonas	1567.1	0.1	0.1	0.2	1.0	1.2
Maranhão	257.4	24.5	26.2	27.5	31.6	34.0
Mato Grosso	802.4	1.1	3.2	6.1	8.9	9.9
Pará	1248.0	3.3	4.3	5.3	10.2	11.3
Rondônia	243.0	0.5	2.7	3.2	12.2	13.2
Roraima	230.1	0.0	0.1	0.2	1.1	1.6
Tocantins	269.9	1.3	3.8	4.2	7.8	8.3
Total	4912.0	2.4	3.4	4.4	7.3	8.0

Note: All areas calculated within legal Amazonia only. The Pará Maranhão estimates include the old 'Bragantina' zone around the northern borders of these states — an area of about 92 000 km².
Source: Reis and Margulis (1990).

Why Does Deforestation Occur?

Popular explanations for Brazilian deforestation tend to emphasize population growth, logging and the poverty that forces small shift and burn farmers to clear new tracts of forest land. But the reality is more complicated.

Population Growth

Table 6.2 shows estimates of net migration up to 1980. Migration to Amazonia certainly increased rapidly in the late 1960s and throughout the 1970s. The estimate of roughly 750 000 migrants in the 1970s needs to be put into perspective. Some 16 million Brazilians migrated to urban centres in the same period. Nonetheless, a gain of even less than a million people is sufficient to damage fragile ecosystems. The data for Rondônia suggest a decline in migration from a peak in 1986. In part, this reflects changing demographic forces: the pool of migrants of the relevant age group began to stabilize in the 1970s and probably peaked because of urbanization and fertility decline. Thus, one of the 'push' factors encouraging migration can be expected to become less important.

Table 6.2   Net migration rates to Amazonia (000s)

	1940–50	1950–60	1960–70	1970–80
Amazonian frontier*	–2	9	16	764

	1977	1980	1984	1986	1988
Rondônia	6	49	153	166	52

* 'Classic' Amazonia plus Mato Grosso.
Source: Martine (1989).

Southgate (1990) has analysed factors giving rise to tropical deforestation in Latin America generally. Using multiple regression analysis, Southgate finds the following linkages between the expansion of agricultural land area and determining factors:

- One per cent change in population growth induces a 0.25 per cent change in agricultural land.
- One per cent change in agricultural export growth induces a 0.03 per cent change in agricultural land.
- One per cent increase in agricultural yields reduces land expansion by 0.20 per cent. That is, if yields rise, they can offset some 80 per cent of the effect of population growth.

Southgate's work suggests that population growth is a major factor in explaining frontier colonization. The particular importance of the study, however, lies in the policy implication that raising yields on agricultural land can, to a considerable extent, offset colonization tendencies. This finding suggests the value of giving priority to yield-raising activity on existing agricultural land and on degraded forest land, together with other actions discussed below.

Land prices

An economic insight into the migration process in Brazil is provided by an analysis of land prices. Table 6.3 shows land prices in absolute and relative terms for selected years. The notable feature is that land prices rose very rapidly in the south until 1986, but the peak in the north occurred in 1982. This means that, up to 1982, the relative attractiveness of selling land in the south and buying it in the north increased, but after 1982 it fell. In 1970, for example, a farmer could buy 1.6 hectares of land in the north for every hectare sold in the south. In 1982, some 15 hectares of northern land could be purchased for one hectare in the south; this change reflected rapid rises in land prices in the south. By 1986–7, the ratio had fallen back to 7 hectares of northern land for one of southern land. High ratios would encourage extensive land uses such as cattle ranching, and would turn small farmers into medium or large landholding farmers.

Table 6.3   Land prices in Brazil

	South	North	South/North
1970	165	100	1.65
1975	679	78	8.70
1980	586	55	10.65
1982	837	56	14.95
1983	766	84	9.12
1986	1409	201	7.00
1987	941	135	6.97

Note: Index of real land prices: 1970=100.
Source: Schneider (1990).

Some of the factors underlying these relative land prices are also interesting and indicative of the economic factors at work. Subsidies to agriculture and ranching had the effect of stimulating the demand for land in the north, as we shall see. Population growth alone does not explain the migration trends.

The land price analysis suggests that, in part, market forces are responsible for migration and hence deforestation. The change in the relative land price suggests that these market forces are playing themselves out, reducing the pressure on Amazonia.

Nutrient mining

Schneider (1990) has suggested that the motivation for migration is to be found in the concept of nutrient mining. While it is popularly thought that nutrients in tropical forests are concentrated primarily in the biomass and not in the soils, the truth is that they are distributed both above and below ground (Whitmore 1990:chapter 8). In the case of Brazilian lowland rain forest, however, the bulk of nutrients tend to be above ground in the biomass.

The capture of the economic value of these above- and below-ground nutrients takes place through various activities. Selective logging extracts the timber value; burning converts plant mineral nutrients to ash, thus improving the nutrients in the soil so that it may support crops; ranching extracts the last remaining soil nutrients. According to this analysis, tropical forests are being treated as exhaustible rather than renewable resources, and nutrient mining is therefore inherently unsustainable as an activity unless there is a substantial reserve to frontier land to turn to, once the mining is complete. It will always pay to invest in frontier expansion if it is cheaper to do so than to raise productivity on existing land. The private cost-benefit comparison is between:

(a) new land with low initial pest incidence (an effect of burning) and requirements for fertilizer (because of the new supply of natural soil nutrients plus the converted biomass nutrients); and
(b) existing or 'old' land, where nutrients need to be purchased and pest control will be required immediately.

The most important factors that bias the choice toward new land in Brazil are: road building, the open-access nature of frontier land, and subsidies.

Road building
There would have been little colonization of Amazonia without federal road-building programmes. As roads are opened, logging can take place and agriculturists can follow. The clearest indicator of the influence of road building is that, when the federal Amazon road-building programme largely came to a halt at the end of the 1980s, it produced a relative shortage of agriculturally productive land in the north and thus forced up the price of land. This effect is seen to some extent in Table 6.3, which shows the rise in land prices in the north as the road-building programme lost momentum in the mid-1980s. Government road policy also switched its emphasis to the paving of existing roads, especially BR-364 through Rondônia; this change increased pressure toward Rondônia and away from the northern areas.

Subsidies and tenure
A great deal of deforestation would be avoided if markets were allowed to function more efficiently. It is because of direct government interference that the price signals are distorted making timber extraction and, more important, clearance (usually by fire) for agriculture profitable. The forms taken by this interference are well-established and have included, in the case of Brazil:

● tax credits whereby the costs of investment in forest land clearance for cattle ranching can be offset against income tax; and
● subsidized credit for crops and livestock development (Mahar 1989, Binswanger 1989, Repetto and Gillis 1988).

Table 6.4 indicates the size of the credits and incentives.

Table 6.4   Livestock incentives in the Amazon

Year	Fiscal incentives ($m)	Livestock credit ($m)	Total ($m)	Real interest rate (%)
1971	345	35	381	−5.8
1975	238	151	389	−13.0
1980	102	99	201	−38.8
1985	153	52	204	−3.8
1987	156	100	256	n.a.

Source: Schneider (1990).

Equally important in the bias towards clearance is the status of land tenure. Forest-dwellers frequently have no secure rights to the land, with the result that outsiders can readily establish rights through clearance. Indeed, in many cases, clearance of the land is a prerequisite for claiming land rights (Southgate *et al.* 1991). In the event of competition for rights, the agricultural colonists invariably win. Providing security of land tenure for indigenous peoples may be one of the most important ways of conserving tropical forests. Conferring security of tenure on colonists, on the other hand, acts like a magnet for outsiders to clear land for agriculture.

The social irrationality of forest clearance for ranching is revealed by the fact that, without subsidies, large-ranch Brazilian beef revenues cover only about one-third of the costs of setting up the ranches as Table 6.5 shows. The subsidy system explains what is privately profitable is socially unprofitable.

Once again, the indicated recent decline in deforestation in the Amazon is consistent with the following policy changes that have been made:

- Tax credits were largely removed in 1988 and 1989. The year 1987 was the last in which tax credits were available to landholders who cleared their land, and this fact may well account for the indicated peak in the rate of deforestation in that year. The rate declined as the tax credits were removed and federal road building in the area virtually ceased.
- Subsidies were also available on land in the south, raising land prices there in the earlier years and thus strengthening the push factor of high land prices.
- The legislation that confirms land ownership through land clearance has been rescinded.
- Subsidized credit has been reduced substantially in scale and level, although a new credit fund has been established for developments in the north, northeast and centre-west areas of the country.

- Agricultural price support schemes that targeted the north have been region-
  alized so that Amazonian agriculture now has less protection from market
  forces than previously. Given high transport costs between the region and
  markets, this change should deter agriculturists.

*Table 6.5   Cost structure of large beef cattle ranch: Brazilian Amazon
(US$ per hectare, 1984)*

Capital investment	
Land cost	31.7
Forest clearance	66.0
Pasture planting	26.4
Fencing	19.4
Cattle acquisition	90.9
Other	7.4
Total	241.8
Operating costs	
Labour	26.2
Herd maintenance	21.0
Pasture maintenance	47.3
Infrastructure	74.3
Other	4.2
Total	173.0
Total all costs	414.8
Total revenues	112.5
Revenues as per cent of costs	27.1

Source: Browder (1988).

The role that subsidies have played is disputed by some authorities. The balance
of opinion suggests that they were highly significant in encouraging deforestation
(Mahar 1989; Reis and Margulis 1990; Browder 1988; Binswanger 1989; Hecht
et al. 1988). Hecht disputes the role that rural credit has played, observing that
official rural credit fell dramatically in classic Amazonia from 1980, but deforestation increased (Hecht 1990: 292).

More recent work at the World Bank suggests that, while the subsidies have
been important in some respects, pure market forces have also encouraged the
growth of the livestock industry (Schneider 1990). The most rapid growth in
livestock numbers on cattle ranches occurred on small farms, which were less
likely to have received government subsidies. Table 6.6 shows some representative

data; these suggest that the smaller the herd size, the faster the growth of herd. Since the subsidy schemes favour large ranches, the economics of small ranching would appear to be profitable. This finding is not inconsistent with Table 6.5 since the figures there are based on a representative sample of large ranches (of some 50 000 ha).

Table 6.6   Classic Amazonia: herd size and rate of growth

Herd size 1985	Total cattle (%) 1985	Growth rate (%) 1980–85
<10	3	72
10–19	4	77
20–49	10	70
50–99	10	51
100–199	12	56
200–499	16	37
500–999	12	18
1000–1999	9	6
2000+	24	20

Source: Schneider (1990).

Nonetheless, the subsidies have unquestionably contributed to deforestation since it is very unlikely that the larger ranches would have been set up at all without them. The fact that the large ranches grew less quickly than the small ones does not indicate that subsidies had no effect on deforestation. As noted, however, the growth of the small farm units does suggest that other factors besides the subsidies are at work. While ranching profitability may be one of these factors, land speculation is another. As long as there are expectations of rising land prices, it may pay to buy the land, hold it in some unprofitable use, and resell at a later date (Fearnside 1990).

Other causal factors

Space forbids more than a cursory treatment of the other factors giving rise to deforestation in the Amazon. Logging has expanded from some 4.5 million m^3 of log production in 1975 to 24.6 million m^3 in 1987. The relevance of logging to deforestation lies not in the area actually logged, but in its role in opening up frontier land for other colonizers. In turn, logging has been facilitated by road building. What appears to be inefficient logging practice — with substantial damage to surrounding trees and forest areas — frequently reflects the simple economics of removing timber from areas that are remote from markets and where land is cheap.

Large-scale mining has also contributed to deforestation. The Greater Carajás Programme includes as its centrepiece the Carajás Iron Ore Project, a huge open-pit mining operation (Hall 1989). While the mine itself has had a modest impact on deforestation and, indeed, has strong environmental controls, the associated developments have had major effects (see also Chapter 9 by da Silva Neto in this volume). Thus the associated iron-ore smelters use charcoal as a fuel and the railway and adjacent townships have generated deforestation. The construction of the hydroelectric dam at Tucuruni has also caused significant forest loss. Tucuruni's electricity is partly sold to Carajás. Other dams have performed badly by conventional financial criteria, notably Balbina, where a disappointingly modest electricity output has been secured despite the flooding of a very large area.

Conclusion on causes

The preceding discussion shows that economic incentives have been instrumental in the deforestation of the Amazon. Road-building programmes (which themselves need proper economic analysis), property rights, subsidies for investment and borrowing, and simple market forces have all combined to influence the rate of forest loss. While logging and other developments have assisted in opening up the Amazon, the main factor has been agricultural colonization. Moreover, the 'population and poverty' explanation for environmental degradation hardly squares with the fact that the recipients of subsidies have been large, not small, farmers. As Hecht states: 'the culprits in setting fires to clear forest are overwhelmingly large-scale landowners and land-grabbers' (1990: 267). Small farmers have undoubtedly played their part, but the true picture is rather different from the popular image.

The Value of the Amazon Forest

We turn now to the economic approach to assessing the value of the tropical forest. It is important to recognize that economic value is different from financial value. The concept that is relevant is 'total economic value'.

Total economic value

Tropical forests have both marketed and unmarketed values. Market values include products such as timber. The watershed protection functions of a forest are not, however, bought and sold in the market-place. Unless incentives are devised whereby the non-market benefits are integrated into the land-use choice mechanism conservation benefits will automatically be undervalued. Very simply, those who stand to gain from, say, timber extraction or agricultural clearance must not consume the non-marketed benefits. This asymmetry of values imparts a considerable bias in favour of the land use that involves development rather than conservation.

The conservation value of the tropical forest is measured by the total economic value (TEV). TEV for a tropical forest is explained in Figure 6.2. TEV includes use and non-use values. Conservation is consistent with some sustainable uses of the forest, for example sustainable timber harvesting.

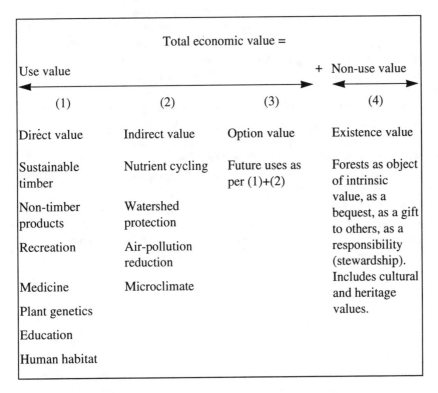

Total economic value =			
Use value			+ Non-use value
(1)	(2)	(3)	(4)
Direct value	Indirect value	Option value	Existence value
Sustainable timber	Nutrient cycling	Future uses as per (1)+(2)	Forests as object of intrinsic value, as a bequest, as a gift to others, as a responsibility (stewardship). Includes cultural and heritage values.
Non-timber products	Watershed protection		
Recreation	Air-pollution reduction		
Medicine	Microclimate		
Plant genetics			
Education			
Human habitat			

Figure 6.2   Total economic value in the tropical forest context

Direct-use values are fairly straightforward in concept but are not necessarily easy to measure in economic terms. For example, minor forest products output should be measurable from market and survey data, but the value of medicinal plants is extremely difficult to measure. Indirect values correspond to the ecologist's concept of 'ecological functions' and are discussed further below.

Option values measure the amount that individuals would be willing to pay to conserve a tropical forest for future use. That is, no use is made of it now but it may be used in the future. Option value is thus like a premium paid to ensure the supply of something, the availability of which would otherwise be uncertain. While it cannot always be assumed that option value is positive, it is likely to be so in the current context.[4]

Existence value measures valuations of the environmental asset unrelated either to current or optional use. Its intuitive basis is easy to understand: a great many people reveal their willingness to pay for the existence of environmental assets by giving donations to environmental charities. Empirical measures of existence value, obtained through questionnaire approaches (the contingent valuation method), suggest that existence value can be a substantial component of total economic value. This finding is even more pronounced where the asset is unique, suggesting high potential existence value for tropical forests and especially for luxuriant moist forests (Brookshire *et al.* 1983, 1985; Schulze 1983).

From Figure 6.2, then, total economic value can be expressed as: TEV = Direct-use value + Indirect-use value + Option value + Existence value.

It is important to note that the components of TEV cannot simply be aggregated. There are trade-offs between different types of use value and between direct- and indirect-use values. In practice, then, the TEV approach has to be used with care.

In order to demonstrate that tropical forests have higher economic value in a conserved state than in a state developed for agriculture or clear-felling, the component parts of TEV need to be estimated. We concentrate on just two of the apparently more intractable elements of TEV: the 'carbon store' function and the size of 'existence value'.

Carbon cycling and the greenhouse effect
In the process of photosynthesis, growing forests absorb or 'fix' carbon dioxide, and give off oxygen. Once grown, forests no longer accumulate carbon from the atmosphere. Mature forests are said to be in a state of approximate carbon equilibrium — that is, they release as much CO_2 as they absorb. The northern hemisphere's temperate and boreal forests may actually exhibit a slight net fixation of carbon, but tropical forests may safely be regarded as being in carbon equilibrium if they are mature, as would be the case for the remaining primary forests.

But while the rate of carbon exchange with the atmosphere is zero for mature tropical forests, these forests lock up or 'sequester' carbon as a stock. This distinction is important since it means that deforestation will release CO_2 into the atmosphere and thus contribute to the greenhouse effect. Indeed, deforestation releases other greenhouse gases such as methane. Tropical forests are major stores of carbon and hence the use made of tropical forest land, and of the timber on the land, is an important factor in global warming.

It is important to realize what is being measured by the carbon-fixing value of a tropical forest. This value is best viewed in the context of the costs and benefits of alternative land use. Consider two basic options: to conserve tropical forests and to clear it for agriculture.

1. Conserving a mature carbon-equilibrium forest avoids any carbon release associated with the alternative land use (agriculture), and hence the damage associated with that carbon release is avoided. It is legitimate, then, to speak of the forest as having a carbon credit equal to the avoided damage.
2. Clearing the forest for agriculture entails deforestation and the release of carbon and other pollutants. The damage associated with that carbon release is therefore a carbon debit to that particular forest land use.

However, it is not legitimate to ascribe both a credit to the conservation option and a debit to the clearance option. That would be double counting since the credit and debit are the obverse of each other. Either conservation is credited with damage avoided, or the agriculture option is debited with the damage incurred by deforestation.

A further complication is that the credit or debit depends on how the timber is removed, how it is subsequently used, and how the deforested land is subsequently managed (Pearce 1991b).[5] Clearance by burning will be associated with a total release of CO_2, and there will be no offsetting credits in terms of the use made of the timber. But if the land is subsequently managed in such a way that carbon is once again fixed — for example by grassland — that rate of fixation has to be offset against the loss of carbon from deforestation. Typically, forests contain 20 to 100 times more carbon per unit of area than do agricultural lands. Thus the offset provided by subsequent land use will be far from sufficient to compensate totally for the loss from deforestation through clearance. The same is true for any downstream reappearance of carbon: by far the greater part of released carbon goes into the atmosphere.

If the forest is clear-felled and all the timber is used to make longlived wood products (housing timber or furniture, for example), the act of deforestation may cause very little carbon release because the carbon remains locked up in the timber products. This type of offset is called 'product carbon offset'. Subsequently, land use may then fix some carbon so that the overall effect of deforestation on carbon release could be very small — zero or even, possibly, negative. This second kind of offset is 'land-use carbon offset'.

In fact, most deforestation occurs through direct clearance or incidental damage. The early 1980 estimates of worldwide deforestation suggested that some 11.1 mhpa (million hectares per annum) of tropical forest were being lost. Of this amount, 7.3 mhpa were being cleared directly for agriculture, usually by burning, while a further 3.8 mhpa were cleared for some combination of agriculture and fuelwood. Selective logging took place on a further 4.4 mhpa. While selective logging is, in principle, consistent with regeneration (and causes little change in the carbon store over time), in practice it tends to be associated with extensive damage to the remaining tree stocks and produces carbon release (World Resources Institute 1989; Repetto 1990). While the extent of net carbon release will vary for each location, in terms of the overall rate of deforestation it is fair to suggest that there is little product carbon offset to the carbon releases caused by deforestation. Both the land-use offset and the product offset tend to be allowed for in the better studies of carbon release.

With due consideration being given for the various offsets, carbon emissions for 1980 caused by deforestation have been estimated to lie somewhere in the range of 0.4 to 2.5 x 10^{15} grams of carbon — i.e. 0.4 to 2.5 gigatonnes per annum (10^{15} g = 1 billion metric tonnes = 1 gigatonne) with a mean figure of 1.8 gigatonne per annum (Houghton *et al.* 1985; Houghton 1990). This compares with CO_2 releases from fossil fuel of 5.3 gigatonnes in 1984. Of this total of 7.1 gigatonnes, around half remains in the atmosphere, the rest being absorbed by the oceans and other sinks. Thus there is a net accretion of some 3.6 gigatonnes in the atmosphere. Tropical deforestation may therefore be contributing about 25 per cent of CO_2 emissions which, in turn, contribute perhaps half of the total greenhouse gases. It may be concluded that tropical deforestation contributes some 10 to 13 per cent of all greenhouse gas emissions. More recent estimates suggest that rates of deforestation have increased and carbon released could be some 2 to 3 gigatonnes per annum (Houghton 1990).

The issue is: What carbon credit should be given to tropical forests for their contribution to avoiding the global warming impact of deforestation, in other words, what is the carbon credit to conservation and hence the carbon debit to clearance? In line with the damage avoided approach to valuation, a tropical forest should be credited with the value of global warming damage avoided by its conservation. Some monetary estimates of global warming damage exist, and they suggest that the damage done, mainly in terms of sea-level rise, could be some $13 per tonne of carbon in 1989 constant dollars (Nordhaus 1990).(See also Chapter 8 by Winpenny in this volume.)

Most of the carbon release from deforestation occurs in the first five years. Focusing on a single year therefore understates the total carbon loss since release occurs beyond the single year. But the analysis of a single year helps to illustrate the orders of magnitude of cost involved. On average, deforestation of one hectare of land contributes some 100 tonnes of carbon to the atmosphere in a single year. At some $13 per tonne in damage, it follows that deforestation causes damage at a rate of some $1300 per hectare. In reality, the damage is higher than this because of the fact that carbon release continues after one year.

If Amazonian deforestation was some 50 000 km^2 per annum in 1988–89 but has fallen to 20 000 km^2 in 1990, the world has saved the carbon releases associated with deforestation of 30 000 km^2. The value of that saving is at least

$1300 per hectare in terms of avoided damage from global warming. The relevant saving is therefore:3 million hectares × $1300/ha = $3.9 billion per annum. This is the sum that Brazil might legitimately claim from the world at large as the benefit of reduced deforestation. Clearly, if deforestation were to cease altogether, the claim could be as much as $6.5 billion. From the standpoint of the developed world, this sum is worth paying if it is less than the cost of removing the carbon dioxide and other greenhouse gases that would be released by the foregone deforestation. From Brazil's standpoint, it is better to receive this sum as compensation for foregone development benefits if it exceeds the value of those benefits. We turn to this issue shortly.

Non-use benefits: existence value

The motivations behind existence value need not concern us unduly.[6] Efforts to estimate existence value are based on contingent valuation studies which essentially use a willingness-to-pay questionnaire approach. No study has been carried out for tropical forests, but Table 6.7 reports estimates of average annual values per person taken from contingent valuation studies for selected animal species and natural amenities. While the studies are limited in number, there is a consistency about the values. The animal values cluster in the range of $5 to $8, with American national symbols — the grizzly bear and the bald eagle — valued at $11 to $15. The Grand Canyon similarly has a high valuation as a piece of major national heritage, compared to the value of cleaning up a river.

Could such values be borrowed for tropical forests? These are unique assets, but generally they are in countries other than rich nations. Allowing for this distance between valuer and the object of value (which applies to the blue whale as well), and the substantial worldwide interest in tropical deforestation, a figure of $8 per adult per annum would seem very conservative. If we take into account only the richest nations of the world, with a population of some 400 million adults (western Europe, North America, Australasia), the valuation would be some $3.2 billion annually.

The opportunity cost of forest conservation is the development benefits foregone. As we have seen, these may not in fact be greater than the benefits of sustainable use of tropical forests. But in order to assess the back-of-the-envelope guesstimate of existence value, one might look at the developmental uses of tropical forests to see what benefits accrue. If we take Amazonia as an example, the entire GNP of classic Amazonia is about 6.4 per cent of Brazil's GNP. In 1980, Brazil's GNP was some $230 billion and Amazonia contributed around $15 billion.[7] On the assumption that each adult person in wealthy countries of the world would be willing to contribute $8 p.a. to an Amazon Conservation Fund, the resulting $3.2 billion would enable the people responsible for more than 20 per cent of the economic output of Amazonia to be compensated for ceasing their activities — assuming that all existing economic activity is unsustainable.

Table 6.7   Non-use values for unique natural assets

Asset	Value per adult (mid-1980 $)
Animal species	
Bald eagle	11
Emerald shiner	4
Grizzly bear	15
Bighorn sheep	7
Whooping crane	1
Blue whale	8
Bottlenose dolphin	6
California sea otter	7
Northern elephant seal	7
Natural Amenities	
Water quality (S. Platte River basin)	4
Visibility (Grand Canyon)	22

Source: Samples (1986).

In practice, Amazon area production of many items (Brazil nuts, latex, fish, crustacea, and others) is consistent with the sustainable use of the forest area. Additionally, many services would remain even if much economic activity ceased. Thus, a total sacrifice of existing development activities is not required. Moreover, the cost-benefit comparison called for here would be unlikely to provide a defence for conserving the whole legal Amazon area.

A closer look at the breakdown of the $15-billion contribution of legal Amazonia to Brazilian GNP in 1980 shows that the broad sectors were as follows:

agriculture	$3 billion
industry	$4 billion
services	$8 billion

Were all mining and mineral processing to cease, as well as ranching, logging and half the crop production, the transfer of resources required would be around

$5.8 billion in 1980 terms. The outline computations above suggest that 55 per cent ($3.2 billion) of this amount could be met by international transfers.

Appropriating Total Economic Value

The concept of total economic value offers a comprehensive framework within which to value tropical forests. Total economic value consists of use values, option values and existence values. Direct-use values include timber and non-timber products and eco-tourism. Indirect-use values include the ecological functions of tropical forests: their watershed protection and mineral cycling functions. Existence value is the value of the forest in itself, unrelated to any use. All these values are related to people. The total economic value approach is highly anthropomorphic. It does not deny other rationales for conserving tropical forests based on rights in nature. Yet it may not be necessary to resort to such moral arguments. Economic arguments alone could well be sufficient to justify a dramatic reduction in deforestation.

One problem with the total economic value concept in the context of a developing country is that means need to be found for appropriating the non-cash elements of this value. In richer countries, a land-use decision can be made that allows non-cash conservation values to outweigh cashable development values. Such land would then be conserved regardless of the fact that net cash flows are lower under the conservation option than under the development option. In other words, traditionally measured GNP is lower under the conservation option than the development option, but unmeasured GNP is greater with conservation. Mechanisms can, but need not, be found for appropriating the non-cash values — for example, entrance charges and user fees. For a developing country, however, the appropriation process is critical. Such countries are unlikely to be able to afford conservation if its benefits show up mainly in non-cash welfare. We return to this point shortly.

There is some evidence that use values alone favour forest conservation. As we have seen, clearance for livestock agriculture, in particular, appears to have no financial rationale. This practice depends on substantial subsidies which themselves introduce major economic distortions. Alternative uses to logging for timber which make use of minor forest products appear to give higher financial rates of return than timber in some areas (Peters *et al.* 1989). Markets fail to allocate forests to their best uses because of inefficient government intervention — notably subsidization — and the absence of secure tenure for small farmers. The recreational use of tropical forests is only now beginning to be realized.

Indirect-use values must be estimated. As yet, little effort has been made to value these indirect functions. As we have seen, some of them are disputed, but there is no question that deforestation followed by unsuitable land use causes significant damage. In addition, tropical forests should be given carbon credits for their role in containing the greenhouse effect. For existing forests, the credit would be for avoided damage by not developing, that is the benefit of conservation. This benefit might total some $1300 per hectare for a single year.

Existence values could be substantial and might easily dominate the use and indirect values. Such a result would be consistent with other findings in the total economic valuation literature. On the assumption that the Amazon forest is valued at an average of $8 per adult in the advanced economies of the world only, existence value could readily amount to $3 billion, or a quarter of the entire gross domestic product (GDP) contribution of classic Amazonia to Brazil's GDP, inclusive of mineral extraction, timber and agriculture. But the cashability issue arises again: how are such values to be appropriated for the benefit of poor countries?

Since much of the option and existence value associated with tropical forests accrues to people outside of the tropically forested countries, appropriation involves cash or other resource transfers from rich to poor countries. Numerous technical co-operation agreements combine elements of such transfers, but the nature of the compensatory agreements needed is rather different. They involve compensation for foregoing development policies of the traditional kind. One would expect such agreements to be associated first with areas where there is comparatively low development value. The receiving country could then ask for relatively modest sums which donor countries would find easier to grant.

Transfers would also have to be based on a realistic interpretation of the foregone development benefits. Making that interpretation raises difficult questions with respect to subsidized activities. Is the compensation to be related to, say, ranching activity foregone and net of subsidies? Or are the subsidies themselves an implicit valuation by the receiving country of the longer-term development benefits thought to be associated with deforestation? If logging is the development option foregone, what logging practice counts as the basis for compensation payments? More familiar complications arise in that the resource transfers have all the hallmarks of environmental conditionality, which has been resisted by many countries. The transfers raise yet further issues of monitoring and control.

But there are precedents. Apart from co-operative ventures such as that between the United Kingdom and the Cameroon on Korup forest, the compensation funds being provided under the Montreal Protocol have the characteristics required. The Protocol's new Multilateral Fund will transfer sums of money to developing countries to compensate them for foregoing the use of CFCs and adopting more expensive substitutes. How far the sums currently under discussion include an element of rent is not clear, but there is a potential for rent capture in such contexts. Debt-for-nature swaps also offer examples of the kind of agreements that might be adopted, and the Global Environmental Facility being prepared by the World Bank is perhaps another.

One thing is clear. If the developed world values tropical forest resources, it must find mechanisms for international transfers to compensate the developing world for foregoing legitimate development projects. But the stress needs to be on legitimacy. The developed world is hardly likely to compensate Brazil, or any other country, for foregoing subsidized activity.[8]

Notes

1. See, for example, World Commission on Environment and Development (1989) (Brundland Commission).
2. For detailed but largely non-technical expositions of the economic approach to the environment see Pearce *et al.* (1989) and Pearce (1991a).
3. Though not to everyone. Julian Simon argues that more people are actually good for us because (a) they stimulate technological change, and (b) a larger 'reservoir' of people means that we shall find more geniuses who can find technical fixes to solve our problems (Simon 1986).
4. The literature on option value is extensive. See Bishop (1982, 1988), Freeman (1985), Plummer (1986) and Johansson (1988). The sign of option value is indeterminate but may be expected to be positive if the future demand for the asset in question (the tropical forest function in this case) is certain, and the supply is uncertain.
5. Much of the literature on the carbon value of tropical forests is misleading in that it fails to take account of (a) uses of the timber culled in deforestation, and (b) the subsequent land use. For an exercise in calculating carbon credits for temperate forests, see Pearce (1991b).
6. Some economists express a concern that such valuations may be counter-preferential or inconsistent with individual preferences, as are acts of duty or obligation. If so, there may be implications for the underlying structure of the welfare economics used to evaluate resource worth; see (Brookshire *et al.* 1986).
7. GNP for Brazil in 1980 was Crz 12 281 billion at 1980 prices and for the legal Amazon region (Amapó, Pará, Roraima, Goiás, Acre, Rondônia, Mato Grosso, Amazonas) it was $ 782 billion. Amazon region's contribution was thus 6.4 per cent in 1980. We have assumed a stable proportion through time. Amazon region's agricultural and ranching GNP was 14.1 per cent of Brazilian agricultural and ranching GNP. (I am indebted to Bernadette Gutierrez for the computations.)
8. This does not imply that the rich world has right on its side. In Europe, farmers are subsidized to overproduce food and some are then paid not to produce food at all in an effort to reduce the surpluses.

References

Binswanger, H. (1989), 'Brazilian Policies that Encourage Deforestation in the Amazon', *World Bank Environment Department Working Paper*, 15. Washington, DC: World Bank.

Bishop, R.C. (1982), 'Option Value: an Exposition and Extension', *Land Economics*, **58**, (1), 1–15.

Bishop, R.C. (1988), 'Option Value: Reply'. *Land Economics*, **64**, 88–93.

Brookshire, D., Eubanks, L. and Randal, A. (1983), 'Estimating Option Prices and Existence Values for Wildlife Resources', *Land Economics*, **59**, 1–15.

Brookshire, D., Schulze W. and Thayer M. (1985), 'Some Unusual Aspects of Valuing a Unique Natural Resource', mimeo, Department of Economics, University of Wyoming.

Brookshire, D., Eubanks, L. and Sarg, C. (1986), 'Existence Values and Normative Economics: Implications for Valuing Water Resources', *Water Resources Research*, **22**, (11), 1509–18.

Browder, J. (1988), 'Public Policy and Deforestation in the Brazilian Amazon', in R. Repetto and M. Gillis (eds), *Public Policy and the Misuse of Forest Resources*, Cambridge: Cambridge University Press.

Fearnside, P. (1990), 'Environmental Destruction in the Brazilian Amazon', in D. Goodman and A. Hall, *The Future of Amazonia: Destruction or Sustainable Development*, London: MacMillan.

Freeman, A.M. (1985), 'Supply Uncertainty, Option Price and Option Value', *Land Economics*, **16**, 176–81.

Goodman, D. and Hall, A. (1990), *The Future of Amazonia*, London: MacMillan.

Hall, A. (1989), *Developing Amazonia: Deforestation and Social Conflict in Brazil's Carajás Programme*, Manchester: Manchester University Press.

Hecht, S. (1990), *The Fate of the Forest*, London: Penguin.

Hecht, S., Norgaard, R. and Possio, G. (1988), 'The Economics of Cattle Ranching in Eastern Amazonia', *Interciencia*, **13**, (5), September–October.

Houghton, R. (1990), 'The Future Role of Tropical Forests in Affecting the Carbon Dioxide Concentration of the Atmosphere', *Ambio*, **19**, (4), 204–9.

Houghton, R., Boone, R., Melillo, J., Palm, C., Woodwell, G., Myers, N., Moor, B. and Skole, D. (1985), 'Net Flux of Carbon Dioxide from Tropical Forests in 1980', *Nature*, **316**, 15 August.

Johansson, P.O. (1988), 'On the Properties of Supply-Side Option Value', *Land Economics*, **64**, 86–7.

Mahar, D, (1989), 'Deforestation in Brazil's Amazon Region: Magnitude, Rate and Causes', in G. Schraamm and J. Warford (eds) *Environmental Management and Economic Development*, Baltimore: John Hopkins.

Martine, G. (1989), 'Internal Migration in Brazil', mimeo, IPEA/IPLAN Brasilia.

Myers, N. (1989), *Deforestation Rates in Tropical Forests and Their Climatic Implications*, London: Friends of the Earth.

Nordhaaus, W. (1990), 'To Slow or Not to Slow: The Economics of the Greenhouse Effect', mimeo, Department of Economics, Yale University.

Pearce, D.W. (ed) (1991a), *Blueprint 2*, London: Earthscan.

Pearce, D.W. (1991b), 'Assessing the Returns to the Economy and to Society from Investment in Forestry', *Forestry Expansion*, Edinburgh: UK Forestry Commission.

Pearce, D.W., Markandya, A. and Barbier, E. (1989), *Blueprint for a Green Economy*, London: Earthscan.

Peters, C., Gentry, A. and Mendelsohn, R. (1989), 'Valuation of an Amazonian Rainforest'. *Nature*, **339**, 29 June, 655–6.

Plummer, M. (1986), 'Supply Uncertainty, Option Price and Option Value', *Land Economics*, **62**, 313–18.

Reis, E.J. and Margulis, S. (1990), 'Options for Slowing Amazon Jungle-Clearing', paper presented to Conference on Economic Policy Reponses to Global Warming, Rome.

Repetto, R. (1990), 'Deforestation in the Tropics', *Scientific American*, **262**, (4), 36–42.

Repetto, R. and Gillis, M. (eds) (1988), *Public Policies and the Misuse of Forest Resources*, Cambridge: Cambridge University Press.

Samples, K. (1986), 'The Validity of the Contingent Valuation Method for Estimating Non-Use Components of Preservation Values for Unique Natural Resources', paper presented to the American Agricultural Economics Association, Reno, Nevada.

Schneider, R. (1990), 'Economic Analysis of Environmental Problems in the Amazon', World Bank, unpublished report.

Schulze, W. (1983), 'Economic Benefits of Preserving Visibility in the National Parklands of the Southwest', *Natural Resources Journal*, **23**, 149–73.

Simon, J. (1986), *Theory of Population and Economic Growth*, Oxford: Blackwell.

Southgate, D. (1990), 'Tropical Deforestation and Agricultural Development in Latin America', mimeo, London Environmental Economics Centre.

Southgate, D., Sierra, R. and Brown, L. (1991), 'A Statistical Analysis of the Causes of Deforestation in Eastern Ecuador', *World Development*, **19**, (9), 1145–51.

Whitmore, T.C. (1990), *An Introduction to Tropical Rain Forests*, Oxford: Clarendon Press.

World Commission on Environment and Development (1989), *Our Common Future*, Oxford: Oxford University Press.

World Resources Institute (1989), *World Resources 1988–89*, New York: Basic Books.

7. The economic value of non-market benefits of tropical forests: carbon storage

Katrina Brown and David Pearce

The fate of the world's tropical forests has attracted worldwide attention. Although the United Nations 'Earth Summit' in Rio de Janeiro in 1992 failed to produce an international convention aimed at the conservation of the world's forests, producing only a vaguely worded statement of 'Forest Principles', pressure continues to slow the current rate of deforestation. The Earth Summit highlighted very different perceptions of the tropical forest problem. The North sees forests as providing a global source of biological diversity and as a sink for carbon dioxide ('the green lungs of the world'). Significant voices in the South argue that developing countries need to exploit natural resources such as forests as part of the process of economic development, as the developed countries have in the past.

While international political consensus on forest conservation is unlikely, the arguments for conservation and sustainable use have shifted in focus from the purely moral to the utilitarian. Economic arguments in particular have focused on the total economic value of tropical forests. One aspect of this total economic value is the role that forests play as carbon stores. As forest land is converted to other uses — crops, livestock, roads, mining — so stored carbon dioxide is released, contributing to the risk of global warming. It follows that land uses which avoid this release should be credited with the value of avoided damage, or, the obverse, carbon-releasing land uses should be debited with the expected damage.

We report estimates of such economic values of carbon storage with special reference to the Amazon rainforest, and we show how carbon credits and debits affect decisions to invest in developmental land uses. That is, carbon storage influences the way in which project appraisal of forest land use should be carried out.

Total Economic Value in the Tropical Forest Context

To focus the analysis, consider a single hectare of tropical forest land. The decision problem is either to develop the land, say by clearing it for agricultural use, or to conserve the land through some combination of sustainable uses. Clearance involves burning. Sustainable use involves concentrating on careful, selective logging, forest products such as nuts, rattan, latex, fruits and some forms of eco-tourism (Peters, Gentry and Mendelsohn 1989; Balick and Mendelsohn 1991; Tobias and Mendelsohn 1990; Pearce and Puroshothaman 1993). But conservation could also be achieved through side payments, or 'bribes' not to develop. Such payments would come from the North.[1]

These conservation options capture the two components of total economic value (TEV). TEV is the sum of use and non-use economic values. Use values are measured by the willingness to pay for the products or services of the forest, where an actual use is involved. Non-use values reflect a willingness to pay unrelated to actual use and are typically classified as the sum of existence and bequest values. Existence value arises where individuals have a concern to see an asset conserved because of altruism, some sense of environmental steward-ship, or empathy. Bequest value arises because of a concern to see the asset conserved for use by future generations (Pearce 1990).

In between use and non-use values is option value, a premium, akin to an insurance premium, to conserve the asset for potential use in the future, even though no use is made of the asset now. We can write:

$$TEV = Value + Non\text{-}use\ value$$

or

$$TEV = E(CS) + OV + EXV + BV \qquad (7.1)$$

where $E(CS)$ is the expected value of the consumer surplus from current and planned use, OV is option value, EXV is existence value, and BV is bequest value.

Since there is some doubt about the credibility of attempts empirically to dif-ferentiate EXV and BV, and OV and $E(CS)$, equation (7.1) can be shortened to

$$TEV = E(CS) + EXV \qquad (7.2)$$

Sustainable use of forest land will therefore capture $E(CS)$, while the idea of resource transfers to compensate for not burning and clearing land will reflect EXV together with any global benefits from indirect uses such as carbon storage.

Returning to the development/conservation choice, developmental uses will be preferred to conservation uses if, in a timeless world:

$$(Bd - Cd) > (Bc - Cc) \qquad (7.3)$$

where B benefits, C costs, d refers to development, and c to conservation or sustainable uses. But Bc is formally equivalent to the TEV of the conservation option. Allowing also for time, we can write the requirement (7.3) as:

$$\sum_t [B_{d,t} - C_{c,t}](1+r)^{-t} > \sum_t [\text{TEV}_t - C_{c,t}][1+r]^{-t} \qquad (7.4)$$

where r is the discount rate.

If markets for land work reasonably well, then the price of land, P_L, should reflect the present value of expected net benefits from the development option. The net benefits of conservation will be reflected in land prices only in so far as the benefits are marketed. Since this will not be the case for non-use values, overall conservation value will not be reflected in land prices. Conservation use values will be reflected in land prices. Actual use will, however, tend to be dictated by central and local economic incentives which, as is well known, tend not to reflect shadow prices (Pearce, Moran and Fripp 1992). Requirement (7.4) now becomes:

$$P_L > pv(\text{TEV} - C_c) \qquad (7.5)$$

where pv denotes present value.

In so far as TEV is a composite of use and non-use values, we wish to test the proposition that one of the indirect use values — carbon storage — exceeds P_L. If it does, or is even close to P_L, the *formal* case for conservation has been made. The *practical* measures needed to implement conservation are, of course, another issue. Global benefits such as carbon storage must be appropriable by the country in question. Indeed, the resource transfer must flow to land users if they are to receive incentives not to clear forest land. One possible mechanism is via the Global Environment Facility — the interim funding agency for resource transfers under the Earth Summit Conventions on climate change and biodiversity.

Here we focus on the estimation of the necessary carbon credits and debits. The first requirement is to obtain an estimate of economic damage per tonne of carbon released into the atmosphere. The second is to estimate carbon releases from a hectare of tropical forest land. The present value of the product of these two magnitudes may then be compared with land prices.

The Economic Value of Storing Carbon

Nordhaus (1991a, 1991b), Cline (1992) and Fankhauser (1992) have produced provisional estimates of global warming damage. In the case of Nordhaus and Cline, the estimates are for the USA and are extrapolated to the rest of the world.

Fankhauser's analysis uses more worldwide information. Nordhaus's estimate suggests damage equal to some 0.25 per cent of gross world product (GWP), while Cline's and Fankhauser's suggest a figure of around 1.1 to 1.5 per cent of GWP. Allowing for omitted categories of damage, Nordhaus suggests that 1 per cent of GWP might be a central estimate, with 2 per cent as an upper bound. Both estimates relate to a 'two times CO_2 concentration' scenario, that is to damage done around 2030 and discounted back to the present. Ayres and Walter (1991) make adjustments to Nordhaus's estimates but unfortunately make use of early drafts of the Nordhaus paper which contains significant errors that are corrected in the final published form.

Table 7.1   Alternative damage costs estimates for global warming

		Cost per tonne carbon equivalent ($ per Ctequ.)	Cost as a proportion of GWP (%)
Nordhaus	(1)	$1.83	0.25
		$7.30	1.0
		$14.60	2.0
	(2)	$66.00	2.0
Cline	(3)	$8.10	1.1
Ayres/	(4)	$15.3–17.5	2.1–2.4
Walter	(5)	$69.3–79.2	2.1–2.4
Fankhauser	(6)	$14.00	1.5

Notes
1. First two estimates as per Nordhaus (1991a, 1991b). Estimate for 2.0 per cent of GWP based on 8 x 0.25 per cent GWP. See (2).
2. Nordhaus alters the discount rate for the high damage estimate from an effective 1 per cent to zero.
3. Cline (1992) does not quote a $ per tonne of carbon figure. We have therefore taken his 1.1 per cent of GWP estimate and scaled up Nordhaus's central estimate.
4. Ayres and Walter quote 2.1 to 2.4 per cent of GWP as their damage estimate, but translate this as $30 to $35 per tCequ. This is because they use an earlier estimate by Nordhaus of $3.3 per tC damage (which they also wrongly believe to be Nordhaus's 'central' estimate) relating to 0.28 per cent GWP damage. Hence they multiply the $3.3 by 2.4/0.28 = 28.3. The $30 to $35 figure then appears to be some rounding of this estimate. For the estimate shown here we multiply Nordhaus's $1.83 estimate by 2.1/0.25 and 2.4/0.25.
5. The estimate here follows the same procedure in (4) but takes Nordhaus's 2 per cent estimate which, it will be recalled, uses a zero discount rate.
6. Fankhauser (1992).

The resulting estimates of primary benefits are shown in Table 7.1[2]. Taking the estimates produced with consistent discount rates, and taking 1 per cent of GWP as the minimum damage, global warming damage would seem to be of the order of \$7 to \$18 per tonne of carbon (tC). If zero discount rates are applicable, then the upper range could be as high as \$80 per tC. For the remainder of this chapter we use a central value of \$10 per tonne carbon as the shadow price of carbon.

Carbon Dynamics in Tropical Forests

We now seek to present a simplified matrix of carbon fluxes under different land use change scenarios.

Land use change, and most particularly deforestation in the tropics, has a significant effect on the global carbon flux. Forests and their soils may store as much as 2000 billion tonnes (Bt) of carbon (C), or 1500 BtC for soils alone (Gribbin 1990).

Deforestation and land use conversion to agriculture are also sources of a number of other gases with a potential warming effect, including methane, nitrous oxide, carbon monoxide, and ozone. We concentrate on emissions of CO_2.

Estimates of aggregate emissions from deforestation differ, as shown in Table 7.2 below, due to different estimates of area of forest cleared, and assumptions as to carbon stored per hectare. The estimates of global emissions range from 0.4 billion tonnes of carbon (BtC) to 2.9 BtC.

Table 7.2   Estimates of global CO_2 emissions from converting tropical forests

Source	Billion tonnes C
Andrasko (1990): (+0.32 as CH_4)	0.4–2.8
World Resources Institute (1990)	2.8
Myers (1989) (mean 1.8)	0.9–2.5
Detwiler and Hall (1988)	0.4–1.6
Sedjo (1989)	2.9
Houghton (1990)	0.4–2.6

Note: It is not always clear if estimates are net of carbon sequestrated by subsequent land use.

Rates of deforestation are believed to have increased in the decade since 1980, probably reaching a peak in 1987–89, and are now declining. Carbon release is more likely now to be in the region of 2 to 3 BtC per year. This would be roughly equivalent to 35 to 50 per cent of current emissions of CO_2 from fossil fuels. Using satellite images, Setzer and Pereira (1991) calculated that biomass burning in Brazilian legal Amazon in 1987 contributed 0.52 BtC. It was possible to detect about 20 million hectares of different types of vegetation burned, of which 8 million were associated with recent deforestation. CO_2 accounted for the 0.47 Bt of carbon emitted (other carbon compounds accounted for the remaining 0.05 Bt).

CO_2 emissions from tropical deforestation are usually calculated by one of two methods: the ecological method and the geochemical balance method. The ecological method calculates net CO_2 emissions from tropical deforestation on the basis of CO_2 sources and sinks in the tropical biosphere. The geochemical method regards the total net emissions of CO_2 from land use change as the upper limit for CO_2 emissions from tropical deforestation, and employs mathematical models to calculate the flux of CO_2 between the biosphere and the atmosphere, and between the oceans and the atmosphere. These models are calibrated by studying the ratio of carbon-13 to carbon-12 and radioactive carbon-14 over a period of time. The results can be used to deduce biospheric carbon fluxes.

We concentrate on the direct measurement of CO_2 sources (the ecological method) and review estimates by various authors. The ecological method calculates the *net* quantity of CO_2 emissions, that is net of subsequent vegetation, on the basis of cleared forest and of secondary vegetation; the density of the biomass of the burned tropical forest, the type of secondary vegetation; the release of CO_2 from the cleared biomass over time and from the soil after deforestation; and the fixation of atmospheric CO_2 in secondary vegetation.

Data are required on the following parameters in order to estimate the quantity of CO_2 emissions attributable to tropical deforestation:

(a) the type of forest being cleared, and the subsequent land use;
(b) biomass density, and carbon storage in the various types of forest, and in the secondary vegetation;
(c) proportion of biomass which is burned;
(d) proportion of biomass which, though burned, is kept in long-term storage;
(e) the rate of CO_2 release in biomass which is neither burned, nor in long term storage.

However, major areas of uncertainty and scientific dispute concern the following:

(a) the extent of deforestation in tropics;
(b) estimates of carbon sequestration and storage in vegetation and soils;
(c) definitions of vegetation types;
(d) subsequent land use and its extent;
(e) end uses of timber and products.

Estimates of the rate of deforestation in tropical regions
The first problem is in defining the different types of forest and vegetation cover; the second is in quantifying the extent of deforestation and land use conversion; a third is in identifying subsequent land use.

Classification of tropical forests
Myers (1990:373) defines tropical forests as:

> evergreen or partly evergreen forests, in areas receiving not less than 100mm of precipitation in any 6 months for two out of three years, with mean annual temperature of 24 plus degrees Celsius, and essentially frost-free; in these forests some trees may be deciduous; the forests usually occur below 1300m (though often in Amazonia up to 1800m, and generally in SE Asia up to only 750m); and in mature examples of these forests there are several more or less distinctive strata.

Such moist forests exist in more than 70 countries of the tropics, but 34 countries account for 7.8 million km², or 97.5 per cent of the present biome. Brazil contains approximately 27.5 per cent of all tropical forests.

Authors distinguish between open and closed forest. FAO (1991) defines forests as being closed when trees of the different stories and the undergrowth cover a large portion of the ground, and if no grass cover exists. Moist evergreen and deciduous forests account for most of the closed forests. The tree crowns of open forests cover at least 10 per cent of the ground surface, which in such forests is typically covered by a continuous carpet to grass. In general, these open forests correspond to dry deciduous forests of the tropics.

The Federal Republic of Germany (1991), for example distinguishes seven classes of tropical forest:

1.   Evergreen moist forest: equivalent to closed evergreen forest or rainforest, 10 degrees north and south of the equator in Amazon/Orinoco basin, Congo/Guinea basin, parts of India, Thailand/Indochina, and eastern Australia.
2.   Predominantly deciduous moist forest: seasonally leaf less, monsoonal and transitional. May border the evergreen moist forest with no clear lines of demarcation. This includes all closed types of high forest which shed leaves of at least the upper layer during a clearly defined dry season, with a lower stand density than evergreen moist forest.
3.   Predominantly deciduous dry forests. Usually found on the edges of deciduous moist forests.
4.   Special sites, including mangrove forests, swamps and flood plains.
5.   Coniferous tropical forests.
6.   Bamboo forests.
7.   Others types of forest.

The first three are the most important types as far as the present study is concerned; in terms of their extent, rate of destruction, and carbon fixing properties.

In addition to classification according to climatic and site-related criteria, forests can also be divided into primary, secondary and logged-over forests depending on their condition. Primary forests are virgin forests whose development has been disturbed only very slightly or not at all by human intervention, so that their physiognomy has been determined exclusively by their natural environment. They are also defined as climax forests, being the final stage of ecological succession. Secondary forest includes all stages of successions which take place on naturally bare land or land that has been cleared. Virgin or natural forest in which trees are felled in a more or less systematic manner and to an extent that the stand structure has been changed, are referred to as logged-over forests. These may be included in the group of secondary forests.

Other authors distinguish between productive and unproductive forests. Brown and Lugo (1984) define unproductive forests due to physical reasons (for example, rough terrain, or flooding), and legal reasons (for example, national parks or reserves). The area in national parks and reserves accounted for only 13 per cent of the total unproductive category.

Estimates of deforestation
Accelerating conversion of tropical forests is occurring for a number of inter-locking socio-economic and political reasons (Wood 1990). These include inequitable land distribution, entrenched rural poverty, and growing populations which push landless and near-landless peasants on to forest lands; government-subsidized expansion into forest regions by plantations growing export crops, timber companies, and cattle ranches; and government-sponsored population relocation to frontier regions.

FAO (1991) estimates, given in Table 7.3, show that 17 million hectares (Mha), out of a total area of 1884 Mha in 1980, of tropical forest were cleared annually between 1981 and 1990, almost exclusively by burning. Preliminary estimates of the forest area and rate of deforestation in 87 countries in the tropics shows that 169.3 Mha were cleared between 1980 and 1990. Tropical Asia had the fastest relative rate of deforestation (1.2 to 1.3 per cent per annum) among the three tropical continents, while its absolute rate was lowest, due to smallest initial forest area. Within continents, West Africa had the fastest rate of deforestation, though tropical Latin America had the largest area deforested, with average annual deforestation of 6.78 Mha.

FAO's results would appear to be substantiated to a degree by those of Setzer of the National Space Research Institute of Brazil (Setzer and Pereira 1991). In 1987, Setzer used satellite imagery to determine that 8 Mha of virgin forest in the legal Amazon were cleared in that year. However, 1987 may have been a year of unusually high deforestation, as it was the last year that tax credits were available to new landowners who cleared their Amazon holdings, and many large landowners may have wished to take advantage whilst they still could. At the same time, Brazil's legislature was discussing taking unimproved land as part of land reform programmes, so again many landowners may have cleared large tracts to retain ownership rights. In 1988 and 1989, tax credits were suspended and later cancelled, some policing and fining of illegal fires was initiated and wet weather discouraged burning. Follow-up studies by Setzer showed a decline in the area burned each year, a 40 per cent drop to 4.8 Mha in 1988, and a further 40 to 50 per cent drop in 1989 to 2.4 to 2.9 Mha. The methodology has been criticized as it uses space photographs of smoke, and smoke may extend beyond the burned area, but would not detect areas deforested but not burned (World Resources Institute 1990). The authors apply a weighting for the amount of vegetation which is forest, and the amount as cerrado (savanna).

Table 7.3   FAO Preliminary Estimates of Tropical Deforestation (million hectares)

Number of countries		Forest area 1980	Annual average loss
Latin America	32	922.9	8.30
Central America	7	77.0	1.35
Caribbean	18	48.8	0.17
Tropical South America	7	797.1	6.78
Asia	15	310.8	3.60
South Asia	6	70.6	0.44
Continental SE Asia	5	83.2	1.35
Insular SE Asia	4	157.0	1.81
Africa	40	650.4	5.03
West Sahel	8	41.9	0.39
East Sahel	6	92.3	0.70
West Africa	8	55.2	1.18
Central Africa	7	230.1	1.47
Tropical Southern Africa	10	217.7	1.14
Insular Africa	1	13.2	0.15
Total	87	1884.1	16.93

Source: FAO (1991)

The range of annual deforestation rates for Brazil's Amazon is between 1.7 to 8.0 Mha per year (Wood 1990), numbers large enough to affect significantly the global rate. Most probably, deforestation accelerated in the early 1980s, peaked in 1987, and declined somewhat in 1988–89 because of changed policies and wetter weather. Bouwman (1990) cites a rate of 0.6 per cent of total global forest area as being cleared for permanent use each year, and suggests that much of this is taking place in the Amazon Basin.

In recent years, remote sensing techniques have ensured greater accuracy in estimates, although these are by no means conclusive. Houghton *et al.* (1985) review some of the earlier estimates and highlight disparities caused by different definitions of vegetation. There remains, however, a certain amount of uncertainty over the true rate of deforestation.

Subsequent land use

Tropical forests are exploited by people for a variety of purposes, including timber extraction, shifting cultivation, permanent agriculture and pasture. Leduc (1985) identifies the immediate causes as slash-and-burn agriculture; commercial timber extraction; cattle raising; fuelwood gathering; commercial agriculture; and additional causes such as large dams, and mining. These various land uses differ in their effect on vegetation and soil, and therefore in the amount of CO_2 released when a unit area of forest is converted.

Much of the clearing in tropical rainforests is for shifting cultivation. Johnson (1991) estimates that 64 per cent of tropical deforestation is as a result of agriculturalists; 18 per cent by commercial logging; 10 per cent by fuelwood gatherers; 8 per cent by ranchers. However, there are different types of shifting cultivation, which may have different effects on carbon fluxes. Davidson (1985) distinguishes two types of shifting agriculture in tropical moist forests. First, the traditional, low intensity form of shifting cultivation which has been practised for many generations, initially involving the clearing of primary forest but afterwards based on a secondary forest fallow system. Secondly, a more destructive form, in which primary forest is cleared and the land cultivated continuously until it is degraded then abandoned.

According to the German Bundestag (1990), shifting cultivation in the tropics remains an appropriate means of land use under the prevailing climatic and soil conditions as long as certain conditions are met

(a) farming must be extensive, with long fallow period, of 12 to 20 years for most fertile soils, but 30 to 100 years for nutrient poor soils, for example those in much of the Amazon basin;

(b) plot size must not exceed 1 to 2 ha, so that it can be readily recolonized by surrounding forest vegetation;

(c)   crop mixtures and mixes should ensure maximum ground cover to avoid soil erosion.

It seems likely that in many parts of the world, shifting cultivation is now posing a threat to forest resources for a number of reasons

(a)   population growth is exceeding the capacity of existing cropland;
(b)   farmers are forced to settle and cultivate unsuitable and poor land;
(c)   land scarcity is further aggravated by ownership and distribution.

Houghton *et al.* (1987) describe typical shifting cultivation as a cycle, which begins with the burning of a plot of forest. Some of the large trees are left standing. Food crops are planted in the ashes and harvested from periods of 1 to 10 years. The yields generally decline over time as the forest grows back and soil fertility is reduced. Some of the surface organic matter is oxidized during the burn and in the earliest years of cropping. The soil organic matter develops again as the forest regrows. The period of fallow, after which the forest may be burned and cleared again, may last from 3 to 80 years depending on the cultural and environmental conditions.

Based on the FAO data, clearing of forests for the different land uses can be broken down as follows : shifting cultivation accounts for 40 per cent of cleared primary forest; permanent cropping and cattle ranching 50 per cent; logging (removes 28 per cent of above ground biomass) 10 per cent. The proportions vary from region to region, with 35 per cent of forest destruction in tropical America attributable to shifting cultivation, 49 per cent in Asia, and 70 per cent in Africa. A total of 31 per cent of forest is cleared for conversion to pasture for cattle in the Americas.

Carbon Dynamics

It is particularly important to distinguish between the active sequestration of CO_2 by trees as they grow, the flow concept and the storage of carbon in forest biomass and soils, the stock concept. Overall, forest ecosystems store 20 to 100 times more carbon per unit area than croplands and play a critical role in reducing ambient CO_2 levels, by sequestrating atmospheric carbon in the growth of woody biomass through the process of photosynthesis. When a forest is cut down, not only does the photosynthesis and therefore active fixing cease, but if the wood and timber is destroyed (most commonly by burning of at least a proportion), then carbon stored by the trees in the past will be released as CO_2. There are still a number of scientific uncertainties, particularly concerning carbon dynamics in representative natural and disturbed tropical forests, and carbon fluxes in tropical soils which may account for one-third of the flux from deforestation.

Biomass

An undisturbed moist tropical forest exhibits net growth for about 100 years after its establishment (Kyrklund 1990), compared with 30 to 40 years of *rapid* growth described by Myers (1989). After this as far as carbon is concerned the forest reaches a state of equilibrium where emission at night equals daytime absorption, and dieback equals growth. Grayson (1989) maintains that existing unmanaged forests contribute no *net* carbon since standing biomass remains the same, and carbon fixed by growth is balanced by carbon released to the atmosphere through death and subsequent rotting.

The CO_2 absorption rate is directly proportional to the growth rate. In commercial, even-aged stands of forest it is simpler to estimate incremental growth and for example in Britain, the Forestry Commission produces yield tables, showing growth rates for most common commercial species (coniferous and deciduous) under a range of different conditions per year. Forest growth can be modelled with an S-shaped logistic curve (Dewar 1990). However, estimating the average growth rate per hectare for natural tropical forest where a wide variety of species may be present, is much more complex for example, as reported by Pearce (1989) one hectare of the Yanomano Forest in Peru was found to contain 283 species of trees, and there were only twice as many individuals as there were species. Table 7.4 shows estimates of growth in tropical forests compiled from various sources, and from different sample sites within the categories. Again there are problems with definition, and in finding a mean rate which can be applied to a range of forests and conditions.

Myers (1990) assumes a working mean figure of 20 t biomass/ha/yr for growth in tropical forest plantation. As Myers notes, there is much variability in figures adduced for growth rates and yields, according to climatic conditions, soil types, and a number of other factors. Myers then assumes that one-half of plant growth is made up of carbon, and that therefore such a plantation can assimilate 10 tC/ha/yr. However, it is not made clear what the nature of the plantation is, and one assumes that such a figure would not apply to an uneven, natural stand. Indeed, Eucalyptus plantations in southern Brazil have been found to have an average growth rate of over 30 t/ha/yr, with occasional top yields of 70 t/ha/yr. Sedjo (1989) applies a universal mean rate of 6.24 tC/ha/yr, which appears to be closer to the expected rate according to data presented in Table 7.4. The Federal Republic of Germany (1991) estimate annual production of dry wood mass in more or less natural tropical forests as between 8 t/ha (evergreen moist forest) and 3 t/ha (moist deciduous forests).

Table 7.4   Biomass production in tropical forests

	DM t/ha/yr	C t/ha/yr
Bolin *et al.* (1986)		
(various sites)		
Tropical rainforest	9.88	4.94
	10.19	5.10
	7.75	3.88
Seasonal forest	7.20	3.60
	7.10	3.55
	5.50	2.75
Cannell (1982)		
Rainforest, Manaus	15.00	7.50
Rainforest, Ivory Coast	24.60	12.30
	17.17	8.58
	12.73	6.36
	14.97	7.48
Jordan (1989)		
Amazon rainforest, mean	12.66	6.33
Slash/burn, after 3 years	5.26	2.62

Note: DM is dry matter; carbon (C) is assumed to be 50 per cent of dry matter.

The estimation of standing biomass can be made by two methods: destructive sampling, and from timber volume estimates. Brown and Lugo (1984) have calculated the carbon content of tropical vegetation using these two methods. In 1982 they calculated tropical forest biomass density by means of destructive sampling, based on the selection of small areas, less than 30 ha, which were clear-felled in order to directly measure the biomass. In 1984 they produced new estimates of the biomass of tropical forest, this time based on volumes. The results summarized in Table 7.4 show that there is a significant difference between the results from the two methods. Brown and Lugo point out that the data base for estimating the biomass or carbon pool in tropical forests is poor at best, and that very few destructive sampling studies have been carried out, and it seems unlikely that those which have been are representative.

In contrast, much more information on standing timber volumes in tropical forest from a broader geographical area and from more and larger plots is available. In 1984 Brown and Lugo used data from FAO detailing stand volumes of forests surveyed in 76 countries, covering 97 per cent of the area that lies in the tropical belt. These are categorized into two broad classes: closed forests, where the forest stories cover a high proportion of the ground and lack a continuous dense ground cover, and open forests in which the mixed broadleaf–grassland tree formation has a continuous dense grass layer and the tree canopy covers more than 10 per cent of the ground. There were further classifications according to degree of disturbance and productivity.

Volume data, in cubic metres are converted to total biomass by assuming a mean wood density of 0.2 t/m^3 (Moore *et al.*, 1981). The ratio of total biomass to usable stem biomass was assumed by the German Bundestag (1990) to be 1.6 for closed forests and 3 for open forests. The density of wood varies over a limited range, and when averaged over a mixed forest the range becomes even smaller. Mid-range is assumed by Marland (1988) as 0.52 t/m^3. Houghton *et al.* (1985) report that the fractional carbon content of wood varies between 0.47 to 0.52 of dry matter (DM).Most authors then assume that 50 per cent of DM is carbon. Sedjo (1989) uses the following conversion factors for converting volume of stemwood to tC: 1 m^3 of stemwood is equivalent to 1.6 m^3 of biomass; 1 m^3 of forest biomass (stem, roots, branches) absorbs 0.26 tC equivalent. Sedjo applies an average figure of forest growth of 15 $m^3/ha/yr$ of stemwood, which therefore means that 1 ha of new forest will sequester 6.24tC/ha/yr ($15 \times 1.6 \times 0.26$).

Brown and Lugo, cited in Detwiler and Hall (1988) show that from volume data, primary closed forest was found to contain 90 tC/ha, and primary open forest 31 tC/ha. Destructive sampling showed primary closed forests consisted of 164 tC/ha, and primary open forest 40 tC/ha. According to Brown and Lugo, the estimates derived from the volume data may be more representative of tropical forests because the volume data are more numerous, and there appears to be a bias in selecting plots with larger vegetation for destructive sampling.

Table 7.5 from Bolin *et al.* (1986) shows a range of estimates derived by this method, again illustrating the variation between different sample sites.

Table 7.5   Estimates of carbon storage in tropical forests

		Rainforest	Seasonal forest
Sites	1	202.35	156.00
	2	187.38	113.33
	3	136.67	63.33

Source: Bolin *et al.* 1986.

Soils

Soil sources of carbon dioxide include respiration of living biomass, and breakdown of dead organic matter. After clearcutting of forest the first will be largely eliminated, but the second will be stimulated by the addition of fresh decomposable organic matter to the soil.

Goreau and de Mello (1988) comment that the rapid decline in carbon-dioxide release from soils after deforestation suggests that respiration of live roots, and of those insects, fungi and bacteria that depend directly on living vegetation for their food, make up approximately three-quarters of carbon-dioxide production in soils.

Over half of the soil organic matter, and thus the carbon, is contained within the top 40 cm of soil profile. The German Bundestag (1990) calculates the average carbon content for closed forests to be 133 tC/ha in the top 100 cm, and 72 tC/ha in the top 40 cm. For open forests, the equivalent estimates are 80 tC/ha in the top 100 cm, and 49 tC/ha for the top 40 cm.

The most useful soil carbon data are those compiled by the German Bundestag, giving the proportions of forested area in each category. These are shown in Table 7.6 below. It shows that in tropical forests the carbon in soil is roughly equivalent, or less, than the above-ground biomass. This contrasts with the temperate case, where soil may contain more carbon per hectare than vegetation.

Table 7.6   Estimates of biomass and soil carbon

Forest category	Area (%)	Biomass (tC/ha)	AGB (%)	Soil (tC/ha)
Lowland rainforest	11	172	83.3	118
Lowland moist forest	19	185	85.5	88
Dry forest	10	146	–	100
Montane rainforest	14	161	81.3	179
Montane moist forest	14	146	88.2	101
Montane dry forest	32	40	70.0	42

Notes:
1. Dry forests correspond to open forest; all others to close forest.
2. AGB is above ground biomass; the percentage of biomass which is above ground not including roots.

Source: Adapted from German Bundestag (1990).

Carbon Changes with Land Use Conversion

Carbon will be released at different rates according to the method of clearance and subsequent land use. With burning there will be an immediate release of CO_2 into the atmosphere, and some of the remaining carbon will be locked in ash and charcoal which is resistant to decay. The slash not converted by fire into CO_2 or charcoal and ash decays over time, releasing most of its carbon to the atmosphere within 10 to 20 years.

Studies of tropical forests indicate that significant amounts of cleared vegetation become lumber, slash, charcoal and ash; the proportion differs for closed and open forests; the smaller stature and drier climate of open forests result in the combustion of a higher proportion of the vegetation.

Houghton *et al.* (1987) maintain that over the long term, a constant rate of deforestation for shifting cultivation will not contribute a net flux of carbon to the atmosphere. Carbon released to the atmosphere during burning balances the carbon accumulating in regrowth. However, this is probably no longer the case, as in recent years the area cleared annually for shifting cultivation has increased, the rotation length has been reduced, and the area of fallow forests may also have decreased as fallow lands are cleared for permanent use. All these trends have increased the net release of carbon from the tropics.

This is illustrated by Uhl's studies (Uhl 1987) of succession following slash and burn agriculture in Amazonia. Due to burning and decomposition of forest wood and root residues, there is a dramatic decline in carbon stocks during slash and burn agriculture. After five years of succession, 86 per cent of the plant mass from the pre-existing forest had disappeared. Biomass accumulation during this time added only 38 t/ha. Total carbon stocks at five years were well below half that of the pre-burn forest stocks. Based on measurement of tree growth and litter production, total above-ground production averaged 12.58 t/ha/yr over the five-year study period, a value almost identical to that measured for mature forest. Pioneer trees grew faster than primary trees.

Soil carbon declines when soil is cultivated as a result of erosion, mechanical removal of topsoil, and increased oxidation. Oxidization is probably responsible for the greatest loss and is the only process which directly affects the CO_2 content of the atmosphere. Again, the scale and timing depends on the use after clearing. Detwiler and Hall (1988) estimate that conversion of forest soils to permanent agriculture will decrease the carbon content by 40 per cent; conversion to pasture decreases content by 20 per cent; shifting cultivation causes a decrease of 18 to 27 per cent; and selective logging seems to have little effect on soil carbon. This assumes that losses caused by permanent agriculture occur over five years; those caused by shifting cultivation occur over two years; and losses due to conversion to pasture occur within a short time. Approximately 35 years of fallow are required to return to the carbon level found under undisturbed forests.

Carbon in Subsequent Land Use

If tropical forestland is converted to pasture or permanent agriculture, then the amount of carbon stored in secondary vegetation is equivalent to the carbon content of the biomass of crops planted, or the grass grown on the pasture. If a secondary forest is allowed to grow, then carbon will accumulate, and maximum biomass density is attained after a relatively short time (45 years according to German Bundestag, 1990). Table 7.7 summarizes the carbon content of soils and biomass in the relevant land uses. These data can be used to calculate the total changes in biomass and soil carbon as a result of land use changes, as shown in Table 7.8. This table illustrates the net carbon storage effects of land use conversion from tropical forests (either closed primary, closed secondary, or open forests), to shifting cultivation, permanent agriculture, or pasture. The negative figures represent emissions of carbon; for example, conversion from closed primary forest to shifting agriculture results in a net loss of 204 tC/ha. The greatest loss of carbon involves change of land use from primary closed forest to permanent agriculture. These figures represent the once and for all change that will occur in carbon storage as a result of the various land use conversions.

Table 7.7   Carbon storage in different land uses (tC/ha)

	Biomass	Soils	Total
Closed primary forest	167	116	283
Closed secondary forest	85–135	67–102	152–237
Open forest	68	47	115
Forest fallow (closed)	28–43	93	121–136
Forest fallow (open)	12–18	38	50–56
Shifting cultivation (year 1)	10–16	31–76	41–92
Shifting cultivation (year 2)	16–35	31–76	47–111
Permanent cultivation	5–10	51–60	56–70
Pasture	5	41–75	46–80

Note: Assumes carbon will reach minimum after five years in cropland, and after two years in pasture.
Source: German Bundestag (1990), Houghton *et al.* (1987).

Table 7.8   Changes in carbon with land use conversion (tC/ha)

	Original C	Shifting agriculture	Permanent agriculture	Pasture
Original		79	63	63
Closed primary	283	−204	−220	−220
Closed secondary	194	−106	−152	−122
Open forest	115	−36	−52	−52

Note: Where range was given in Table 7.7 a mid-point is used here. Shifting agriculture represents carbon in biomass and soils in second year of shifting cultivation cycle.

The estimates in Table 7.8 show emissions of carbon if all the biomass is lost. This may be true if burnt, but not if used for timber. When calculating the net effects of deforestation on carbon flux, it is important to also consider the end uses of timber cleared from the forest. This may contain the bulk of biomass carbon, and although removed from the growing site, the carbon may not be released to the atmosphere as CO_2; it may remain stored for some time depending on the use, and the life of timber products produced. A model developed by Dewar (1990) describes carbon storage in vegetation (especially forests) and in products removed from vegetation (timber, grain). This illustrates the relation between carbon storage, vegetative growth, rotation length, and the carbon retention properties of products. This enables management strategies to be examined with respect to their effect on carbon storage (see also Thompson and Matthews 1989). This issue is not examined further in the present study which concentrates solely on effects of land use strategies on vegetation and soil carbon.

Table 7.8 shows that the largest loss of carbon from both biomass and soils occurs with a change of land use from tropical forest to permanent agriculture. This change also degrades the environment in many other ways, including loss of soil fertility and erosion. Conversion to pasture involves changes of a similar magnitude, though if the emissions of methane from cattle grazing this pasture were included, this conversion may have more serious consequences in terms of greenhouse gas emissions. The conversion of tropical forests to shifting agriculture produces considerable emissions of CO_2 and soil and biomass take many years to recover their carbon store. These results are necessarily generalized, and it must be stressed that empirical evidence from individual experimental sites may provide different data. In particular, different practices of shifting agriculture will affect the carbon flux in differing ways. Some methods of shifting agriculture may be less damaging to the environment than others.

More research is now being conducted into less damaging cultivation practices. For example, Southworth *et al.* (1991) have developed a model which simulates tenant farmer colonization and its effects on deforestation and associated carbon losses. The model is used to contrast the typical pattern of colonist land use in Rondônia, Brazil, with a system of sustainable agriculture. Sustainable agriculture is simulated to resemble the activities of a group of immigrant Japanese farmers who have settled in eastern Brazil. In this system, farmers clear plots of 10 ha each in the first two years of settlement. Annual crops are planted in the first and second years; annual and perennial crops intercropped in the third year so that carbon recovery is initiated. After ten years of intercropping, the land is left fallow for eight years. The intercropping acts to increase the rate of succession, and no significant carbon loss or gain is assumed to take place during this period.

The dual role of forests both as a source of greenhouse gases and as a sink for CO_2 gives rise to a number of forest-related options aimed to ameliorate greenhouse gas concentrations in the atmosphere; curb deforestation; reforestation; and sink enhancement. Of these the first should be given priority, given the range of services provided by tropical forests.

The Cost-benefit Model: Results

The representative estimates in Table 7.8 now permit us to test the results of the cost-benefit model set out earlier. There it was suggested that a global value of $10 per tonne carbon might be indicative of global warming damage. Note that, since the source of CO_2 emissions is immaterial as far as warming effects are concerned, this global damage figure is applicable to any source of carbon emissions. From Table 7.8, then, we can conclude that converting an open forest to agriculture or pasture would result in global warming damage of, say $300 to $500 per hectare; conversion of closed secondary forest would cause damage of $1000 to $1500 per hectare; and conversion of primary forest to agriculture would give rise to damage of about $2000 per hectare. Note that these estimates allow for carbon fixation in the subsequent land use.

How do these estimates relate to the development benefits of land use conversion? We can illustrate with respect to the Amazon region of Brazil. Schneider (1992) reports upper bound values of $300 per hectare for land in Rondônia. Fearnside (1985, 1991) reports carbon loss rates of some 105 to 125 tonnes per hectare for conversion of primary forest to pasture, well below the representative figures given in Table 7.8. But taking these apparently low emission figures suggests carbon credit values of $1050 to $1250 per hectare, three to four times the price of land in Rondônia.[3]

The policy implications of this kind of analysis are clear. If the world is serious about combating global warming and biodiversity loss, it will pay to direct policy in a cost- effective manner at the cheapest options first. The analysis here suggests, strongly, that one of the cheapest options is to reduce tropical deforestation via some form of international transfer based on incentives not to burn the forests for clearance. Exactly how these incentives could be designed is a complex and separate issue, but there is scope for the Global Environment Facility to encourage such reductions in deforestation through its investment portfolio, and for tradeable burning rights to be experimented with.

Notes

1. For variants of this idea involving 'tradeable development rights' see Katzman and Cale (1990); Sedjo, Bowes and Wiseman (1990); and Schneider (1992).
2. Comparisons are hazardous since Ayres and Walter (1991) relate their judgemental estimates to earlier versions of Nordhaus's papers which gave damage as $3.3 to $37.0 per tonne of carbon

equivalent, figures that are revised in Nordhaus (1991a, 1991b). Neither do Ayres and Walter make the units (CO_2 or C) clear, but they appear to be CO_2 as carbon.
3.   Schneider (1992) suggests a ratio of seven times based on a reading of Nordhaus's work on the damage costs of global warming (Nordhaus 1991a, 1991b). But Schneider has (a) used the earlier, incorrect drafts of Nordhaus's paper, and (b) has assumed Nordhaus's damage estimates relate to CO_2 rather than carbon.

References

Andrasko, K. (1990), 'Global Warming and Forests : An Overview of Current Knowledge'. *Unasylva*, 163, 3–11.

Ayres, R. and Walter, J. (1991), 'The Greenhouse Effect: Damages, Costs and Abatement', *Environmental and Resource Economics*, **1**, (3), 237–70.

Balick, M. and Mendelsohn, R. (1991), 'Assessing the Economic Value of Traditional Medicines from Tropical Rain Forests', *Conservation Biology*, **6**, (1), March, 128–30.

Bolin, B., Doos, B.R., Jager, J. and Warrick, R. (eds) (1986), *The Greenhouse Effect, Climate Change and Ecosystems*, Chichester: John Wiley.

Bouwman, A.F. (1990), 'Land Use Related Sources of Greenhouse Gases', *Land Use Policy*, 7, pp. 154–64.

Brown, S. and Lugo, A.E. (1984), 'Biomass of Tropical Forest: A New Estimate based on Forest Volumes', *Science*, 223, pp. 1290–3.

Cannell, M.G.R. (1982), *World Forest Biomass and Primary Production Data*, London: Academic Press.

Cline, W. (1992), *The Economics of Global Warming*, Cambridge: Cambridge University Press.

Davidson, J. (1985), 'Economic Use of Tropical Moist Forests', *The Environmentalist*, Supplement 9.

Detwiler, R.P. and Hall, C.A. (1988), 'Tropical Forest and the Global Carbon Cycle', *Science*, 239, pp. 42–7.

Dewar, R.C. (1990), 'A Model of Carbon Storage in Forests and Forest Products', *Tree Physiology*, 6, pp. 417–28.

Fankhauser, S. (1992), 'A Point Estimate of Global Warming Damage', Centre for Social and Economic Research on the Global Environment, University College London, London.

Fearnside, P.M. (1985), 'Brazil's Amazon Forest and the Global Carbon Problem', *Intercienca*, 10.4.

Fearnside, P.M. (1991), 'Greenhouse Gas Contributions from Deforestation in Brazilian Amazonia', in J.S. Levine (ed.), *Global Biomass Burning: Atmospheric, Climatic and Biospheric Implications*, Cambridge, Mass: MIT Press.

Federal Republic of Germany, (1991), *FRG Tropical Forest Report*, Bonn, March.

Food and Agriculture Organisation (1991), unpublished deforestation data, October, Rome: FAO.

German Bundestag (edited), (1990), *Protecting the Tropical Forests: A High Priority International Task*, Bonn: Bonner Universitats Buchdruckerei.

Goreau, T.J. and de Mello, W.Z. (1988), 'Tropical Deforestation: Some Effects on Atmospheric Chemistry', *Ambio*, 17.4, pp. 275–81.

Grayson, A.J. (1989), Carbon Dioxide, Global Warming and Forestry', *Forestry Commission Research Information Note 146*, Forestry Commission: Alice Holt.

Gribbin, J. (1990), *Hothouse Earth, The Greenhouse Effect and Gaia*, London: Transworld Publishers Ltd.

Houghton, R.A. (1990), 'The Future Role of Tropical Forests in Affecting Carbon Dioxide Concentration of the Atmosphere', *Ambio*, **19**, (4), 204–9.

Houghton, R.A., Boone, R.D., Melillo, J.M., Palm, C.A., Woodwell, G.M., Myers, N., Moore III, B. and Stole, D.L., (1985), 'Net Flux of Carbon Dioxide from Tropical Forests in 1980'. *Nature*, 316, pp. 617–20.

Houghton, R.A., Boone, R.D., Fruci, J.R., Hobbie, J.E., Melillo, J.M., Palm, C.A., Peterson, B.J., Shaver, G.R., Woodwell, G.M., Moore, B., Skole, D.L. and Myers, N. (1987), 'The Flux of Carbon from Terrestrial Ecosystems to the Atmosphere in 1980 due to Changes in Land Use: Geographical Distribution of the Global Flux'. *Tellus*, 39B, pp.122–39.

Johnson, B. (1991), *Responding to Tropical Deforestation*, Godalming: Worldwide Fund for Nature UK.

Jordan, C.F. (ed.) (1989), 'An Amazonian Rainforest: The Structure and Function of a Nutrient Stressed Ecosystem and the Impact of Slash and Burn Agriculture'. *UNESCO Man and Biosphere Series Volume 2*, Paris: UNESCO.

Katzman, M. and Cale W. (1990), 'Tropical Forest Preservation Using Economic Incentives: a Proposal of Conservation Easements', *BioScience*, **40**, (11), 827–32.

Kyrklund, B. (1990), 'The Potential of Trees and the Forestry Industry in Reducing Excess Carbon Dioxide', *Unasylva*, 163, pp. 12–14.

Leduc, G. (1985), 'The Political Economy of Tropical Deforestation'. in H.J. Leonard, (ed.) *Divesting Nature's Capital: The Political Economy of Environmental Abuse in the Third World*, New York: Holmes and Meier.

Marland, G. (1988), *The Prospect of Solving the CO₂ Problem Through Global Reforestation*, US Department of Energy Carbon Dioxide Research Division Report TR039, February.

Moore, B., Boone, R.D., Hobbie, U.E., Houghton, R.A., Melillo, J.M., Peterson, B.J., Shaver, G.R., Vorosmarty, C.J. and Woodwell, G.M., (1981), 'A Simple Model for Analysis of the Role of Terrestrial Ecosystems in The Global Carbon Budget', in Bert Bolin (ed.), *Carbon Cycle Modelling*, Scope 16, Chichester: John Wiley.

Myers, N. (1989), 'The Greenhouse Effect: A Tropical Forestry Response', *Biomass*, **18**, (1), 73–8.

Myers, N. (1990), 'Tropical Forests', in J. Leggett (ed.) *Global Warming, The Green Peace Report*, Oxford: Oxford University Press.

Myers, N. and Goreau, T.J. (1990), 'Tropical Forests and the Greenhouse Effect: A Management Response', *Climatic Change*, **19**, (1–2), 215–26.

Nordhaus, W. (1991a), 'To Slow or Not to Slow: the Economics of the Greenhouse Effect', *Economic Journal*, **101**, (407), July, 938–48.

Nordhaus, W. (1991b), 'A Sketch of the Economics of the Greenhouse Effect', *American Economic Review, Papers and Proceedings*, **81**, (2), 146–50.

Pearce, D.W. (1990), 'An Economic Approach to Saving the Tropical Forests', in D.Helm (ed.), *Economic Policy Towards the Environment*, Oxford: Blackwell.

Pearce, D.W., Moran D. and Fripp, E. (1992), *The Economic Value of Biological and Cultural Diversity*, Report to the World Conservation Union, Centre for Social and Economic Research on the Global Environment, University College, London.

Pearce D.W. and Puroshothaman S. (1993), 'Protecting Biological Diversity: the Economic Value of Medicinal Plants', in T. Swanson (ed.), *Biodiversity and Botany: the Values of Medicinal Plants*, Cambridge: Cambridge University Press.

Pearce, F. (1989), *Turning Up the Heat: Our Perilous Future in the Global Greenhouse*, London: Palladin.

Peters, C.M., Gentry, A.H. and Mendelsohn, R. (1989), 'Valuation of an Amazonian Rainforest', *Nature*, **339**, 29 June, 655–6.

Schneider, R. (1992), *Brazil: an Analysis of Environmental Problems in the Amazon*, Report No.9104-BR. World Bank, Latin American and Caribbean Region, Washington, DC.

Sedjo, R.A. (1989), 'Forests to Offset the Greenhouse Effect', *Journal of Forestry*, **87**, (7), 12–15.

Sedjo, R.A., Bowes M. and Wiseman, C. (1991), 'Toward a Worldwide System of Tradeable Forest Protection and Management Obligations', Resources for the Future, Energy and Natural Resources Division, Paper 91–16.

Setzer, A.W. and Pereira, M.C. (1991), 'Amazonia Biomass Burnings in 1987 and an Estimate of Their Tropospheric Emissions', *Ambio*, **20** (1), 19–22.

Southworth, F., Dale, V.H. and O'Neill, R.V. (1991), 'Contrasting Patterns of Land Use in Rondonia, Brazil: Simulating the Effects on Carbon Release', *International Social Science Journal*, November 1991, pp. 681–98.

Thompson, D.A. and Matthews, R.W. (1989), 'The Storage of Carbon in Trees and Timber', Forestry Commission Research Information Note 160, Edinburgh.

Tobias, D. and Mendelsohn, R. (1990), 'The Value of Recreation in a Tropical Rainforest Reserve', *Ambio*, **20**, 91–3.

Uhl, C. (1987), 'Factors Controlling Succession following Slash and Burn Agriculture in Amazonia', *Journal of Ecology*, **75**, 377–407.

Wood, W.B. (1990), 'Tropical Deforestation: Balancing Regional Development Demands and Global Environmental Concerns', *Global Environmental Change*, **1**, (1), 23–41.

World Resources Institute, (1990), *World Resources 1990–91*, Oxford: Oxford University Press.

8. The relevance of global climatic effects to project appraisal

J.T. Winpenny

It is now accepted by many, though by no means all, scientists that certain man-made processes are responsible for a rise in global temperatures. Another set of factors is causing the depletion of the earth's atmospheric ozone layer. There is growing understanding of the activities responsible for these phenomena.

Global climatic effects are classic externalities. Their perpetrators experience a negligible cost from their actions, but make everyone worse off. At present those responsible for global warming or depletion of the ozone layer, and the consumers of their products, do not directly bear any of the costs incurred by international society from their actions. The issue addressed here is whether it is feasible to attribute such costs directly to projects, and if so, how.

Although they are similar in principle to the more familiar localized externalities (such as the effect of soil erosion on downstream farmers and industrial air pollution on urban residents), global externalities possess features which complicate any straightforward attribution to projects.

In the first place there is still great uncertainty over the extent of global warming, and even, in some scientifically respectable quarters, about whether it exists at all. Secondly, the incremental effect from new activities is not easy to disentangle from the 'commitment' implied by historical actions, given the natural lags in the climatic system. Thirdly, the distribution of the costs (and benefits) from global warming is very uneven, and important parties may even stand to gain by it.

At the time of writing, the state of knowledge about these global environmental issues is very fluid, and research continues. Meanwhile, international diplomatic efforts are in train to agree preventative actions and the necessary systems of controls, incentives and sanctions. This chapter first describes the phenomena in question, briefly reviews their likely causes and effects, considers some influential attempts to quantify global climatic costs, and ends by suggesting how global externalities can be attributed to projects.

Greenhouse Effect

The presence of greenhouse gases (technically, radiatively important gases (RIGs)) in the earth's atmosphere keeps the planet over 30°C warmer than it would otherwise be. These gases are carbon dioxide (CO_2), nitrous oxide (N_2O), methane (CH_4), tropospheric ozone (03), and chlorofluorocarbons (CFCs). They allow short-wave visible radiation to enter the atmosphere, but absorb and reradiate (that is, trap) long-wave thermal radiation, hence the greenhouse analogy.

In theory, past emissions of these gases have committed the earth to a warming of 1–2.5°C over pre-industrial levels. In practice, a rise of about 0.5°C has been observed during the past century, almost half of which has been since 1965. The majority view of scientists is that by 2020 global mean temperatures will have risen to 1.8°C above pre-industrial levels (range 1.3 to 2.5°C), with an increase in global mean precipitation and evaporation of 3 per cent.

By 2070 the range of temperature increase is likely to be 2.4 to 5.1°C (best estimate 3.5°C), and precipitation 7 per cent greater. Snow cover and sea ice areas may be smaller.[1]

These changes in temperature will be greater in higher latitudes than at the Equator, thus North America, USSR and Europe will be more affected than tropical regions.

The most obvious result of such warming would be a rise in sea level due to the thermal expansion of the oceans and melting of some land ice. The sea level is rising at 1.6 to 3.3cm per decade, one-quarter of which is due to the thermal expansion of the oceans and the rest to the melting of glaciers and snowfields. Between now and 2030 the sea is predicted to rise by about 20cm (range 10 to 32cm) and by 2070 by 45cm (range 33 to 75cm).

Depletion of Ozone Layer

Ozone is present in the atmosphere up to a height of about 60 km. At lower levels it is one of the greenhouse gases, but at higher levels it is a filter for ultra-violet radiations from the sun. It prevents the most dangerous ultraviolet wavelengths reaching the earth's surface, where they would otherwise cause sunburn, snow blindness, skin cancer, ageing and wrinkling of skin, and other effects on plant and animal life.

Certain trace gases help to break down atmospheric ozone, including nitrogen oxides, water vapour, chloroform, methane and CFCs. CFCs, used mainly in aerosols, foam-blowing agents and refrigeration, are especially important in this process.

The concentration of the trace gases, and in particular the CFCs, in the atmosphere is increasing, mainly as a result of industrial activity. Although the presence of ozone at lower atmospheric levels is increasing, there are signs of some (as yet small) reduction at upper levels. The most definite evidence of a weakening in the ozone layer comes from observations in the Antarctic, which record a reduction by 40 per cent since 1957, most of which has occurred since

1977.[2] There is considerable scientific uncertainty about chemical and physical effects in the atmosphere, and what causes them. Another problem is that CFCs take some time to rise to the level where they damage the ozone layer. Hence there are considerable lags in the process, and, by the same token, the phenomenon will continue long after the emission of CFCs has been reduced or eliminated.

Causes

The relative contribution of different RIGs to global warming depends on the rate at which they are emitted, and the lifetime of each gas, amongst other factors. It has been estimated that the cumulative effect of 1990 emissions on 'global warming potential' over 100 years is as follows for the different gases: carbon dioxide 61 per cent; methane 15 per cent; nitrous oxide 4 per cent, CFCs 9.4 per cent in total, others 10.6 per cent.

Another way of viewing the relative responsibility of the different gases is to ask what reductions in the current level of emissions would be necessary to stabilize concentrations at current levels. The figures are: carbon dioxide 60–80 per cent; methane 15 to 20 per cent, nitrous oxide 70 to 80 per cent; CFC 11 70 to 75 per cent; CFC 12 75 to 85 per cent; and HCFC 2240 to 2250 per cent (IPCC 1990).

Taking into account the origins of the various gases, global warming can be roughly attributed to the following main activities: energy use (direct and indirect) 49 per cent, deforestation 14 per cent, agriculture 13 per cent, and industry 24 per cent (quoted in Trexler *et al.*, 1990).

On a geographical basis, emissions of carbon dioxide from burning fossil fuel — the largest single contributor to global warming — is heavily concentrated in developed and industrializing countries: the USA (25 per cent), USSR (20 per cent), western Europe (15 per cent), China (10 per cent) and Japan (6 per cent). Developing countries apart from China contributed only 15 per cent in 1985.

However, this is likely to change rapidly, as developing countries industrialize and increase their per capita energy use — currently only one-sixth that of industrialized countries. One estimate has industrialising developing countries emitting 50 per cent of all carbon dioxide within a matter of several decades (Trexler et al., 1990). These figures leave out the contribution of developing countries to CO_2 emissions from deforestation, which is estimated to be between 20 and 33 per cent.

Effects

If the temperature changes described earlier do come about, they are likely to have the following kinds of effect (COMSEC 1989; Trexler *et al.* 1990; IPCC 1990).

A rise in sea level
This rise is estimated at 33 to 75cm by 2070. Some have higher estimates — 40 to 120cm (Trexler *et al.* 1990) — while the more pessimistic scenarios predict rises of several metres. The worst outcome would be melting of the west Antarctic ice sheet, which would cause a rise of seven meters. Even the more modest predicted rises would totally submerge some island groups (such as the Maldives and some Pacific Atolls), erode barrier islands, and inundate many coastal wetlands and estuaries. There would be saline intrusion into ground-water supplies. Low-lying coastal hinterlands, which include many of the world's most productive and densely-settled areas, would be lost to the sea.

A number of the other effects discussed below stem from a rise in sea level.

Effects on vegetation
There would be a quickening of the hydrological cycle, leading to a slight increase in global rainfall and changes in the timing and distribution of regional rainfall. The timing and location of monsoons would probably change. Rainfall would probably decline in mid-continental regions and increase in coastal and high-latitude regions. Combined with higher evaporation, this would spell growing water shortages in important food-producing areas.

The predicted climatic changes would occur at a much faster rate than historical changes, and it is unlikely that vegetation would have time to adapt smoothly. Some species would be reduced or die out, whilst others would spread rapidly. The growth of some plants would be stimulated by the higher temperatures and greater supply of carbon dioxide, but so would weeds and insect pests.

Increased incidence of natural disasters and other extreme events
Hurricanes and typhoons would probably increase in frequency and intensity, since they draw their energy from ocean heat, which would increase. Weather patterns would become more extreme, with more frequent droughts, early frosts, cold periods, storms, storm surges, and so on. It is particularly difficult to predict the local distribution of these effects because of the little-understood interaction between the oceans and the climatic zones, and the outcome for major ocean circulatory systems (such as the Gulf Stream).

Social and economic effects
Energy use would change. In temperate latitudes there would be less use for heating and more for air conditioning. The net effect would probably be to increase the use of energy and power. The fishing industry would be disrupted by the shifts in the boundary between land and sea, the loss of breeding grounds in wetlands and estuaries, and the alterations in species composition due to these changes and the rise in sea temperatures.

The net effect on food supply and commercially-important crops is hard to predict, but it is safe to expect a need for major adaptations. Crop zones could migrate by hundreds of kilometres. Forests could be especially at risk as people migrate and adjust to new agricultural systems. Water would become an increasing constraint in a number of important agricultural areas.

Tourism and recreation would be affected, as many islands and beaches were lost and weather conditions became more unpredictable. Winter sports would suffer. Many important habitats (wetlands, forests, wildlands) would be lost or invaded. Changes in climate and vegetation, along with population movements, would stretch the adaptation of species up to and beyond their natural limits.

The loss of densely-settled coastal lowlands and islands would set in motion migration to other parts of the same country and to other countries. `Ecological refugees' would increase in numbers. There would be major needs for new infra- structure — housing, transport, water supplies, health care, education, and so on.

For its part, the depletion of the ozone layer would affect human health, the growth of vegetation and marine life, and the longevity of materials. The dangerous part of the spectrum of ultraviolet radiation which is mainly absorbed by the ozone layer is the UVB. If more of this is allowed to penetrate to the earth's surface, both localized and generalized (melanoma) skin cancer is likely to increase, mainly among white-skinned people living in lower latitudes. One estimate is that a 1 per cent depletion of the ozone layer would increase the incidence of skin cancer by 2 per cent (or 6000 cases in the USA per year). This assumes no change in human behaviour. If CFC emissions could be stabilized, it has been estimated that 1.65 million cases of non-melanoma skin cancer could be prevented (UNEP/GEMS 1987).

Increased exposure to UVB would also tend to suppress the efficiency with which the body's immune system works. An increased incidence of skin infections might be one outcome of this. Plant and tree growth may suffer, since UVB damages chemicals involved in photosynthesis. Certain crops have been identified as particularly sensitive — cotton, peas, beans, melons, cabbage and soya. Grass and trees may be similarly affected.

Ultraviolet rays penetrating deep into clear water threaten single-celled algae. Working through the marine food-chain, this would affect edible fish. There might also be direct effects on fish larvae. Ultraviolet radiation also increases the degradation of many synthetic materials, for instance paint, glazing, car roofs and plastics used in building, such as PVCs. Other possible effects include more eye complaints and more incidence of smog.

Costs of Global Warming

In spite of the great uncertainties about the existence, size and effects of these global phenomena, some attempts have been made to estimate their economic costs. One approach is to estimate greenhouse damage costs assuming no action were taken to control emissions. Another type of estimate is that of the costs of mitigating the effects accompanying global warming, such as by raising sea defences. A third type assesses the costs of abatement — curbing the emissions of greenhouse gases at source.

The first type of study is analogous to taking the effect on production (EOP) approach to the economic valuation of environmental effects, while the second and third are akin to the replacement cost (RC) and preventive expenditure (PE) methods (Dixon *et al.* 1988; Winpenny 1991). In principle, if the values from EOP are less than those from PE/RC, the policy conclusion is that it is cheaper to let the effects happen. Alternatively, if the costs of abatement (PE) are less than EOP or RC, it is rational to curb emissions at source.

At a more refined level, the 'optimal' amount of abatement can be estimated, at a point where the cost of abating the marginal unit of greenhouse gas equals the damage that it causes (Nordhaus 1990). This type of calculation does, however, depend on far greater confidence in the effects, and firmer estimation of their costs, than anyone now possesses.

The two studies considered here (Nordhaus 1990, and Ayres and Walter 1991) combine estimates of the economic damage from the greenhouse effect and certain defensive measures against sea-level rise. Other studies, not considered in detail here, estimate the national costs of abatement at source (notably Manne and Richels 1990).

Taking Nordhaus's work first, the sectors of the US economy are divided into categories according to how sensitive they are judged to be to climatic changes. Agriculture, forestry and fisheries are judged to be most sensitive, and contribute 3.1 per cent to GNP, while sectors of 'moderate' sensitivity include construction, water transport and utilities, accounting for a further 10.1 per cent of GNP. Other sectors are taken as largely unaffected by climatic change.

No firm view is taken of the net effect on agriculture, which could be plus or minus $10 bn, according to whether the stimulus from extra carbon dioxide were enough to offset the losses from other factors. The main quantified damage is from the consequences of sea-level rise on the need to protect the more valuable property and open coasts by levees and dykes.

The total US coastline is taken to be 20 000km and the average cost of protection $5m per km. However, there would also be land losses, estimated to be 77 ha per km of coastline, or 15 540sq km in total. The lost land is assumed to be worth $5000 per ha. The coastal defence works ($5.7bn) plus the land losses ($0.48 bn) are converted to an annual equivalent loss of $6.18 bn per year.

The other main quantified damage is from a net increase in the consumption of energy. This results from offsetting the reduced demand for space heating (savings of $1.16 bn) against the increased demand for air conditioning ($1.65 bn).

The total economic damage from these two sources is $6.67 bn in 1981 prices, or 0.28 per cent of US GNP. It is recognized that many items are omitted from this estimate, and an upper bound of ten times higher than this is suggested, which would amount to about 2 per cent of US GNP.

Worldwide Estimate

These estimates for the USA are scaled up by a factor of 8.1 to illustrate what the effect on global income might be in 2050 if the US costs could be taken as typical (global income is projected to be $26 trillion by 2050 in 1981 prices). On this basis, most likely annual world damages from global warming were projected to be $54 bn in 2050 with an upper limit of $520 bn. Related to expected emissions by then of 16.9 bn tons of CO_2 equivalent, a 'marginal shadow emission damage' figure of $3.3 per ton of CO_2 equivalent is derived (or $36.9 per ton in the worst case).

The above figures, grossed up for the world as a whole, are adjusted by Ayres and Walter (1991) to allow for a rather greater range of effects. Coastal land losses are increased to $2.5 trillion, reflecting the same unit value of land but a much greater hinterland area at risk. Coastal protection costs are estimated to be in the range $2.5 to $5 trillion, derived from applying a unit cost of $5mn per km to a total world coastline of 0.5 to 1.0 m km. Some estimate is also made of the cost of resettling refugees, amounting to $0.5 to $1.0 trillion (250 million people displaced, at $1000 to $2000 per head representing direct resettlement costs and lost output for two years).

The total costs of the above reworking amount to $5.5 to $8.5 trillion worldwide, assumed to be spread over 50 years. On an average annual basis they are equivalent to 0.7 to 1.0 per cent of gross world income — greater than Nordhaus's best estimates, but within his range of error.

The original study by Nordhaus was prepared as a first attempt to apply cost-benefit analysis to compare the costs of various kind of abatement actions with the expected greenhouse damage costs, as a means of deciding what kinds of abatement actions were justified. It contains many disclaimers and qualifications, and it is worth stressing some of its limitations.

Both the studies by Nordhaus and Ayres and Walter rely heavily on effects stemming from sea-level rise. Apart from energy use, the many other possible effects of global warming discussed earlier are not treated. It is quite likely that global warming would have its greatest effects on agriculture in developing countries, rather than the damage caused by the rise in sea levels (IPPC 1990).

The global estimates are obtained by extrapolating the US figures to the world as a whole, which assumes the same economic structure and damage pattern in the global economy in 2050 as prevailed in the USA in 1981. It is obviously impossible to predict the state of technology, and therefore consumption patterns, by the middle of the next century.

Although the use of a wide range of values (where the worst case is ten times the best estimate) is useful in suggesting upper bounds on national damages, it is of little help in fixing a shadow marginal damage level per ton of emission.

Neither set of estimates does justice to the loss of consumer surplus from reduced enjoyment of environmental services — wildlife, forests, coastlines, and so on — or the possible irreversible losses to future generations.

In short, these two studies are best viewed as pre-feasibility exercises in assessing the costs and benefits of abatement policies, illustrating the method, the type of data needed, and 'orders of magnitude' estimates of some of the more easily identified effects.

There is clearly great scope for further work in confirming the physical effects involved, and assessing the likely damage costs in economies with radically different features from those of the USA.

Attribution to Projects

To accurately ascribe global climatic costs to a project, the project analyst needs information on:

(a) the likely future effects of global warming; and responsibility for those effects (types of emission, timing, location);
(b) the incremental effect of current actions, compared with the commitment to warming caused by past activities;
(c) estimates of the economic cost of the effects at various future dates, discounted to the present; and
(d) the means to assign responsibility, and thus costs (benefits), to individual projects.

This is a tall order. Any valuation method relying on the direct attribution of costs and benefits is unreliable in the present state of our knowledge, since the global environmental costs resulting from a particular project are subject to enormous estimation problems. This is true whether we are considering estimators based on direct effects or those based on defensive measures.

In present circumstances, it is more practicable to consider the attribution problem in a context where a ceiling (or target, or quota) for the emission of greenhouse gases is accepted or imposed. This could be at international, national, or local level.

To simplify the discussion, assume that a national ceiling is agreed for each country, and that these could be monitored and enforced. (At the time of writing many countries have accepted such a target for CFC gases, and there is active international discussion of the feasibility of agreeing ceilings for greenhouse gases.)

A proposed project (such as a thermal power station) or activity (such as continued burning of tropical forest) might use up part of this emission quota. This would force other sources of emissions to cease, or undertake abatement, either now (if the country was already up to quota) or at some time in the future (if the country was still within its ceiling, in which case the cost would be discounted). In principle, the cost of this abatement action, wherever and whenever it fell, would be the economic cost attributable to the offending project. In other words, within a national emissions ceiling, a project which threatens to increase emissions should be debited with the marginal cost of abating that volume of emissions.

If economic policymakers were rational, they would try to ensure that the marginal amount of abatement was done at least national economic cost. How this was achieved would depend on the circumstances of each country. In countries where the main emitters were the industrial and power sectors, it might be feasible to create national 'bubbles' for each greenhouse gas, and to allow emitters to trade permits to emit within these ceilings (akin to tradeable permits used in the context of air pollution).

This would not be an appropriate solution for countries where a significant part of emissions came from forest or grassland burning, farming, households and vehicles. In some cases a carbon tax might be part of a package of measures, imposed at a level calculated to achieve the national emissions target. This would depend on estimates of the elasticities of demand and supply in the main emitting sectors.[3]

Marginal Abatement

Marginal abatement costs can be estimated by constructing a 'savings curve', relating the cost of abating a unit of carbon-dioxide emission to the volume of abatement, and ranking the various options in ascending order of cost (analogous to ranking sources of electricity generation in merit order).

In one such exercise for developing countries, ERL (1990) gave a high cost-effectiveness ranking to fuel efficiency measures in industry, and power station rehabilitation. The management of natural forest, and various kinds of refor-estation also came out well when their other environmental benefits were taken into account. At the other extreme, fuel switching in power generation was considered a high-cost abatement option.

The marginal abatement cost can only be determined with some knowledge of the feasible alternatives open to each country, and it is unwise to generalize. In some cases, the cessation of forest burning would be the most cost-effective course, but only if this were enforceable. Curbing methane emissions by taking land out of rice cultivation is unlikely to be the most feasible or cost-effective option in many rice-producing countries.

Whatever the empirical outcome, the cost of national abatement required because of the creation of a project should be included as a 'shadow project' when that scheme is being appraised. It is only by coincidence that this would be equal to the cost of abatement if the project entity had to undertake it itself.

Projects that reduce greenhouse gas emissions, or which absorb carbon, have positive benefits equivalent to the avoided costs of abatement on others. The analogy is with energy efficiency and power-saving projects.

Firms and public utilities responsible for greenhouse gas emissions sometimes undertake their own 'compensatory projects' (such as thermal-power stations and car manufacturers planting trees in other countries to absorb carbon created by their own activities). Although some of these schemes are gimmicks, to the extent that they result in genuine abatement offsets, they internalize global costs and represent shadow projects made real.

Certain activities have national, international and global effects. Industrial and power-station emissions cause national air pollution, and acid rain in neighbouring countries, and contribute greenhouse gases. The same is true of the burning of tropical forest, and the annual firing of grasslands. Their positive equivalents are projects to control air pollution, and so on, which are undertaken for national benefits, but which also have international and global gains.

Provided the incidence of costs and benefits can be sorted out into national and global categories, this is not an insuperable objection to the method proposed. A coal-fired power station in India, for instance, would be appraised partly for its national net benefits (a combination of economic and environmental effects) and partly for its effect on greenhouse gas emissions.

If India were party to an agreement to limit its national emissions, part of the cost of that power station, to be included as a shadow project, would be the marginal abatement cost imposed on the economy. If this shadow project were very costly, this would influence the decision as to whether to proceed with the project.

The valuation principles discussed here should help in assessing the respective economic values of national and international environmental effects, which will be important elements in future international environmental diplomacy.

Conclusion

The effect on global climate of the production of greenhouse gases and CFCs is under active investigation. Efforts are intensifying to produce estimates of allowing, preventing, and abating these emissions at source. Estimates so far available are interesting illustrations of the scale of possible benefits, but they are incomplete, and offer a wide range of values which makes them unreliable bases for attributing costs to the responsible projects.

Appraisers are on better ground in a scenario in which national ceilings, targets or quotas are accepted. It is then legitimate to debit projects with the national opportunity cost of their actions, namely, the cost of keeping within national ceilings, or the national marginal abatement cost. There is, so far, little empirical evidence on these costs, but where it is available it should be included as a shadow project in the appraisal. Activities which reduce greenhouse gas emissions should receive corresponding credit, equal to the avoided cost of abatement.

Notes

1. Data in this section are drawn from IPCC (1990); Trexler, Mintzer and Moomaw (1990); and Arrhenius and Waltz (1990).
2. Data from UNEP/GEMS (1987).
3. See Manne and Richels (1990) for US estimates.

References

Arrhenius, E. and Waltz, T.W. (1990), 'The Greenhouse Effect: Implications for Economic Development', *World Bank Discussion Paper,* No. 78, Washington, DC: World Bank.

Ayres, R. and Walter, J. (1991), 'The Greenhouse Effect Damages, Costs and Abatement', *Environmental and Resource Economics,* **1**, 237–70.

COMSEC (1989), 'Climate Change: Meeting the Challenge', report by a Commonwealth Group of Experts, London: Commonwealth Secretariat.

Dixon, J., Carpenter, R.A., Fallon, L.A., Sherman, P.B. and Manipomoke, S. (1988), *Economic Analysis of the Environmental Impact of Development Projects,* London: Earthscan Publications.

ERL (Environmental Resources Ltd) (1990), 'Assessing the Cost-Effectiveness of Selected Options to Reduce CO_2 Emissions in Developing Countries', Report to ODA, February.

Intergovernmental Panel on Climate Change (IPCC), (1990), *Climatic Change, the IPCC Scientific Assessment,* Report from Working Group 1, Cambridge University Press.

Manne, A.S. and Richels, R.G. (1990), 'CO_2 Emissions Limits: an Economic Cost Analysis for the USA', *The Energy Journal,* **11**, (2), 51–74.

Nordhaus, W.D. (1990), 'To Slow or Not to Slow: The Economics of the Greenhouse Effect', mimeo, Department of Economics, Yale University.

Trexler, M.C., Mintzer, I.M. and Moomaw W.R. (1990), 'Global Warming: An Assessment of its Scientific Basis, its Likely Impacts, and Potential Response Strategies', January, Washington DC: World Resources Institute, paper presented to workshop on the Economics of Sustainable Development organized by UN Economic Commission for Europe and US Environmental Protection Agency.

UNEP/GEMS (1987), 'The Greenhouse Gases', UNEP/GEMS Environmental Library No. 1, and 'The Ozone Layer', UNEP/GEMS Environment Library No. 2 United Nations Environment Programme, Nairobi.

Winpenny, J.T. (1991), *Valuing the Environment: A Guide to Economic Appraisal,* London: HMSO.

9. Environmental effects and the Carajás iron-ore project, Brazil

Alfredo Lopes da Silva Neto

The Carajás Iron-ore Project

In the late 1960s the iron-ore deposits of the Carajás Mountain (*Serra dos Carajás*) were discovered in Brazil's north region by geologists who were surveying the south of the state of Pará for a subsidiary of the United States Steel (USS).[1] They soon realized that the measured and inferred reserves added up to 17.8 billion tons of iron-ore with an average of 66.08 Fe. Even iron-ore experts were impressed by the dimension and high quality of the discovered reserves that can last up to 360 years at the rate of exploitation of 50 million tons per year (mtpy) (Santos 1986: 294–9).

Faced with such huge reserves the Brazilian government urged the Brazilian public enterprise *Companhia Vale do Rio Doce* (CVRD) to form a joint venture with the USS to explore these large deposits of high-quality iron-ore. Thus, the *Amazônia Mineração SA* (AMZA) with 51 per cent of shares belonging to CVRD and the other 49 per cent to USS was set up to design and implement a project to explore the Carajás Mountain's iron-ore. However, in the mid-1970s the USS struggled with a serious downturn in the steel market and CVRD decided to buy AMZA's shares that belonged to that American enterprise in 1977 (Santos 1986: 300).

CVRD designed the Carajás project to produce up to 35 mtpy of iron-ore. This is the project's full capacity that can be expanded in the future if the demand for iron-ore justifies this. Like CVRD's other productive structure in Brazil's southeast region, the Carajás project is a complex formed by mine, railway, port and two town sites. Further, this infrastructure is complemented by an airport and an access road that links the mine site to the regional road network. These two components were added to the project due to the lack of support infrastructure in the region where the mine is located.

The Project's Economic Evaluation

The Carajás project came on stream in 1986 and its full capacity was achieved in 1989 when 34.5 million tons (mt) of iron-ore were exported and 0.5 mt were sold for local pig-iron producers. Therefore, the main direct effect that resulted from the project's implementation is foreign exchange generation. Apart from this, one of the project's components (the Carajás Railway — EFC) has created other effects such as passenger and general cargo transport services. These project by-products have brought important benefits to the regional economy because the EFC crosses a vast area of the national territory (890 km) that is barely equipped with other transport infrastructure.

Table 9.1   Carajás project's NPV and IRR (US$ million—December 1979 real terms)

Resources flow (1980/2015)	Present value at 10% Total
I. Inflow (.1.+.2.)	12 720.8
.1. Operating results (/.1. – /.2.)	12 354.6
/.1. Revenues	15 742.9
/.2. Operating costs	3 388.3
.2. Terminal value	366.2
II. Outflow (.1.+.2.+.3)	2 897.8
.1. Working capital	78.9
.2. Investment costs (/.1.+...+/.6.)	1 951.3
/.1. Mine	284.8
/.2. Railway	987.1
/.3. Port	150.8
/.4. Town sites	105.4
/.5. Project management	410.1
/.6. Other capital costs	13.1
.3. Replacement costs	867.6
III. NPV[1]	283.9
IV. IRR	11.24%

Source: da Silva Neto (1992:chapter 3).

Note:
[1] Discount rate: 10 per cent representing the opportunity cost of capital.

The project is evaluated in detail in da Silva Neto (1992). The evaluation at constant market prices resulted from a mix of ex-post and ex-ante cost-benefit analysis. Thus, since the project was already implemented at the time of the appraisal, actual data for investment costs and revenues during the five initial years of its operational phase (1986–90) could be used. The Carajás project's feasibility studies provide data for operating and replacement costs as well as iron-ore prices over the future operating life of the project (1990–2015). On the other hand, the appraisal was complemented by sensitivity and risk analysis that considered alternative estimates for the iron-ore prices and operating costs. This procedure was followed because these two variables play an essential role in the uncertainties that surround the project's future operations. Table 9.1 summarizes the base case estimates of the project's NPV and IRR.

Identification of the Carajás Project's Environmental Impact

Iron ore is a non-renewable natural resource. Thus, an iron-ore project creates a link between the economic and the environmental system that often results in several forms of environmental degradation such as water and air pollution as well as soil erosion.[2] The extent of the environmental damage that a mining project can bring about to its environment is a function of the following characteristics;

(a) the size of the mine facilities;
(b) the mine location;
(c) the mineral or minerals extracted; and
(d) the method of mining that is adopted (Down and Stocks 1977; Financial Times 1990; Winpenny 1991: 203–7).

Therefore, each mining project has a different potential to affect its physical environment.

The relationship between the Carajás project and its physical environment is complex due to three main reasons. First, the project's output comes from a large surface mine located in a tropical rainforest. As a result, the project involves directly two components of the environment system: a non-renewable resource (iron-ore) and a renewable resource (tropical rainforest). Further, two of the project's components (mine and port) are also a potential source of environmental damage to water and air.

Second, the EFC crosses regions of different ecosystems: tropical rainforests, palm forests, savannah areas and wetlands. Thus, the project's environmental damage can occur at the mine site, at the right-of-way of the railway, (a corridor with a width of 80 m throughout the railway extension) or at the port site.

Third, forward linkages generated by the Carajás project amplify its area of influence. The project's environmental impact is not restricted to the area encompassed by the project's main components (mine, railway and port). Instead, it should be analysed in a much broader area. However, the magnitude of this area is still a controversial matter.

The Carajás project's environmental effects can be divided into two main components. Direct environmental effects have resulted from the project's implementation and they affect only the Carajás project's area of direct influence, i.e., the area of the mine concession, the right-of-way of the EFC and the area of the port site. Indirect environmental effects were created by the project's forward linkages. This process is occurring within a much larger area of Brazil's eastern Amazon region. These two components are discussed in turn.

Direct Environmental Effects

Physical environment

Environmental damage caused by mining activity is not a recent issue for CVRD because since 1942 it has been operating another important mining complex (mine, railway and port) in Brazil's southeast region. This means that CVRD has been dealing with environmental problems for many years and has developed some expertise in this area (Goodland 1985:5–35). In fact, CVRD's previous experience with environmental problems was the origin of the enterprise's decision to include special features in the design of the Carajás project. For example, the environmental planning and management of the project was assigned to a special division set up for this specific purpose. CVRD's Environment Division was staffed and equipped to design a project to compensate for the environmental damage that would be brought about by the Carajás project. This environment compensating project (ECP) was appraised in parallel with the main project (Goodland 1985:19).

In the early 1980s, CVRD decided to reinforce its environmental planning capability. The enterprise established the Environmental Study and Advisory Group (GEAMAM). This special administrative unit was formed by nine Brazilian scientists who are experts in problems of the Amazon region. Further, to give more effectiveness to their recommendations, they report directly to CVRD's chairman (Freitas 1984:280–9).

The ECP devised by CVRD was monitored by the World Bank from design to implementation and ex-post evaluation. Further, this multilateral lending agency provided firm support to CVRD's environmental initiatives, mainly to the independent bureaucratic structure of GEAMAM (CVRD 1989:8).

Resources for environmental prevention were allocated according to the potential environmental damage of each of the project's components. The railway and the mine together received 82 per cent of the ECP budget. This resource allocation was justified by the fact that they are the most important potential source of direct environmental damage. Table 9.2 illustrates this allocation pattern.

Table 9.2   *CVRD's expenditures with the ECP (US$ million — December 1979 real terms)*

Items	Costs	Percentage
1. Mine	18.6	27.7
2. Railway	36.4	54.2
3. Port	2.8	4.2
4. Town sites	6.2	9.2
5. Ecological research	3.2	4.8
Total	67.2	100.0

Source: CVRD (1986).

CVRD organized the ECP as follows.

Mine
(a) Two sedimentation lakes were built to store the polluted water that results from the iron-ore beneficiation process. This preventive measure intends to avoid any pollution caused by the project to the Amazon basin.
(b) Around the mine site, air quality is sampled at six collection points on a monthly basis. Water quality is also monitored through the physical, chemical and biological analysis of samples taken from 40 locations inside and near the mine site (Freitas 1986:18).

Railway
To prevent soil erosion the areas that had their original vegetation removed during the railway construction were replanted through a hydroseeding process.

Port
(a) Control and monitoring of water and air pollution in the port area occurs regularly. For the monitoring of water, a total of 14 sampling stations were set up in the port area. Further, nine stations were established to monitor air quality in the port area and three stations in the neighbouring city of São Luís.
(b) Two waste-water treatment plants were built in the port area; one is a conventional sewage treatment plant for domestic effluents and the other is a decantation and stabilization plant.
(c) A meteorological station was built at the port. Its purpose is to gather data to undertake a more detailed analysis of atmospheric pollution problems in the port area.

Town sites
(a) Domestic sewage from the Carajás's town site is treated in stabilization ponds.
(b) A botanical and zoological park was established to preserve plant and animal native species. The botanical park at the Carajás's town site is located in a 100-hectare area. This facility is equipped with research installations, including a herbarium and a seed laboratory (Nepomuceno 1987:297–306).
(c) A programme of environmental education was established by CVRD. This initiative tries to improve awareness among the enterprise's employees and their families of the need for a more positive attitude regarding environmental conservation.

Ecological research
(a) CVRD financed a survey project to study the flora, fauna and archaeology of the Carajás Mountain region. This project was carried out by the Emilio Goeldi Museum (*Museu Emilio Goeldi*), a Brazilian research institution specializing in the study of the natural and ethnological history of the Amazon region.
(b) An ecological reserve was set up in the area that surrounds the mine facilities. In this buffer zone no mine activity will be undertaken. This area (210 750 ha) is representative of the richness of the tropical forest vegetation. Therefore, it will be preserved from deforestation and it is an ideal area for future ecological research.

In an economic evaluation, the costs of the ECP should be added to the investment costs of the main project. In the case of the Carajás project, the cost of the ECP was equivalent to only 3.4 per cent of the project's investment costs. The additional expenditure with environmental protection had a small impact on the project's rate of return which is reduced from 11.24 per cent to 10.95 per cent . Table 9.3 illustrates this result.

Table 9.3   Impact of the ECP (US$ million — December 1979 real terms)

Items	Without ECP	ECP	With ECP
Investment costs	1951.3	67.2	2018.5
IRR (per cent)	11.24	–	10.95

Note: The maintenance costs of the specific facilities of this compensating project are included in the Carajás project's resource flows as an item of its operating costs.

Source: da Silva Neto (1992)

Human environment

The Carajás project's area of influence is the homeland of 14 000 Amerindians that live in more than 130 villages and represent 15 different tribal groups. The project has affected directly the Amerindians' welfare because the EFC crosses three Amerindian reserves.

However, here the project's indirect impact is much more relevant because both the Amerindians' land and their traditional culture have suffered enormous pressure following the project's implementation. This negative environmental impact has resulted from the growth of the population and economic activity in the project's area of influence. This indirect effect would be fatal for the Amerindians' cultural and economic survival if no form of compensation were devised (Treece 1990:264–87).

This problem was addressed only when the project was already being implemented because the project's original design had ignored this kind of environmental damage. The incentive to deal with this environmental effect resulted from the World Bank's direct intervention in the Carajás project's implementation in the early 1980s. This attitude is one of the earliest evidences of the new approach adopted by the World Bank towards project environmental impacts.[3]

In fact, the loan agreement between CVRD and the World Bank required the former to devise a special compensating project whose objectives were defined as follows:

(a) to prevent the immediate impact of the project on the Amerindian culture;
(b) to mitigate long-term environmental effects;
(c) to allow the Amerindians to acculturate at their own pace and in the style they desire (Goodland 1985:22).

Therefore, resources were allocated to this special sub-project (Amerindian Protection Project — APP) and CVRD was urged to implement the two compensating projects together — this one and that designed to cope with direct environmental demand. To carry out this assignment, CVRD signed a contract with the Indian National Foundation (*Fundação Nacional do Indio* — FUNAI), the Brazilian government agency in charge of Amerindian welfare.[4]

Table 9.4 illustrates the main expenditures made by CVRD to implement the APP. The modest results achieved by CVRD with this project are reflected in the fact that at the end of 1988 only 25 per cent of the project's resources were allocated to the project's priorities, while education received only 0.7 per cent. Meanwhile, 60 per cent of the budget was utilized to finance FUNAI's public works, equipment, maintenance and personnel.[5]

Table 9.4   Expenditures with the APP (US$ million — December 1979 real terms)

Items[1]	Costs	Percentage
Land demarcation	1.5	15.5
Health	1.0	10.3
Infrastructure improvements	2.4	24.3
Equipments	1.3	13.3
Maintenance	1.3	13.3
Personnel	0.9	8.9
Education	0.1	0.7
Administration	0.3	2.6
Total	8.8	88.9
Technical reserves (in 1989)	1.1	11.1
Total	9.9	100.0

Source: CVRD/FUNAI.
Note: [1] Expenditures realized from 1982 to 1987.

The costs of the APP are also added to the Carajás project's actual investment costs (US$ 2018.5 million) that already include the costs of ECP (US$ 67.2 million). Table 9.5 shows that the impact of this additional cost on the Carajás project's IRR is very small.

Table 9.5   Impact of the APP (US$ million — December 1979 real terms)

Items	Without the APP	APP	With the APP
Investment costs	2018.5	9.9	2028.4
IRR (%)	10.95	–	10.91

Source: da Silva Neto (1992)

Amerindians are tribal people who do have a great social and economic vulnerability to the Carajás project's implementation. Therefore, the reduction of 0.37 per cent (from 10.95 to 10.91 per cent) in the Carajás project's IRR is a social cost that is justified according to the CBA principle of compensation payment to project losers.

The compensating project approach: strength and drawbacks
CVRD implemented two compensating projects to avoid environmental damage in the Carajás project's area of influence. To evaluate the effectiveness of the

two compensating projects one should verify to what extent environmental externalities were avoided. It seems that three conditions are essential for a non-biased evaluation.

First, one must have access to all data collected by CVRD since the implementation of the compensating projects. These data come from the analysis of the water samples collected on a regular basis at the mine and port site. The results of the air quality control are also important. Further, one must verify if CVRD implemented the suggestions of the Emilio Goeldi Museum's research. Finally, one must also verify the effectiveness of the ecological reserve, botanical and zoological park established by CVRD near the mine site.

Second, an extensive fieldwork is necessary to interview the potential project's losers. In other words, those who would suffer either loss of income or social welfare with the Carajás project's environmental damage should be heard. Third, this evaluation should be undertaken by an independent regulatory agency.

In 1989, the World Bank's Operations Evaluation Department (OED) carried out an ex-post evaluation of the two compensating projects that fulfilled the three conditions summarized above. Evidence provided by the OED's report suggests that the main objectives of the ECP were achieved (OED 1990:103–19). Similar evidence is provided by the European Communities Court of Auditors (ECCA 1991: chapter 3) and by other analysts that know the Carajás project (Hall 1991:166–7; Margullis 1990:15–18).[6]

CVRD's experience with the APP should also be evaluated carefully. The available evidence suggests that the APP was able to improve the Amerindians' welfare in two basic areas: health care and land demarcation (OED 1990:124–5). However, the Amerindians' welfare is an issue that is much more complex and some losses are non-quantifiable in monetary terms. For example, it is impossible to measure and evaluate changes in the Amerindians' lifestyles or loss of their historical as well as religious sites. These losses can only be evaluated in qualitative terms and one of the limits of CBA should be acknowledged (Dixon 1991:189–200).

CVRD's attempt to avoid the Carajás project's environmental damage is a practical application of a technique advocated by the environmental economics literature. This experience has shown that many environmental damages can be avoided if they are included in the early phases of the project cycle. The main strength of the compensating approach is that it internalizes environmental externalities that are added as additional cost estimates to the project's resource flows.

However, this approach also raises important questions and shortcomings that deserve special attention. First, both compensating projects implemented by CVRD must be maintained during the project's long lifetime. Indeed, post-implementation maintenance will require a firm commitment by CVRD's management to environmental protection in the long term. Otherwise, environmental damage will occur later during the project's operational phase and all the initial effort may be lost.

Second, and much more important, is the fact that preventive expenditures implemented at a project level are project specific. These expenditures can avoid environmental damage only within the confines of a particular project (the so-called project area of influence). However, they can do nothing to prevent environmental damage outside this area. This is a relevant constraint to the effectiveness of the compensating project approach. In this sense, this technique is only a second-best solution to the environmental problems that are being analysed (Pezzei 1989:58–9).

It has been argued that environmental protection requires the definition and implementation of policies at a macro-level. On the one hand, these policies tend to be less effective in solving specific problems than preventive expenditures implemented at a project level. On the other hand, they can reach all the economic agents that cause environmental degradation (Dixon 1991:196).

CVRD's experience with the two compensating projects in Brazil's north region is a good example of this argument. In fact, the two compensating projects implemented by CVRD have tried to avoid several forms of environmental degradation such as deforestation, soil erosion, air and water pollution, as well as deterioration of tribal people's welfare.

Unfortunately, all of these forms of environmental damage are also present outside CVRD's area of concession. They can be attributed to other economic agents (farmers, cattle ranchers, gold prospectors, etc.) that are not concerned with environmental protection issues. For example, one of the worst forms of environmental degradation in Brazil's north region is deforestation that is being caused indirectly by the Carajás project. However, the compensating projects implemented by CVRD can do nothing to avoid this form of environmental degradation.

Indirect Environmental Effects — Forward Linkages

Several pig-iron smelters and ferrous-alloy plants have been and are being set up in the Carajás project's area of influence since the late 1980s. This is the result of input availability, fiscal incentives and subsidized credit created by the Greater Carajás Programme (*Programa Grande Carajás* — PGC).

These industrial projects have a direct link with the Carajás project because CVRD is the sole supplier of iron-ore for all industrial projects approved by the PGC. This link is reinforced by the EFC that transports both the main input (iron-ore) and the output (pig-iron and metal alloy) from the production sites to the port.

Without the availability of iron-ore and the transport service provided by the EFC no pig-iron producer could set up plants in that region. This forward linkage generated by the Carajás project must be examined carefully for the purposes of this analysis.[7]

The revenues created both by the sales of iron-ore for the internal market and transport service provided by the EFC are a small component of the Carajás project's direct benefits and were included in the project resource flows for appraisal. However, these forward linkages referred to above may have created indirect costs that have not yet been included. The available evidence shows that these indirect costs are environmental externalities that should be added to the Carajás project's economic evaluation. Therefore, the next sections try to identify and evaluate this indirect effect (Hall 1991:166–80; Anderson 1990; Fearnside 1987, 1989a, 1990a).

Pig-iron projects — the extent of the problem

Table 9.6 shows that the output of the pig-iron and metal-alloy projects approved by the PGC can reach up to 2.2 million tons per year (tpy). In this total is included the production of the three geographical sub-regions that form the Carajás project's area of influence, i.e., the western, central and eastern zones.

Table 9.6   Forward linkage (thousand tons per year)

Pig-iron projects: located in	Productive capacity[1]		
	Effective	Planned	Total
Western zone	180.00	742.20	922.20
Central zone	109.00	696.00	805.00
Eastern zone	54.00	397.50	451.50
Total	343.00	1835.70	2178.70

Note: [1] *Effective* refers to the annual productive capacity of the pig-iron projects that are already on stream. *Planned* refers to the annual productive capacity of those projects that were approved by the PGC but that are not yet implemented.

Source: da Silva Neto (1992).

In most countries that produce pig-iron the source of fuel that is used for smelting the iron-ore is coke (a product of coal carbonization). However, a constraint to pig-iron production in Brazil's north region is the shortage of coal in that part of Brazil's territory. Then, pig-iron producers use charcoal as the industrial source of fuel instead of coke. In addition, they have been using the fuelwood provided by the native forest as the main input to produce charcoal.

As a result, pig-iron production and indirectly the Carajás project are linked to deforestation. The extent of this environmental damage is directly proportional to the magnitude of the regional metal production but the problem must be qualified.

First, the production of charcoal for industrial use in Brazil's north region began in 1988 when the first pig-iron plant came on-stream. However, environmental problems that result from this economic activity are not recent in Brazil. For example, in the country's southeast region (where the bulk of the steel industry is located) charcoal production has been one important source of environmental degradation (Ackerman and Almeida 1990:661–8).

Second, the with/without project framework requires that deforestation caused by the charcoal production must be isolated from other causes of deforestation in Brazil's eastern Amazon region. This is the first step to estimate the extent of deforestation that can be indirectly attributed to the Carajás project.[8]

Charcoal production — demand for and supply of fuelwood

Table 9.6 also shows that the pig-iron productive capacity in the Carajás project's area of influence can be broken down into both effective and planned. This outlook results from the fact that whilst 21 projects have been approved by the PGC, only five have been implemented.[9]

Da Silva Neto (1992) shows that charcoal production can reach up to 2.0 million tpy (0.91 x 2.2 million tons) if all the pig-iron projects approved by the PGC are implemented.[10] As a result of this charcoal production, 16.0 million steres of fuelwood (2.0 x 4.72 x 1.71) can be demanded per year. This estimated demand for charcoal and fuelwood will only become effective when all projects come on-stream.

The estimate of fuelwood supply is a much more complex issue because the native forests of the Carajás project's area of influence are not homogeneous. The available source of data for this estimate is a survey of the forestry resources of the eastern Amazon's region that clarified many doubts about the capacity of that forest to supply fuelwood (UFRRJ 1986).[11]

UFRRJ (1986) gives estimates of the stock of fuelwood supply in each one of the three zones that form the Carajás project's area of influence. They are equal to the product of the forest size (km^2) in each zone multiplied by the related fuelwood productivity per hectare (steres/hectare). The estimated fuelwood supply (measured in 10^6 steres/zone) of the western, central and eastern zones together totals 1.8 billion steres.

Annual deforestation

As a general rule, charcoal producers in Brazil invest their capital neither in conservation practices, such as forest management, nor in reforestation projects. This implies that native forests can be treated as a non-renewable resource that is subject to a rate of depletion or rate of deforestation. This can be derived from the comparison between the estimated annual demand for fuelwood (a flow) and the equivalent supply of fuelwood (a stock). The rate of deforestation quantifies the impact of fuelwood production on the native forest.

Annual deforestation is another measure of forest extinction. This indicator can be defined as a function of the rate of deforestation and the size of the area covered by the native forest in each of the three zones.

Both the rate of deforestation and the annual deforestation that can result after the implementation of all projects approved by the PGC were estimated.[12] Table 9.7 shows that the eastern zone will suffer the worst impact of deforestation, because its native forests are smaller than the central and western zones' forests.

Table 9.7 Annual deforestation caused by charcoal production

Deforestation	Zones			Total
	Western	Central	Eastern	
(A) Fuelwood supply (10^6 steres)	955.8	782.4	24.5	1 762.7
(B) Fuelwood demand (10^6 steres)	6.8	5.9	3.3	16.0
(C) (B/A) = Rate of deforestation (%)	0.7	0.8	13.5	–
(D) Forested area (Km^2)	64 037	42 001	4 225	110 263
(E) (C x D) = Annual deforestation ($km^{2)}$	455.6	316.7	569.1	1 341.4

Source: Calculated from data in da Silva Neto (1992).

Table 9.7 can also be used to forecast the annual deforestation that will result if all projects approved by the PGC come on stream. In such a scenario, a large tract of the Amazonian forest may be extinct in a few decades. For example, if the projected annual deforestation (1341.4 km^2 per year) were realized, all the natural forests of the Carajás project's area of influence ($110 \ 263 \text{ km}^2$) may disappear in 82 years. This industrialization process is clearly non-sustainable because it destroys its own natural resource base.

The economic cost of this environmental degradation should be estimated and included in the Carajás project's cost flows. A first approach to the problem would be the estimate of the economic value of the forest that is being destroyed. However, any such estimate is surrounded by methodological problems.[13]

A second approach takes into account not the economic value of the forest but the costs of preventive expenditures that can be implemented to avoid deforestation caused by charcoal production. The next section adopts this approach and discusses alternative procedures that consider both the characteristics of the Carajás project's area of influence and the magnitude of the environmental problem that has been identified.

Alternatives to deforestation

The pig-iron and metal-alloy projects that were submitted to the PGC's appraisal were designed without any regard to forest preservation. In this sense, project planners considered the tropical forest as a cheap source of charcoal, nothing more than this. This short-term perspective could not even foresee that the extinction of the forest curbs pig-iron production itself in the long term. As a result of this project planning failure, these industrial projects are clearly non-sustainable.

Therefore, the only alternative to deforestation caused by charcoal production is a re-evaluation of all industrial projects already appraised by the PGC. The main objective of this re-evaluation would be the addition of preventive expenditures into each project.[14]

The suggested re-evaluation is a two-tier process. At project level it is a serious possibility because, as already stated, from the 21 projects approved by the PGC only five have been implemented. At the macro level there is evidence that the Brazilian government is increasingly concerned with the environmental degradation brought about by development projects.[15]

In fact, the deforestation of the Amazon region has increased environmental awareness both in Brazil and abroad. This can be measured by the increasing amount of research that has taken into account the effects of deforestation. Second, the international media has also emphasized the issue (Time 1989:44–50). Finally, and much more important, development agencies such as the World Bank and the Inter-American Development Bank (IDB) have also expressed their concern about environmental degradation in the Amazon region.[16]

As a result of this new trend the Brazilian government is already undertaking a re-evaluation of all pig-iron projects already approved by the PGC in the late 1980s (Brazil 1990a, 1990b, 1990c, 1991a, 1991b, 1991c). To be effective any revision should take into account that there are three alternatives to the fuelwood supplied by the native rainforest. First, the fuelwood may be provided by sustainable forest management. Second, reforestation projects may also be a source of fuelwood supply. Third, imported coal may substitute for charcoal as the source of fuel to produce pig-iron. The next three sections discuss such possibilities.

Forest management

In principle, all the necessary charcoal demanded by the pig-iron projects can be provided by natural forest management. This means that fuelwood for charcoal production can be extracted from the forest without the consequent forest destruction. In other words, sustainable forest management occurs if the rate of deforestation is inferior to or equal to the rate of regeneration. This is a classical condition for sustainable forest management that has received much attention in the natural resource economics literature (Fisher and Krutilla 1975; Fisher and Peterson 1976; Fisher 1981).

What are the economic possibilities of the implementation of sustainable forest management in the Carajás project's area of influence? Cunha (1988: 212–17) analyses a theoretical model in which a firm that maximizes profits exploits a renewable natural resource, and the above condition for sustainable forest management is a restriction that the firm has to face. The model shows that the rate of deforestation that maximizes profits and the rate of regeneration are not compatible. The latter is a function of biological factors that cannot be changed by human intervention. The former is a function of economic variables such as the price of the wood, operating costs and the rate of discount. Since the two rates are independently determined only by coincidence they can be equal unless the government intervenes to force producers to pay the full costs of the resources they use.

In the case of the pig-iron projects approved by the PGC, the scale of the demand for fuelwood (see Table 9.7) increases the possibility of deforestation. Further, in the Amazon region there is no tradition of sustainable forest management practices (Fearnside 1989b:69). In short, sustainable forest management is an alternative that should be discarded in the short term because of the sheer size of the demand for fuelwood required by the pig-iron projects. It seems that forest management is not a suitable alternative, even in a situation of reduced demand for fuelwood, because of the dichotomy between the rate of deforestation and the rate of forest regeneration.

However, in the long term, forest management may be used to complement other sources of fuelwood supply. This may happen provided that forest management practices can be improved as a result of applied research that provides evidence on the yield of sustainable forest management practice. Such research is essential because it can both increase the scientific knowledge of the complex ecosystems that characterize tropical rainforests and provide useful guidelines for policy formulation.

Reforestation

There are in Brazil's eastern Amazon region large areas that are already completely degraded and that have a low opportunity cost. They are not suitable for agriculture practices (without high costs of fertilization) and some areas are occupied by low productive pastures. The reforestation of these areas can both provide fuelwood for charcoal production and improve environmental conditions through the prevention of soil erosion.

It has been demonstrated that in some special circumstances reforestation projects for industrial purposes are economically viable. Indeed, they are adopted in several countries (FAO 1979). However, a reforestation project linked to an industrial project is a complex issue that needs to be analysed carefully. First, reforestation projects are characterized by long maturation periods. The first harvest can take up to seven years if the plantation is formed by fast-growing trees. Second, biological production processes tend to be characterized by a great deal of heterogeneity within a given ecosystem. This means that the volume and the quality of the output is uncertain. Third, available evidence shows that homogeneous plantations in tropical regions are highly vulnerable to a variety of pests and diseases. This possibility is heightened by the lack of knowledge of the Amazon ecosystem (Fearnside 1988:23; Gregersen and Contreras 1979:2).

As far as the pig-iron projects are concerned, the main problem with reforestation is uncertainty of supply. In other words, reforestation may not be a reliable source of fuelwood supply on the scale required by those projects. The native forest will always be threatened if the reforestation projects are adopted as the source of fuelwood supply to the pig-iron projects. This will happen because in case of a harvest failure the industrial process cannot wait for the new harvest that can take several years.

Coke
Since the 18th century most steelmakers in western Europe and in other parts of the world have used coke to produce pig-iron and other steel products. In principle, the projects approved by the PGC can use coke instead of charcoal because there is a large international market for coal. However, it is alleged that the PGC's planners have not considered this option for three reasons:

1. coke is more expensive than charcoal;
2. the use of coke will reduce the net effect of pig-iron production on the balance of payments;
3. imports of coke will eliminate the employment generated by charcoal production (Cagnin 1988).

However, these arguments can be maintained only in the absence of any commitment towards the preservation of the Amazon forest. Otherwise, it should be clear that the Brazilian society will always have to pay a price to preserve that forest. Table 9.8 shows the price (December 1979 prices) of three alternative sources of blast furnace fuel that can be employed to produce pig-iron.

Table 9.8 Prices of charcoal and coke (US$/ton)[1]

Alternative source of fuel	Costs
Charcoal (origin: native forest)[2]	18.53
Charcoal (origin: reforestation)[2]	38.44
Coke[3]	41.69

Source: SEPLAN/PGC (1989: 306–22).

Notes:
[1] The original data (December 1989) were deflated to December 1979 and converted to the US dollar at the official exchange rate.
[2] The price does not include transport costs from the charcoal plants to the pig-iron plants.
[3] Domestic prices = CIF price + local costs + subsidy.

The choice of one of these sources implies different trade-offs. Earlier estimates made by the PGC have found that the cost of charcoal derived from the native forest (US$ 18.53/ton) can create the biggest rate of return to the pig-iron producers (*ceteris paribus*) (SEPLAN/PGC, 1989:309–10). In principle, this alternative can also bring about the highest net effect to the Balance of Payments because all the output can be exported and no input is imported. Further, this alternative can increase the level of employment due to the regional charcoal production. In practice, it was argued in the previous sections that this choice of fuelwood supply can destroy the forest that surrounds the Carajás project's area of influence in a few decades.

The PGC also estimated that the choice of charcoal derived from reforestation (US$ 38.44/ton) reduces the rate of return of pig-iron projects (SEPLAN/PGC 1989: pp.309–10). This alternative presents two positive aspects. First, it does not require any import of fuel for the blast furnaces and, therefore, it does not reduce the impact of the pig-iron projects on the balance of payments. Second, it can increase the regional level of employment due to the reforestation projects.

As discussed above there are problems with the reforestation projects which cannot guarantee a reliable supply of fuelwood due to the magnitude of the fuelwood supply required by the pig-iron projects.

The use of coke is the most expensive alternative. The PGC estimated that the cost of imported coke (US$41.69/ton) is the worst alternative if only financial considerations are included in the analysis. However, if the criterion of sustainable development is taken into account, the use of coke can guarantee that the pig-iron projects will not cause deforestation.

The Impact of Pig-iron Production on the Carajás Project's Rate of Return

The production of pig-iron in the Carajás project's area of influence brought about direct benefits that affect the project's rate of return. The evaluation of these benefits can be measured by the revenues that are generated by the transport and sales of iron-ore (input for pig-iron projects) and transport of output (pig-iron) produced by those projects. The revenues that were yielded by these activities are already included among the Carajás project's direct benefits in Table 9.1.

However, it is necessary to evaluate the revenues that will be generated until the end of the Carajás project's operational lifetime (from 1991 to 2015). These revenues will result from the demand for iron-ore and transport services created by the pig-iron projects.

It was already emphasized that the PGC has been re-evaluating these projects in the face of the environmental problems already discussed. As a result of this process several projects were cancelled by the Brazilian government because they have not fulfilled the new environmental requirements (Brazil 1990b, 1990c, 1991b). Therefore, it will be assumed that no more pig-iron projects will come on-stream from 1991 to 2015. This assumption means that the effective production of pig-iron in the Carajás project's area of influence will be maintained at 343 thousand tons per year (see Table 9.6).

This level of production generates a demand for iron-ore and transport service that will be extended from 1991 to 2015. By assumption, this demand will not increase in this period and, therefore, it is only necessary to estimate these revenues (in December 1979 real terms) and include the results in the Carajás project's flow of benefits.

The evaluation of the costs to avoid deforestation caused by the pig-iron projects must be linked to the Carajás project because this environmental damage was indirectly created by the mining project. In other words, this deforestation is an indirect cost caused by the Carajás project and, therefore, in an economic evaluation should be included among that project's costs.[17]

The evaluation of this cost deforestation is based on the theoretical principle of the compensation payment to the losers of a development project. In fact, this compensation payment would be equivalent to another preventive expenditure to avoid environmental degradation in the Carajás project's area of influence. In other words, this additional expenditure should be added to the actual costs of the two compensation projects that were already analysed.[18]

The quantity of coal that would be imported is directly related to the quality of the coking coal. In average terms the carbonization of one ton of coking coal yields 0.75 tons of coke. Further, 0.987 tons of coke is demanded to produce one ton of pig-iron. This implies that 451.4 thousand tpy of coking coal must be imported to produce 343 thousand tpy of pig-iron.

The price of coal estimated by the PGC (US$41.69/ton) from Table 9.8 is used to evaluate the total expenditure on the imported coal from 1991 to 2015. As a result, here it is estimated that US$18.8 million per year is the total expenditure on imports of coal. This is the estimated cost to avoid the environmental degradation indirectly caused by the Carajás project. The project's IRR falls from 10.91 to 10.65 per cent when this additional indirect cost is included in its flow of costs. This fall in the Carajás project's IRR can be easily explained by the project's cost structure. It should be remembered that the bulk of expenditures on the project are investment costs that occurred during the project's implementation phase.

On the other hand, the estimated cost of coal imports is equivalent to 3.3 per cent of the estimated annual foreign exchange that the project will generate (US$555.3 million). Further, this expenditure is spread over a period of 25 years (from 1991 to 2015). This fact also explains the small impact of these additional costs on the project's IRR since they are discounted at the rate of 10 per cent.

The impact on the Carajás project's rate of return would be quite different if, according to the original schedule, the 21 pig-iron projects approved by the PGC would be implemented until the year 2000. As a result, in that year the effective capacity to produce pig-iron in the Carajás project's area of influence would reach the total planned capacity, that is 2.2 mtpy (see Table 9.6). Assuming that two pig-iron projects would come on stream per year from 1991 until 1999 it is possible to estimate both the imports of coal required to produce that amount of pig-iron and the value of these imports (see Table 9.9).

The Carajás project's rate of return is reduced from 10.91 to 9.6 per cent when the price of the imported coal is allocated to its resource flows as an additional project's cost. Considering that the discount rate is 10 per cent (da Silva Neto 1992) this implies that the project's NPV becomes negative as a result of the inclusion of environmental costs. In other words, although the Carajás project has the capacity to generate a significant amount of direct and indirect benefits, the Brazilian economy would be worse off as a result of the project's implementation. This result shows that large projects can generate important environmental costs that should be carefully evaluated and included in the procedures of project economic evaluation. In this case it is important to ensure that the additional 21 pig-iron projects do not go ahead because even if their environmental consequences are compensated by coal imports the cost of these imports brings the Carajás project's IRR below the estimated discount rate.

Table 9.9   *Requirements of coal to produce pig-iron in the Carajás project's area of influence*

Year	Number of pig-iron projects	Coal		
		Effective capacity (ttpy)[1]	Imports of coal (ttpy)[2]	Costs per year (US$ thousand December 1979 real terms)[3]
1991	05	343.0	451.4	18 818.4
1992	07	732.0	963.3	40 160.5
1993	09	915.2	1 204.4	50 211.6
1994	11	1 085.2	1 428.1	59 538.5
1995	13	1 258.2	1 655.8	69 029.9
1996	15	1 728.2	2 274.3	94 816.0
1997	17	1 931.2	2 541.5	105 953.4
1998	19	2 035.2	2 678.3	111 659.3
1999	21	2 178.7	2 867.2	119 532.3

Notes:
[1] Source: da Silva Neto (1992).
[2] Technical relation: 1.32 tons of coal is required to produce one ton of pig-iron.
[3] Price of coal: US$41.69/ton.

Conclusion

The compensating project approach was followed by the Carajás project's planners to avoid environmental damage both to the project's physical and human environment. CVRD drew on its own experience in the mining sector to protect the Carajás project's physical environment. Several measures were taken to avoid environmental damage within its area of concession (411 000 ha). On the other hand, the initiative to protect the project's human environment is attributed to the World Bank. This is evidence of the important role that this institution may have in the implementation of the sustainable development concept in developing countries.

Environmental externalities can be created directly by large projects or indirectly by their forward linkages. The Carajás project is a clear illustration of this later argument. The pig-iron (and metal-alloy) projects approved by the PGC are forward linkages that are generating a serious form of environmental degradation. These industrial projects were conceived to use charcoal derived from the native forest as the source of blast furnace fuel. This industrialization process is non-sustainable because it will result in the extinction of the native forests in the Carajás project's area of influence. This form of environmental degradation is irreversible because the ecological functions of tropical forests cannot be replaced.

From an economic point of view, the environmental degradation created by the pig-iron projects are inconsistent with the conservationist effort of CVRD. There is no point in preserving the environment within that enterprise's area of concession if outside, in a much larger area, the same environment is being irreversibly degraded.

The only way to correct this failure of project planning is an immediate revision of the projects approved by the PGC. However, this is only possible if the Brazilian government incorporates environmental protection among its long-term objectives. The incorporation of the sustainable development criterion in project analysis is not a simple question of trade-offs. Conversely, this concept should be tackled as a long-term strategy in which the interests of future generations are taken into account. From this perspective, coke is the best fuel substitute for charcoal because it guarantees that deforestation caused by the pig-iron projects can be avoided.

It is also suggested that the total expenditure on coal imports should be included in the Carajás project's cost structure for the purpose of its economic evaluation. This argument is justified on the grounds that this project is indirectly the origin of the alleged deforestation. The impact of this preventive expenditure is the reduction of the project's IRR (from 10.91 to 10.65 per cent or from 10.91 to 9.6 per cent depending upon whether plans for pig-iron expansion are allowed to go ahead) that can be translated mainly in an immediate loss in foreign exchange. However, this is only an apparent effect because in the long term a sustainable industrialization process may more than compensate this negative impact on the balance of payments.

Finally, it should be remembered that deforestation in Brazil is caused by several factors. In fact, deforestation caused by industrialization is only the most recent and is not the most important cause. It is also suggested that the problem of deforestation should be first tackled at the macro-economic policy level. In practice, the Brazilian government must make a clear and firm commitment towards this objective. As a result of this policy, project planners should incorporate the government guidelines into their appraisals. Further, not only large projects should include environmental protection into their appraisal. The rich environment of the Amazon forest will only be preserved if those guidelines are followed by all projects that are being implemented in that region.

Notes

1. Iron-ore is only one among several other minerals that were discovered in the Carajás Mountains. Other important deposits of different minerals were also measured: manganese (70.10^6 tons), copper (1200.10^6 tons), zinc ($8.5.10^6$ tons), bauxite (48.10^6 tons), nickel (100.10^6 tons), tin (100.10^3 tons), gold (100 tons) and tungsten (1.10^6 tons) (Santos 1986: 352–3).

2. A mining project reduces the physical stock of natural capital. By definition, this economic activity is non-sustainable. However, the environmental economics literature does not offer any practical guideline to evaluate this possible form of environmental damage, i.e., the reduction of the physical stock of natural capital (Pearce 1988: 3–11; Barbier 1989a: 188, 1989b; Dasgupta and Maler 1990: 10).

3. Only in the late 1980s did the World Bank institutionalize its policy towards environmental problems brought about by development projects (World Bank 1988).

4. The APP was submitted to the World Bank in June 1982. Early in that year the World Bank rejected the first proposal submitted by FUNAI. Largely for this reason, CVRD hired a team of consultants to monitor the reformulation of the compensating project's design and its future implementation. Then, two priorities were identified for Amerindian protection: land demarcation and health care (Ferraz and Castro 1987: 30–3; Treece 1987: 44–57).

5. CVRD realized that FUNAI was using the project's resources mainly to expand its own administrative structure rather than to improve the Amerindians' basic social services. At the beginning of 1989, the enterprise still had US$1.1 million remaining in the project's budget. Then, CVRD's managers decided that those resources would be allocated mainly to land demarcation, an issue that Amerindians judge extremely important to their welfare (Freitas and Genes 1987: 257–64).

6. Deforestation in the area that is being mined is an environmental degradation that no compensating project can avoid. To remove the ore from the soil, the mining enterprise needs to clear the area that surrounds the surface mine. This is an inevitable consequence of this production process that can only be repaired through revegetation of the mined area after the depletion of the ore deposits.

7. The pig-iron projects are only one of the several forward linkages created by the Carajás project, see da Silva Neto (1992) for further details.

8. Industrialization is only the most recent source of deforestation in the Amazon region. It has been suggested that cattle ranching, agribusiness, lumbering, slash-and-burn agriculture and construction of hydroelectric dams are much more important causes of environmental degradation in the region. See: Mahar (1989: 87–116); Fearnside (1990a:179–225, 1990b: 213–26); Pearce *et al.* (1990: chapter 9); Hall (1991: chapter 4); Browder (1988: 247–97); Binswanger (1989); Barbier (1989a: chapter 6); Cunha (1988:181–239); Cowell (1990); Shoumatoff (1990); and Hecht and Cockburn (1989).

9. The pig-iron projects that have come on-stream are: Cia. Siderurgica do Para (COSIPAR), Siderurgica Maraba (SIMARA), Siderurgica Vale do Pindare, Viena Sideerurgica do Maranhao and Maranhao Dusa SA (MARGUSA).

10. The following technical relationships were utilized to estimate the demand for fuelwood in the Carajás project's area of influence:

    (a) 0.91 ton of charcoal = 1 ton of pig-iron
    (b) 4.72 tons of fuelwood = 1 ton of charcoal
    (c) 1.71 steres of fuelwood = 1 ton of fuelwood.

    A stere is usually defined as a cubic metre of fuelwood, including air spaces. These coefficients were originally estimated by SUDAM/CODEBAR (1986), and Brazil/PRODIAT (1982).

11. The forests of the Carajás project's area of influence were classified in three main groups:
    1. *Unexploited forests* are primary forests that have not suffered any human intervention. They provide the greatest productivity of fuelwood per hectare and are more abundant in the western zone.
    2. *Logged forests* have a smaller capacity to produce fuelwood because the best wood has already been extracted by the lumber industry.
    3 *Savannahs* are secondary forests that are common in areas already degraded, or neutral formations that are more relevant in the eastern and central zones.

    UFRRJ's survey encompassed 150 km from each side of the Carajás Railway through all its extension, that is, a total of 250 000 km^2. The forestry inventory estimated that 44 per cent of the surveyed area (110 263 km^2) was covered by natural forests. Further, UFRRJ's survey also estimated that fuelwood productivity per hectare (steres/hectare) is not constant in the region. Instead, it varies from one forest group to another and from one of the region's zone to another due to the diversity that characterizes tropical rainforests.

12. The procedure adopted by Anderson (1990:1191–205) to estimate the rate of deforestation was followed closely.

13. For a summary of these methodological problems see da Silva Neto (1992:chapter 2).

14. It should be remembered that preventive expenditures can be implemented by a compensating project, or by changes in the original project design, such as changes in technology or inputs.

15. Since the late 1980s the Brazilian government has changed into commitment towards environmental protection. The main institutional measure has been the establishment of the Special Environmental Secretariat (*Secretaria Especial do Meio Ambiente*). This environmental planning unit is attached directly to the office of the President and is in charge of all environmental affairs in Brazil. In addition, the enforcement of environmental protection measures is in the hands of the National Environment Agency (IBAMA), that is the executive branch of the Special Environment Secretariat (Hall 1991:296–9).

16. The World Bank fund a major conservation programme in Brazil. The so-called National Environmental Project aims to strengthen national conservation agencies and to support Brazil's National Environmental Programme (*Programa Nacional do Meio-Ambiente*) (Coronel 1991:3; Hall 1991:300).

17. From the point of view of a financial analysis this argument is not applicable. However, in an economic evaluation what matters are the net benefits (direct plus indirect benefits minus direct plus indirect costs) created by development projects. From this wider approach to project analysis, the forward linkage created by the Carajás project is the origin of both a benefit and an indirect cost.

18. Any compensation payment has distributional consequences that must be analysed. In the case of the compensation payment that is suggested, it is assumed that the government intervenes in a rational way to defend the interests of the future generations. If nothing is done to halt the on-going deforestation process they will be the losers because they will not have the benefits of the rainforest. On the other hand, the imports of coal are a burden to the present generation and distributional effects will arise whoever pays for these imports.

References

Ackerman, F. and Almeida, P.E.F. (1990), 'Iron and Charcoal. The Industrial Fuelwood Crisis in Minas Gerais', *Energy policy,* September.

Anderson, A. (1990), 'Smokestacks in the Rainforest: Industrial Development and Deforestation in the Amazon Basin', *World Development*, **18**, (9).

Barbier, E.B. (1989a), *Economics, Natural Resource Scarcity and Development*, London: Earthscan.

Barbier, E.B. (1989b), 'The Contribution of Environmental and Resource Economics to an Economics of Sustainable Development'. *Development and Change,* **20**.

Binswanger, H.P. (1989), *Brazilian Policies that Encourage Deforestation in the Amazon*, Environment Department Working Paper No.·16, Washington, DC: World Bank.

Brazil/PRODIAT (1982), *Diagnóstico da Bacia Araguaia-Tocantins. Recursos naturais*, Brasília: Ministério do Interior.

Brazil (1990a), *Decree No· 99,353, (Decreto-Lei No. 99,353)*, Brasília: Presidência da República.

Brazil (1990b), *Ministerial Decree No· 120, (Portaria No. 120),* Brasília: Regional Development Secretariat.

Brazil (1990c), *Ministerial Decree No· 121, (Portaria No. 121)*, Brasília: Regional Development Secretariat.

Brazil (1991a), *Ministerial Decree No 145, (Portaria No. 145)*, Brasília: Regional Development Secretariat.

Brazil (1991b), *Ministerial Decree No 301, (Portaria No. 301)*, Brasília: Regional Development Secretariat.

Brazil (1991c), *Ministerial Decree No 302, (Portaria No. 302)*, Brasília: Regional Development Secretariat.

Browder, J.O. (1988), 'Public policy and deforestation in the Brazilian Amazon', in R. Repetto and M. Gillis (eds), *Public Policies and the Misuse of Forest Resources*, Cambridge: Cambridge University Press.

Cagnin, J.U. (1988), *Exploração Econômica da Amazonia: Perspectivas Para a Região de Carajás*, Brasilia: mimeo.

Coronel, L. (1991), 'Global Environment Facility. First Projects to be Financed by Bank-Implemented $1.5 Billion Fund', *Environment bulletin*, **3**, (2).

Cowell, A. (1990), *The Decade of Destruction: the Crusade to Save the Amazon Rain Forest*, New York: Henry Holt.

Cunha, A.S. (1988), 'Economia dos Recursos Naturais: o Caso do Desmatamento na Amazônia', in A.S.P. Brandão (ed.), *Os Principais Problemas da Agricultura Brasileira: Análise e Sugestões*, Rio de Janeiro: IPEA/INPES.

CVRD (1986), *Impacto Ambiental e Desenvolvimento Sócio-Econômico ao Longo da Estrada de Ferro Carajás*, CVRD, vol. I, mimeo, Rio de Janeiro.

CVRD (1989), *Carajás Iron-Ore Project. Environmental Management Program. Briefing Paper and Photos*, CVRD, mimeo, Rio de Janeiro.

da Silva Neto, A.L. (1992), *A Cost-Benefit Analysis of a Large Mining Project in Brazil*, unpublished PhD thesis, University of Bradford.

Dasgupta, P. and Maler.K. (1990), 'The Environment and Emerging Development Issues', Paper produced for the World Bank Annual Conference on Development Economics, Washington, mimeo.

Dixon, J.A. (1991), 'Economic Valuation of Environmental Resources', in J.T. Winpenny, (ed.), *Development Research: The Environmental Challenge*, London: ODI.

Down, C.G. and Stocks, J. (1977), *Environmental Impact of Mining*, London: Applied Science Publishers.

ECCA (1991), *Relatorio Sobre a Gestao Contabilistica e a Gestao Financeira da Comunidade Europeia do Carvao e do Aco*, (Portuguese version), Luxembourg: ECCA.

Economist, The (1989), 'Costing the Earth (a survey of the environment)', 2 September.

FAO (1979), *Economic Analysis of Forestry Projects: Case Studies*, FAO Forestry Paper No.17 – Sup,1, Rome: FAO.

Fearnside, P.M. (1987), 'Deforestation and International Economic Development Projects in Brazilian Amazonia', *Conservation Biology*, **1**, (3).

Fearnside, P.M. (1988), 'Jari at Age 19: Lessons for Brazil's Silvicultural Plans at Carajás', *Interciencia*, **13**, (1), papers.12–24.

Fearnside, P.M. (1989a), 'The Charcoal of Carajás: A Threat to the Forests of Brazil's Eastern Amazon Region', *Ambio*, **18**, (2).

Fearnside, P.M. (1989b), 'Forest Management in Amazonia: The Need for New Criteria in Evaluating Development Options', in *Forest Ecology and Management*, **27**, papers 61–79.

Fearnside, P.M. (1990a), 'Environmental Destruction in the Brazilian Amazon', In: D. Goodman and A. Hall (eds) *The Future of Amazonia. Destruction or Sustainable Development?*, London: Macmillan.

Fearnside, P.M. (1990b), 'The Rate and Extent of Deforestation in Brazilian Amazonia', *Environmental Conservation*, **17**, (3).

Ferraz, I. and Castro, E.V. (1987), 'Projeto Carajás e os Povos Indígenas: Expectativas e Realidade', *Pará desenvolvimento*, Nos 20–21.

Financial Times (1990), 'Open Cast Mining', issue of March 20.

Fisher, A.C. (1981), *Resources and Environmental Economics*, Cambridge: Cambridge University Press.

Fisher, A.C. and Krutilla, K.V. (1975), 'Resource conservation, Environmental Preservation and the Rate of Discount', *Quarterly Journal of Economics*, **79**, (3).

Fisher, A.C. and Peterson, F.M. (1976), 'The Environment in Economics: A Survey', *Journal of Economic Literature*, **14**, (1).

Freitas, M.L.D. (1984), 'Brazil's Carajás Iron-Ore Project — Environmental Aspects', in CEMP, *Environmentally Sound Development in the Energy and Mining Industries*, Aberdeen: Aberdeen University.

Freitas, M.L.D. (1986), 'Metodologia de Avaliação Ambiental Aplicada para um Caso de Enfoque Preventivo. Projeto ferro Carajás', *Espaço, ambiente e planejamento*, **1**, (1).

Freitas, M.L.D. and Genes, K.A. (1987), 'Comunidades Indígenas na Região de Influência da Estrada de Ferro Carajás', in SEMA/IWRB/CVRD, *Desenvolvimento Econômico e Impacto Ambiental em Áreas de Trópico Úmido. A Experiência da CVRD*, Rio de Janeiro: CVRD.

Goodland, R. (1985), 'Brazil's Environmental Progress in Amazonian Development', in J. Hemming (ed.), *Man's Impact on Forests and Rivers*, Manchester: Manchester University Press.

Gregersen, H.M. and Contreras, A.H. (1979), *Economic Analysis of Forestry Projects*, FAO Forestry Paper No.17, Rome: FAO.

Hall, A.L. (1991), *Developing Amazonia. Deforestation and Social Conflict in Brazil's Carajás Programme*, Manchester: Manchester University Press.

Hecht, S. and Cockburn, A. (1989), *The Fate of the Forest: Developers, Destroyers and Defenders of the Amazon*, London: Verso.

Mahar, D.J. (1989), 'Deforestation in Brazil's Amazon Region: Magnitude, Rates and Causes', in J.J. Warford and G. Schramm (eds.), *Environmental Management and Economic Development*, Washington: World Bank.

Margullis, S. (1990), *Avaliação do Projeto Grande Carajás*, mimeo, Rio de Janeiro.

Nepomuceno, L.C. (1987), 'Atividade da CIMA/Carajás', in SEMA/IWRB/CVRD, *Desenvolvimento Econômico e Impacto Ambiental em Áreas de Trópico Úmido. A Experiência da CVRD*, Rio de Janeiro: CVRD.

OED (1990), *Environmental Aspects of Selected Bank-Supported Projects in Brazil. Environmental Aspects and Consequences of the Carajás Iron-Ore Project*, mimeo,Washington, DC: World Bank, OED.

Pearce, D.W. (1988), *Cost-Benefit Analysis*, London: Macmillan.

Pearce, D.W., Barbier, E. and Markandya, A. (1990), *Sustainable Development. Economics and Environment in the Third World*, London: Edward Elgar.

Pezzei, J. (1989), *Economic Analysis of Sustainable Growth and Sustainable Development*, Environment Department Working Paper No.15, Washington, DC: World Bank Publication.

Santos, B.A.S. (1986), 'Recursos minerais', In: J.M.G. Almeida Jr (ed.), *Carajás: Desafio Político, Ecologia e Desenvolvimento*, São Paulo: Editora Brasiliense/CNP.

Scott, D.A. and Roth, P.G. (1987), A Avifauna da Baixada Maranhense', in SEMA/IWRRB/CVRD, *Desenvolvimento Econômico e Impacto Ambiental em Áreas de Trópico Úmido. A Experiência da CVRD*, Rio de Janeiro: CVRD.

SEPLAN/PGC (1989), *Plano Diretor do Corredor da Estrada de Ferro Carajás. Relatório Sintese*, Brasilia: SEPLAN.

Shoumatoff, A. (1990), *The World is Burning*, Boston: Little and Brown.

Silva, M.F.F. (1987), 'Estudos Botânicos em Carajás', in SEMA/IWRRB/CVRD, *Desenvolvimento Econômico e Impacto Ambiental em Áreas de Trópico Úmido. A Experiência da CVRD*, Rio de Janeiro: CVRD.

SUDAM/CODEBAR (1986), *Problemática do Carvão Vegetal na Área do Programa Grande Carajás*, Belém: SUDAM/CODEBAR.

Time (1989), 'Playing with Fire', 18 September.

Treece, D. (1987), *Bound in Misery and Iron: the Impact of the Grande Carajás Programme on the Indians of Brazil*, London: Survival International.

Treece, D. (1990), 'Indigenous People in Brazilian Amazonia and the Expansion of the Economic Frontier', in D. Goodman and A. Hall, (eds), *The Future of Amazonia. Destruction or Sustainable Development?*, London: Macmillan.

UFRRJ (1986), *Diagnose Florestal da Area de Influência da Estrada de Ferro Carajás: Sumário Executivo*, Rio de Janeiro: UFRRJ.

Winpenny, J.T. (ed.). (1991), *Values for the Environment. A Guide to Economic Appraisal*, London: HMSO.

World Bank (1988), *Environment and Development: Implementing the World Bank's New Policies*, Development Committee Pamphlet No. 17, Washington, DC: World Bank.

10. Fuzzy multigroup conflict resolution for environmental management

G. Munda, P. Nijkamp and P. Rietveld

Evaluation models serve to judge the feasibility and desirability of alternative courses of action (for example new projects), based on political choice and plausibility criteria. Plan and project evaluation has become an important component of modern public planning and administration. It should be noted that different kinds of evaluation can be distinguished in a policy analysis; one of the important discriminating characteristics is between monetary and non-monetary evaluation. A monetary evaluation is characterized by an attempt to measure all effects in monetary units, whereas a non-monetary evaluation utilizes a wide variety of measurement units to assess the effects. Cost-benefit analysis and cost-effectiveness analysis are well-known examples of a monetary evaluation (Nijkamp *et al.* 1990).

The history of plan and project evaluation before World War II showed first a strong tendency towards a financial and monetary trade-off analysis. Later on, much attention was focused on cost-effectiveness principles. Especially after World War II, cost-benefit analysis gained increasing popularity in public policy evaluation, by using willingness to pay notions, consumer surplus principles and shadow prices.

The hypotheses underlying monetary evaluation methodologies took for granted rational choice behaviour based on a one-dimensional well-defined performance indicator. The use of such conventional optimization models has been criticized from many sides. Furthermore, in the past decades, the degraded state of the natural environment has become another key issue in evaluation, because of the externalities involved and it is increasingly taken for granted that environmental and resource problems generally have far-reaching economic and ecological consequences, which cannot always be encapsulated by a market system. The limits inherent in conventional evaluation methodologies and the necessity of analysing conflicts between policy objectives in the case of environmental externalities have led to a need for more appropriate analytical tools for strategic evaluation (Nijkamp 1980).

Multiple-criteria evaluation techniques aim at providing such a set of tools. In fact, in the last two decades, it has been understood that welfare is a multi-dimensional variable which includes, *inter alia*, average income, growth, environmental quality, distributional equity, supply of public facilities, and accessibility. This implies that a systematic evaluation of public plans or projects has to be based on the distinction and measurement of a broad set of criteria. These criteria can be different in nature: private economic (for example, investment costs, rate of return), socio-economic (employment, income distribution, access to facilities), environmental (pollution, deterioration of natural areas, noise), energy (use of energy, technological innovation, risk), physical planning (congestion, population density, accessibility, etc.), and so forth.

Generally, ecosystems are used in several ways at the same time by a number of different users. This complies with the definition of multiple use. Such situations almost always lead to conflicts of interest and damage to the environment. The consequences range from suboptimal use due to unregulated access, to degradation of resource systems due to limited knowledge of the ecological process involved (Costanza, 1991). Thus, in the area of environmental and resource management and in policies aiming at an ecologically sustainable development, many conflicting issues and interests emerge. As a tool for conflict management, multi-criteria analysis is then an important evaluation method, which has demonstrated its usefulness in many environmental management problems (Archibugi *et al.* 1990).

In the context of conflicting interests, it is also noteworthy that there is an interference from local, regional or national government agencies, while there is at the same time a high degree of diverging public interests and conflicts among groups in society. At an intraregional level many conflicting objectives may exist between different actors (consumers, firms, institutions), which can formally be represented as multiple objective problems and which have a clear impact on the spatial organization of a certain area (for example, industrialization, housing construction, and road infrastructure construction). At a multi-regional level various spatial linkages exist which affect a whole spatial system through spatial interaction and spillover effects (for example, diffusion of environmental pollution, and spatial price discrimination) and which in a formal sense can be described by means of a multiple objective programming framework. At a super-regional level various hierarchical conflicts may emerge between regional government institutions and the central government or between regional branches and the central office of a firm, which implies again a multiple objective decision situation.

From an operational point of view, the major strength of multi-criteria methods is their ability to address problems marked by various conflicting interests. Multi-criteria methods can provide systematic information on the nature of these conflicts so as to make the trade-offs in a complex situation more transparent to decision makers (Nagel and Mills 1991).

Qualitative Multi-criteria Methods for Environmental Management

During the 1970s and the beginning of the 1980s a great number of multi-criteria methods were developed and used for different policy purposes in different contexts (Bana e Costa 1990; Nijkamp *et al.* 1990). The following distinctions can be made regarding the contexts and the scope of multi-criteria evaluation methods:

1. discrete versus continuous methods;
2. multi-person versus single-person evaluation;
3. single-step versus multi-step evaluation procedures;
4. qualitative versus quantitative information.

We will elaborate the latter feature of multi-criteria methods first.

It has been argued that the presence of qualitative information in evaluation problems concerning socio-economic and physical planning is a rule, rather than an exception (Nijkamp *et al.* 1990). Thus there is a clear need for methods taking into account qualitative information. In multi-criteria evaluation theory, a clear distinction is made between quantitative and qualitative methods. Essentially, there are two approaches for dealing with qualitative information: a direct and an indirect one. In the direct approach, qualitative information is used directly in a qualitative evaluation method; in the indirect approach, qualitative information is first transformed into a cardinal form, then one of the existing quantitative methods is used. Cardinalization is especially attractive in the case of available information of a 'mixed type' (both qualitative and quantitative data). In this case, the application of a direct method would usually imply that only the qualitative contents of all available (quantitative and qualitative) information is used, which would give rise to an inefficient use of this data. In the indirect approach, this loss of information is avoided; the question is, of course, whether there is a sufficient basis for the application of a certain cardinalization scheme. A multi-criteria method that may use mixed information is the EVAMIX procedure. Another useful method for dealing with mixed information is the so-called REGIME method; this method is based on pairwise comparison operations.

Another problem related to the available information is the uncertainty contained in this information. Ideally, the information should be precise, certain, exhaustive and unequivocal. But, in reality, it is often necessary to use information which does not have these characteristics and hence there is a need to face uncertainty of a stochastic and/or fuzzy nature. In fact, if the available information is insufficient or delayed, it is impossible to establish exactly the future state of the problem faced, so that then stochastic uncertainty is created.

Fuzzy uncertainty does not concern the occurrence of an event but the event itself, in the sense that it cannot be described unambiguously. This situation is very common in human systems. Spatial systems, in particular, are complex systems characterized by subjectivity, incompleteness and imprecision (Zadeh 1965; Zimmermann 1986,1987).

Therefore, the combination of different levels of measurement with the different types of uncertainty has to be considered. Recently, a discrete multi-criteria method whose impact (or evaluation) matrix may include either crisp, stochastic or fuzzy evaluations of the performance of an alternative a_n with respect to a criterion g_m has been developed by the present authors (Munda *et al.* 1992b).

From a methodological point of view, two main issues had to be faced:

1. the problem of equivalence of the procedures used in order to standardize the various evaluations (of a mixed type) of the performance of alternatives according to different criteria;
2. the problem of comparison of fuzzy numbers typical of all fuzzy multi-criteria methods.

This method will now briefly be described here. It can be subdivided into four main steps:

1. Definition of a fuzzy region of satisfactory alternatives.
2. Comparison of fuzzy sets.
3. Pairwise comparison of alternatives.
4. Evaluation of alternatives.

Definition of a fuzzy region of satisfactory alternatives

Given a 'consistent family' of mixed evaluation criteria $G = (g_m)$, $m = 1, 2, \ldots\ldots$, M, and a finite set $A = (a_n)$, $n–1, 2, N$ of potential alternatives (actions), a region of satisfactory alternatives can be obtained by defining a fuzzy interval of feasible and acceptable values for each criterion.

From an operational point of view, in public decision-making a single point-value solution (e.g. weights) tends to lead to deadlocks in the evolution of the decision process because it imposes too rigid conditions for a compromise. On the contrary, when a higher degree of flexibility is allowed, the definition of a fuzzy region of satisfactory solutions could in principle make more room for mutual consensus. A natural and flexible way of defining such a region is by means of linguistic propositions.

In traditional mathematics, variables are assumed to be precise, but when we are dealing with our daily language, imprecision usually prevails. Intrinsically, daily languages cannot be precisely characterized on either the syntactic or semantic level. Therefore, a word in our daily languages can technically be regarded as a fuzzy set. In order to allow a formal analysis, a mathematical translation of the linguistic propositions is needed. This can be done by means of possibility theory (Leung 1988).

Comparison of fuzzy sets

In general, fuzzy approaches to multi-criteria evaluation include the following limitations:

(a) most of them are limited to the use of triangular fuzzy numbers;
(b) the shape of the membership function is not taken into consideration or only a part of it is used, which gives rise to a loss of information;
(c) a general problem concerns the 'sensitivity' (degree of discrimination[1]) of the solutions.

Some authors claim that a low degree of discrimination is a negative feature; on the contrary, others believe that in a fuzzy context, an attempt to reach a high degree of precision of the results is somewhat artificial. We share this latter position. In public decision-making in general, and in environmental problems, in particular, we often face the desire not to be confronted with single unambiguous and (sometimes) imposed fixed solutions, but with a spectrum of open feasible solutions each having its own merits.

The present authors have recently developed a new distance metric that is useful in the case of continuous membership functions allowing also a definite integration. This will briefly be described here.

If $\mu_{A1}(x)$ and $\mu_{A2}(x)$ are two membership functions, we can write

$$f(x) = c_1\mu_{A1}(x) \qquad (10.1)$$

and

$$g(y) = c_2\mu_{A2}(x) \qquad (10.2)$$

where $f(x)$ and $g(y)$ are two functions obtained by rescaling the ordinates of $\mu_{A1}(x)$ and $\mu_{A2}(x)$ through c_1 and c, such that

$$\int^2 f(x) \, dx = \int g(y) \, dy = 1 \qquad (10.3)$$

Thus our semantic distance is the following:

$$S_d (f(x), g(y)) = \iint |x - y| f(x) \, g(y) \, dydx \qquad (10.4)$$

It is easy to show that this distance satisfies the properties of non-negativity and symmetry; the proof of the triangle inequality and a Monte Carlo type numerical procedure for the computation of such a distance can be found in Munda *et al.* (1992a). It has to be noted that without the absolute value sign, equation (10.4) becomes a function of the sign, thus allowing the computation of the possibility degree of a fuzzy set to be greater than another one (preference index).

From a theoretical point of view, the following main conclusions can be drawn from the above observations:

(a)   the absolute value metric (simple difference) is a particular case of this type of distance (preference index);
(b)   by applying this preference index, the problem of the use of only one side of the membership functions, common to most of the traditional fuzzy multi-criteria methods, is overcome.

Pairwise comparison of alternatives

Evaluation normally requires a judgement of the relative performance of distinct alternatives based on dominance relationships. Six different fuzzy relations are considered here:

1.   much greater than ($\gg$)
2.   greater than ($>$)
3.   approximately equal to ($\cong$)
4.   very equal to ($=$)
5.   less than ($<$)
6.   much less than ($\ll$)

The use of such relations is inspired by the same philosophy as the definition of a 'pseudo-criterion' (Roy 1985), but here, according to fuzzy principles, no precise boundary is established, thus allowing a focused use of each single evaluation criterion for different preference modelling situations. Furthermore, the decision maker is not asked to evaluate thresholds (which is always a difficult and perhaps arbitrary process), although the choice of the membership functions contains always some degree of arbitrariness.

Given such information on the pairwise performance of alternatives according to each single criterion, it is necessary to aggregate these evaluations in order to take into account all criteria simultaneously; this is done by taking into account the degree of compensation introduced in the model, and a measure of the 'incertitude' of the evaluations given by the entropy concept.

Evaluation of alternatives

The information provided by a 'fuzzy preference relation' can be used in different ways, for example, the degree of truth (T) of statements such as: 'according to most of the criteria

- a is better than b,
- a and b are indifferent,
- a is worse than b',

can be computed by means of proportional linguistic quantifiers and approximate reasoning rules.

Pairwise evaluations can be used directly by the decision maker(s) in order to isolate a set of satisfactory solutions. Alternatively, if in a given decision environment there is a need to carry out further elaborations in order to get a ranking of the alternatives (in a complete or partial pre-order), this can also be done by using further elaborations of approximate reasoning taking into account the entropy levels and the relations with all the other actions.

However, it has to be noted that all results obtained can provide 'justifiable' or 'defensible' decisions to policy makers, but in real-world environmental decision-making, it is necessary to interact with many actors (often each single actor is represented by complex organizations like town councils, trade unions, different associations and so on) each of them having different goals and values. Therefore, since, real-world problems are generally not direct win-lose situations and a certain degree of compromise is needed, a procedure aimed at supporting real environmental policy-makers would ideally consider this problem of different (and often conflicting) evaluations. Multi-criteria evaluation techniques cannot solve all these conflicts, but they can help to provide more insight into the nature of these conflicts and into ways to arrive at political compromises in case of divergent preferences in a multi-group or committee system. For this aim, the possibilities of coalitions between different interest groups whose preference patterns do not show significant differences has to be explored. This will briefly be reviewed in the next section.

Coalition Formation Theory: a Concise Overview

The aim of coalition formation theory is to predict a set of coalitions which are likely to be formed in a given political situation. There are two basic schools of thought among those who have applied game-theoretic principles to the study of political coalition formation. The two opposing positions can be referred to as 'size theory' and 'policy theory' (Holler, 1984).

Size theory originated from Neumann and von Morgenstern's (1947) 'minimal winning coalitions', and was modified by Riker (1962) and Gamson (1962) into 'the size principle'. Size theorists assert that parties prefer governments of which they are a member and which are 'as small as possible'. Size theorists argue that when a government coalition is voted into office it thereby gains control over a fixed sum of benefits which are then subdivided among its constituent members (with non-members receiving nothing). Therefore, the smaller the coalition, the more benefits are available per member.

'Policy theorists' such as Leiserson (1966), and De Swaan (1973) argue that the benefits to the political parties which are generated by a particular government come primarily from the policies implemented by the government. Since government policies are public goods, the benefits that a party may receive from different governments are not necessarily related to the size of the governments. Instead, these benefits are related to the preferences of that party for the policies of one government compared with those of the other.

There are two major variants of 'policy theory': 'Minimal range theory' and 'Policy distance theory' (Holler, 1984).

Minimal range theory asserts that a particular party will prefer a government coalition of which it is a member and which has a small 'range'. Range can be defined as the distance in the policy space between the policy positions of the two most extreme members of a coalition. The argument underlying the minimal range hypothesis is that the smaller the range of the government, the closer the government policy is likely to be to the policy position of any one of its members. The minimal range hypothesis predicts thus government coalitions whose range is as small as possible, given that they must form a majority.

De Swaan (1973) makes the assumption that a coalition government selects its policies by a majority rule. For instance, thinking of the policy space as a line, this assumption leads to the conclusion that the policies chosen by a particular coalition government will be the policies of the party that is at the median of the coalition. According to the policy distance hypothesis, a party will prefer to belong to a coalition for which the policy position of the median member is close to its own position.

In policy distance theories, the construction of the predicted set of coalitions proceeds in two distinct steps: first, each actor establishes his preference ordering among the various possible coalitions, and then individual preferences are used to select a subset of all possible coalitions, i.e. the set of predicted coalitions. In general, the results of policy distance theory are less clear cut than minimal range theory, because it tends to predict that any of a relatively large number of coalitions is possible in a given period, whereas minimal range theory predicts a more restricted set of possibilities.

The cornerstone of the theory of co-operative n-person games (Moulin 1988; Shubik 1983) is the characteristic function. The idea is to capture in a single numerical index the potential worth of each coalition of players (the representation of a coalition's worth by a single number implies freely transferable utility).

Games are defined as inessential if no profitable grounds exist for co-operation among players. They are essential if some members of coalitions, at least, do strictly better by sticking together. Mathematically, the characteristic function, traditionally denoted by v, is a function from subsets of players to the set of real numbers. A general property of characteristic functions is that the function v is superadditive (any set of players can do at least as well in coalition as in any subcoalition), formally,

$$v(S \cup T) \geq v(S) + v(T) \tag{10.5}$$

which holds whenever S and T have no members in common.

A special class of games, which may be thought of as 'games of control' are important tools in the modelling of organizational and group decision processes. They are called *simple games* and are distinguished by the property of having just two kinds of coalitions, namely, winning and losing. In the presence of transferable utility, they are c-games, and after suitable normalization they give rise to a special single type of characteristic function:

$$v(S) = \begin{cases} 0 & \text{if S is losing} \\ 1 & \text{if S is winning} \end{cases} \tag{10.6}$$

Fuzzy Cluster Analysis in Coalition Formation Theory

Any political situation is characterized by an information set, composed by descriptive data and actors' behavioural rules, represented by assumptions that describe the way each actor uses the descriptive information in order to establish his own preferences.

Since, generally real-world problems are not direct win-lose situations (simple games), but a certain degree of compromise is needed, the assumption typical of voting theory, that actors' preferences are fixed can be relaxed, and also strategic aspects may be introduced.

In real-world situations of public decision analysis two main cases can be distinguished (Stewart 1991):

1. Broad commonality of goals (i.e., differences among parties are revealed through various trade-offs which they perceive to be most in their interest).
2. Direct conflict of goals (i.e., a case where public policy involves an explicit division of resources among different sectors of the society or where attitudes have led to unreconcilable strong antagonisms, for example environmentalists versus industrialists).

Given these considerations, it is possible to construct a model (performing as a 'simulation model') whose main aim is to give relevant information on the structure of the decision problem at hand. For example, the authority in charge of a decision can try to forecast the possible behaviour of the relevant interest groups. The following main assumptions are made:

1. only a set of well defined actions has to be taken into account;
2. the actors evaluate the different actions by means of 'linguistic declarations' (good, not very good);
3. the actors are often groups too, but we take for granted that it is possible to obtain their evaluations independently from the way they are derived (in any case, to give a linguistic evaluation of each action can be easier than to supply a complete ranking of all actions).

Given a conflict indicator, a fuzzy cluster algorithm can be used in order to have an idea of the coalitions (minimizing such an indicator) that are 'possible'. It should be noted that the formal structure of the model is:

units=actors   attributes=actions.

Thus we have to evaluate the similarity among actors given the evaluations of the different actions. By using the semantic distance described above as conflict indicator, a similarity matrix (achieved by means of the simple transformation s=1/1+d) for all possible pairs of actors can be obtained, so that the following clustering procedure is meaningful.

On an axiomatic basis, cluster analysis can be distinguished in deterministic, stochastic and fuzzy. By taking into consideration the 'clustering criteria', the following distinction exists (Anderberg 1973; Bezdek 1980; Hartigan 1975):

(a) hierarchical methods,
(b) graph theoretic methods,
(c) objective functional methods.

The hierarchical clustering approach, in particular, allows an evolutionary view of the aggregation process and can easily be dealt within fuzzy terms.

However, in a fuzzy environment a problem exists, i.e. the relation between the concepts of partition and equivalence class. In a crisp environment, the choice of treatment of data in terms of partitions or equivalence relations is a matter of convenience, since the two models are fully equivalent (philosophically and mathematically). On the contrary, fuzzy equivalence relations and partitions are philosophically similar, but their mathematical structures are not isomorphic (e.g. the notion of transitivity is unique for crisp relations but has taken several proposed forms in the fuzzy case). In the Appendix to this chapter we present the technical details of a fuzzy clustering procedure which can be used for an analysis of coalition formation.

In the next section, the applicability of this procedure for the analysis of possible coalitions in conflicting environmental management problems will be illustrated by means of a real-world land-use planning problem.

Environmental Management and Fuzzy Conflict Analysis: Illustration by means of a Land-Use Problem

The application used in this section is based on a previous case study which used ordinal information and multi-dimensional scaling techniques (Nijkamp 1980). It concerns a study on environmental management in the Netherlands.

The southern part of Limburg (a province in the south-eastern part of the country) is the major centre of the Dutch cement industry owing to the special physical structure and condition of the soil in this area. The production of cement is based on the raw material marl. The marl winning takes place by extracting this raw material from so-called marl-pits. This is an open-air activity which destroys more or less completely the original physical structure of the area concerned. There is a company with almost absolute dominance in the Dutch cement industry. This company has a concession to extract marl on one of the hills in south Limburg, but this concession may finish in the near future; thus alternative areas have to be explored. Among the new possible areas, the most appropriate one is the Plateau van Margraten; this is a rather flat area which is used for agriculture and for some recreation. It has a unique physical structure and it is a characteristic area in the landscape of the region. Designation of this area for marl winning would fundamentally affect its social and ecological value; on the other hand, if the authorities would refuse to grant permission for marl winning to the company, this would lead to an almost total destruction of the national cement industry and to serious unemployment effects for this already weak economic region. This situation clearly demonstrates the sharp conflict between environmental and economic interests.

A first meaningful step toward an evaluation analysis for this land-use problem is to identify a set of feasible and relevant alternatives. These alternatives are:

1. An implementation of the original plans of the company (i.e., a concession for the total area). This guarantees the future position of the national cement industry and also favours employment and welfare in the region. Agriculture suffers from some negative impacts, while the negative social impacts (for example, for recreation) are high. Finally, the environmental damage is very high.

2. The use of an alternative area (the Rasberg area, in the same region) for marl winning. But this area is much smaller and the physical condition of the soil restricts profitable cement production at present prices. On the other hand, the ecological damage is less serious.
3. The provision of a concession for one half of the area (Plateau van Margraten). This leads to less agricultural losses, while the environmental damage is also lower. The economic impacts are less favourable than those of the first alternative.
4. A new concession for marl winning on the present area. This is only a short-term solution which is less attractive from an economic point of view (note that in this case, one would need a multi-period approach, but this is too complex for illustrative purposes).
5. Import of marl from the Plateau van Vroenhoven, an area in Belgium. This solution may be attractive from a social and environmental point of view (at least from a national standpoint), but it is less attractive from an economic point of view. For simplicity, we ignore the environmental impact of transport of marl.
6. A restructuring of the company so that it becomes a trade and research organization for cement instead of a production unit for cement. This will lead to a certain loss of employment, while the future need for such an organization is unclear.
7. A closedown of all productive activities of the company. This may be favourable from the viewpoint of environmentalists and recreationers, but it will lead to serious economic problems for the region.

These alternatives are to be judged on the basis of various evaluation criteria. Three main groups of criteria can be distinguished, namely economic, social, and environmental. These three classes can be subdivided into various components.

- *Economic criteria*

  1. employment in agriculture
  2. employment in cement industry (including marl winning)
  3. agricultural production
  4. national production of marl
  5. value added in cement industry

- *Social criteria*

  6. residential attractiveness
  7. recreational attractiveness (daily)

8. tourist attractiveness
9. congestion created in transportation infrastructure

● *Environmental criteria*

10. quality of physiological structure
11. diversity and scarcity of eco- and bio-components
12. consistency with existing landscape components
13. consistency with existing cultural-historical components.

It appears that concerning the information on the diverse plan impacts the degree of uncertainty is high, so that quantitative information on these impacts is often not available. A representation of such impacts in fuzzy terms seems very appropriate. A multi-criteria fuzzy evaluation matrix related to the above-mentioned seven alternatives and 13 criteria is presented in Table 10.1.

Table 10.1   Evaluation matrix for a fuzzy land-use problem

criteria	a_1	a_2	a_3	a_4	a_5	a_6	a_7
				Alternatives			
g_1	moderate	moderate	good	good	excellent	excellent	excellent
g_2	excellent	excellent	moderate	moderate	good	moderate	bad
g_3	moderate	moderate	good	good	excellent	excellent	excellent
g_4	excellent	excellent	moderate	moderate	moderate	bad	bad
g_5	excellent	moderate	bad	bad	good	good	bad
g_6	moderate	moderate	bad	bad	good	good	bad
g_7	good	good	good	excellent	excellent	excellent	excellent
g_8	moderate	moderate	good	excellent	excellent	excellent	excellent
g_9	moderate	moderate	moderate	excellent	excellent	excellent	excellent
g_{10}	moderate	moderate	moderate	excellent	excellent	excellent	excellent
g_{11}	good	good	good	excellent	excellent	excellent	excellent
g_{12}	bad	moderate	good	excellent	excellent	excellent	excellent
g_{13}	moderate	good	good	excellent	excellent	excellent	excellent

In addition to this fuzzy evaluation matrix, an assessment of the priority structures of the diverse interest groups is required. The number of interest groups distinguished in this study is six. These groups are:

1. the board of directors of the company
2. the employees of the company
3. the farmers' association in Limburg
4. the recreational association for south Limburg

5.   the environmental federation in Limburg
6.   the residents of the area around the Plateau van Margraten.

In Table 10.2 the linguistic evaluations of the alternative plans according to each interest group are presented. These evaluations were assessed on the basis of personal inquiries, interviews, talks with interest groups, and study of available material.

Table 10.2   Fuzzy evaluations of alternatives according to each interest group

Interest groups	Alternatives						
	a_1	a_2	a_3	a_4	a_5	a_6	a_7
1	very good	good	moderate	bad	fairly good	fairly bad	very bad
2	very good	good	moderate	bad	fairly good	very bad	very bad
3	very bad	fairly bad	moderate	good	very good	good	moderate
4	very bad	fairly bad	fairly bad	good	fairly good	good	very good
5	very bad	bad	fairly bad	moderate	fairly good	good	very good
6	very bad	good	bad	good	good	good	very good

By applying our fuzzy multi-criteria procedure for each pair of actions, the following degrees of truth (expressing the credibility of the pairwise comparison results) of a linguistic evaluation are obtained:

a_1 is better than a_2	$\tau = 0$	a_1 is better than a_3	$\tau = 0$
a_1 and a_2 are indifferent	$\tau = 1$	a_1 and a_3 are indifferent	$\tau = 0$
a_1 is worse than a_2	$\tau = 0$	a_1 is worse than a_3	$\tau = 0$
a_1 is better than a_4	$\tau = 0$	a_1 is better than a_5	$\tau = 0$
a_1 and a_4 are indifferent	$\tau = 0$	a_1 and a_5 are indifferent	$\tau = 0$
a_1 is worse than a_4	$\tau = 1$	a_1 is worse than a_5	$\tau = 1$
a_1 is better than a_6	$\tau = 0$	a_1 is better than a_7	$\tau = 0$
a_1 and a_6 are indifferent	$\tau = 0$	a_1 and a_7 are indifferent	$\tau = 0$
a_1 is worse than a_6	$\tau = 1$	a_1 is worse than a_7	$\tau = 1$
a_2 is better than a_3	$\tau = 0$	a_2 is better than a_4	$\tau = 0$
a_2 and a_3 are indifferent	$\tau = 0$	a_2 and a_4 are indifferent	$\tau = 0$
a_2 is worse than a_3	$\tau = 0$	a_2 is worse than a_4	$\tau = 1$
a_2 is better than a_5	$\tau = 0$	a_2 is better than a_6	$\tau = 0$
a_2 and a_5 are indifferent	$\tau = 0$	a_2 and a_6 are indifferent	$\tau = 0$
a_2 is worse than a_5	$\tau = 1$	a_2 is worse than a_6	$\tau = 1$

a_2 is better than a_7	$\tau = 0$	a_3 is better than a_4	$\tau = 0$
a_2 and a_7 are indifferent	$\tau = 0$	a_3 and a_4 are indifferent	$\tau = 0$
a_2 is worse than a_7	$\tau = 1$	a_3 is worse than a_4	$\tau = 1$
a_3 is better than a_5	$\tau = 0$	a_3 is better than a_6	$\tau = 0$
a_3 and a_5 are indifferent	$\tau = 0$	a_3 and a_6 are indifferent	$\tau = 0$
a_3 is worse than a_5	$\tau = 1$	a_3 is worse than a_6	$\tau = 1$
a_3 is better than a_7	$\tau = 0$	a_4 is better than a_5	$\tau = 0$
a_3 and a_7 are indifferent	$\tau = 0$	a_4 and a_5 are indifferent	$\tau = 1$
a_3 is worse than a_7	$\tau = 1$	a_4 is worse than a_5	$\tau = 0$
a_4 is better than a_6	$\tau = 0$	a_4 is better than a_7	$\tau = 0$
a_4 and a_6 are indifferent	$\tau = 1$	a_4 and a_7 are indifferent	$\tau = 1$
a_4 is worse than a_6	$\tau = 0$	a_4 is worse than a_7	$\tau = 0$
a_5 is better than a_6	$\tau = 0$	a_5 is better than a_7	$\tau = 0$
a_5 and a_6 are indifferent	$\tau = 1$	a_5 and a_7 are indifferent	$\tau = 1$
a_5 is worse than a_6	$\tau = 0$	a_5 is worse than a_7	$\tau = 0$
a_6 is better than a_7	$\tau = 0$		
a_6 and a_7 are indifferent	$\tau = 1$		
a_6 is worse than a_7	$\tau = 0$		

It is clear that almost all linguistic evaluations are quite unambiguous. This is caused by four factors:

1. the number of criteria in favour of an action;
2. the degree of compensation allowed in the aggregation process;
3. definition of the membership function of the linguistic operators;
4. aggregation operator chosen for the approximate reasoning operations (in this application we have used the 'min' operator which is known as a representation of the logic 'and', and therefore is completely non-interactive, since a high value cannot compensate a low one).[2]

It has to be noted that between actions a_1 and a_3, and a_2 and a_3, none of the possible situations satisfies the minimum requirement requested by the linguistic operator 'most'; this can be interpreted as a difficulty in the comparison which might bring about an incomparability relation.

On the basis of the above pairwise comparison between alternatives, we arrive at the following final ranking of alternatives:

$$(a_4, a_5, a_6, a_7) > (a_1, a_2, a_3).$$

This means that we obtain two subsets of alternatives. The best subset contains a_4, a_5, a_6 and a_7. On the basis of the pairwise comparison results, it is not possible, however, to rank the alternatives within the two subsets.

A higher degree of discrimination can be obtained by means of a complex procedure whose details can be found in Munda *et al.* (1992b). The result of such a procedure is the following

$$a_6 \rightarrow a_5 \rightarrow a_4 \rightarrow a_7 \rightarrow a_1 \rightarrow a_2$$
$$\searrow a_3$$

This (ordinal) ranking appears quite stable. In fact, only two incomparability relations are present, that is between a_1 and a_3, and between a_2 and a_3. (It is interesting to note that these results are consistent with the information given by the pairwise linguistic evaluations.) Finally, it has to be noted that this ranking includes a higher degree of discrimination than the pairwise linguistic evaluations, because it is a function of the relation of each alternative with all other ones, and no 'minimum requirement threshold' like in the linguistic quantifiers is introduced.

However, since a weighting of criteria is not assumed and no consideration is given to the 'minority principle' (like the discordance index in the ELECTRE methods) such a procedure must be integrated with conflict minimization methods which allow policymakers to seek for 'defensible' decisions that could reduce the degree of conflict (in order to reach a certain degree of consensus) or that could have a higher probability of being accepted by certain groups of decision makers.

Taking into consideration the possibility of coalitions among the different interest groups, the following results can now be obtained.

Table 10.3   Similarity matrix for all possible pairs of interest groups

	Groups					
	1	2	3	4	5	6
1	1	0.729	0.426	0.399	0.403	0.403
2	0.729	1	0.410	0.386	0.390	0.390
3	0.426	0.410	1	0.675	0.584	0.569
4	0.399	0.386	0.675	1	0.729	0.672
5	0.403	0.390	0.584	0.729	1	0.595
6	0.403	0.390	0.569	0.672	0.595	1

By applying the semantic distance as defined in (10.4), after the transformation $s = 1/1+d$, the similarity matrix shown in Table 10.3, for all possible pairs of interest groups, is obtained. It means, for example, that the highest similarity occurs for interest groups 1 and 2, and for groups 4 and 5. These interest groups have a relatively high correspondence of goals, accordingly. The reverse holds true for interest groups 2 and 4 where the lowest degree of similarity is found.

Application of the clustering procedure presented in the Appendix leads to the following results. As long as the similarity degree α required for a coalition is higher than .729, there will be no coalition formation. Two coalitions will be formed when α is between .729 and .675(1 and 2), and (4 and 5). When the similarity degree is reduced to .675 and .672, interest groups 3 and 6 join the last coalition, respectively. The conflict of interest between the remaining coalitions (1, 2) versus (3, 4, 5, 6) is considerable as can be inferred from the low similarity degree associated with a grand coalition. (See figure 10.1.)

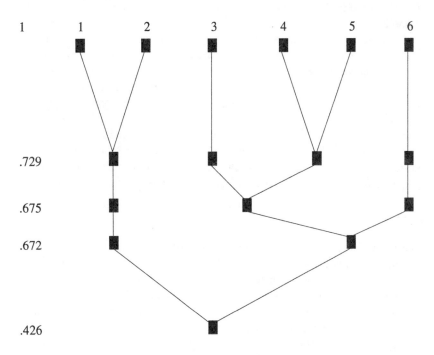

Figure 10.1   Dendrogram of the coalition formation process

These results are quite well in agreement with prior expectations about the attitudes and behaviour of the interest groups. The interests of the company and of its employees seem to run fairly parallel. The agricultural interest group seems to take an intermediate position, but it joins quite soon the coalition made by the recreation and environmental groups. The priority patterns of the recreation group and the environmental group bear a very close correspondence. The residential group presents a more individualistic character since it can be considered a clear case of a 'NIMBY' (never in my back yard) syndrome; in any case, it is closer to the interests of the recreation and environmental groups than to those of the economic groups.

It is interesting to note that the alternatives strongly supported by interest groups 1 and 2 (a_i, a_2) have bad environmental impacts. All the alternatives considered 'good' from an environmental point of view are more or less well-accepted by interest groups 3, 4, 5 and 6. Among the actions of this group, a_6, a_5, and a_4 are clearly compromise solutions in nature while a_7 is a too extreme solution (closedown of all productive activities) but which clearly has a high performance from a social and environmental point of view; a_5 is the only alternative which minimizes the conflicts. Both a_6 and a_4 will be rejected strongly by interest groups 1 and 2.

Up till now a weak element in this analysis is the lack of strategic considerations leading to new coalitions or alliances. In fact, the clustering algorithm only indicates the groups whose interests are close in comparison to the others. This is more or less in agreement with the hypotheses underlying the 'minimal range theory'. This theory is quite plausible in the case of 'broad commonality of goals'. On the contrary, in the case of 'direct conflict of goals', game-theoretic elements such as the notion of 'power' need to be introduced. Furthermore, attaching to each interest group the same weight can be an oversimplification of a real-world situation. Such an introduction of strategic elements in this analysis of coalitions should be undertaken in future research.

Conclusion

We have illustrated how qualitative multi-criteria methods can be used in evaluation problems with conflicting objectives related to economic and environmental impacts. It is shown how fuzzy set approaches can be used to generate a ranking of alternatives in order of attractiveness according to the preference of a decision maker. As long as there is only one decision maker, this approach is directly applicable. In this case, multi-criteria methods have a normative orientation in the sense that they are an aid to the decision maker to find out which alternative is most attractive given his or her preference structure.

In the case of more than one decision maker, such a normative approach is still useful for each decision maker or interest group to determine the most preferred alternative. But the final decision to be taken cannot be determined in this case only on technical grounds. It depends among others on relative power, and decision rules and practices. The second part of this chapter no longer has a normative orientation. It addresses the question to what extent decision makers have different evaluations of the alternatives. This gives the approach an analytical orientation: the analysis of similarity of interests is an input for the analysis of the formation of coalitions. In this chapter we have shown that fuzzy cluster analysis is a useful tool to study the coalition formation process.

Appendix

We start the discussion on fuzzy cluster analysis with the definition of a *crisp equivalence relation.*

Let $X = (x_1, x_2, ...xn)$ be any finite set. Then an nxm matrix $R=[r_{ij}]$ $[r(x_i, x_j)]$ is a crisp equivalence relation on XxX if

$$r_{ii} = 1 \quad 1 \leq i \leq n \qquad \text{(reflexivity)}$$

$$r_{ij} = r_{ji} \quad 1 \leq i \neq j \leq n \qquad \text{(symmetry)}$$

$$\begin{cases} r_{ij} = 1 \\ \\ r_{jk} = 1 \end{cases} \Rightarrow r_{ik} = 1 \forall i, j, k$$

$$\text{(transitivity)}$$

Let R be a fuzzy binary relation with $\mu_R(x_i, x_j)$ indicating the degree to which two elements x_i and x_j are similar (similarity matrix). The relation R is obviously reflexive and symmetric, thus it is called a resemblance relation.

A fuzzy relation is a *similitude relation* if it has the following properties:

$$\mu R(x_i, x_j) = 1 \quad \forall (x_i, x_j) \in XxX \qquad \text{(reflexivity)}$$

$$\mu_R(x_i, x_j) = \mu_R(x_j \, x_i) \, \forall (x_i, x_j) \in XxX \qquad \text{(symmetry)}$$

$$\mu_R(x_i, x_k) \geq \max \min \, [\mu_R(x_i, x_j), \mu_R(x_j \, x_k)]$$

$$\forall (x_i, x_j), (x_j, x_k), (x_i, x_k) \in XxX \text{(max-min transitivity)}$$

Note that compared to the notion of transitivity in conventional analysis, the present notion defines a weak transitivity of similarity.

If one wants to derive a set of equivalence classes (and not simple partitions) there is a need for the similarity matrix being at least max-min transitive. As is known (Leung 1988), a method to transform an intransitive similarity matrix into a transitive one is to derive the transitive closure $\Re$ of R. The max-min transitive closure of a fuzzy binary relation R is

$$\Re = R \cup R^2 \cup R^3 \cup \ldots\ldots$$

where $R^2 = R^\circ R$ is the max-min composition of R.

The element $\mu\Re(x_i, x_j)$ indicates the max-min transitive similarity of x_i and x_j.

A standard operation for two fuzzy relations is the *max-min composition:* given two relations R(x, y), S(y, z) defined on XxY and YxZ, respectively, the max-min composition of R and S, denoted as $R^\circ S$, is defined by

$$\mu_{R\circ S}(x, z) = \underset{y \in Y}{\text{max-min}} \; [\mu_R(x, y), \mu_S(y, z)]$$

$x \in X, y \in Y$ and $z \in Z$.

By using the notion of max-min composition, one is allowed to derive new fuzzy relations. A transitive closure can be obtained by means of the following theorem.

Let R be any fuzzy binary relation. If for some k, the max-min composition $R^{k+1}=R^k$, then the max-min transitive closure is

$$\Re = R \cup R^2 \cup R^3 \cup ,\ldots\ldots\ldots, \cup R^k$$

Knowing that a fuzzy set A can always be decomposed into a series of α-level sets A_α, the similitude relation $\Re$ can be decomposed into

$$\Re = \cup \; \alpha\cdot\Re\alpha$$
$$\alpha \in [0, 1]$$

where

$$f_\Re(xi, xj) = \begin{cases} 1 \text{ if } \mu_\Re\left(x_i, x_j\right) \geq \alpha \\ 0 \text{ if } \mu\Re(xi, xj) < \alpha \end{cases}$$

and

$$\alpha_1 > \alpha_2 \Rightarrow \Re_{\alpha 1} \subset \Re_{\alpha 2}$$

Since $\mathfrak{R}_\alpha$ is reflexive, symmetric and transitive in the sense of ordinary sets, then it is an equivalence class of level α. Within each α-level equivalence class, the similarity of any two units is no less than α.

Note that the equivalence classes obtained are ordinary disjoint sets. In fact, in order to have non-mutually exclusive equivalence classes, it is necessary to assume the use of a min-addition transitive distance matrix (which is a stronger assumption than max-min transitivity).

It can be proved that the following four algorithms generate the same partition (Miyamoto 1990):

(a) the single linkage method
(b) the connected components of an undirected fuzzy graph
(c) the transitive closure of a reflexive and symmetric fuzzy relation, and
(d) the maximal spanning tree of a weighted graph.

Then the following consequences can be drawn:

1. Since the connected components are independent of the numbering of the vertices, the algorithm is independent of the ordering of the inputs, and therefore it is stable.
2. No *reversal* exists in the dendrogram (reversal meaning that the merging levels are not monotonically decreasing, and thus a cut of the dendrogram may produce ambiguous results).
3. One is not obliged to use only the Euclidean metric (for example, like in the 'centre of gravity' procedures), but any distance measure (even if it does not respect the triangular inequality property) can be used; thus the method is quite general.

As an illustration of the application of the max-min composition we use the following similarity matrix as a starting point:

	1	2	3	4	5	6
1	1	0.729	0.426	0.399	0.403	0.403
2	0.729	1	0.410	0.386	0.390	0.390
3	0.426	0.410	1	0.675	0.584	0.569
4	0.399	0.386	0.675	1	0.729	0.672
5	0.403	0.390	0.584	0.729	1	0.595
6	0.403	0.390	0.569	0.672	0.595	1

By using the notion of max-min composition, the following new fuzzy relations are derived:

$$R^2$$

	1	2	3	4	5	6
1	1	0.729	0.426	0.426	0.426	0.426
2	0.729	1	0.426	0.410	0.410	0.410
3	0.426	0.426	1	0.675	0.675	0.672
4	0.426	0.410	0.675	1	0.729	0.672
5	0.426	0.410	0.675	0.729	1	0.672
6	0.426	0.410	0.672	0.672	0.672	1

$$R^3$$

	1	2	3	4	5	6
1	1	0.729	0.426	0.426	0.426	0.426
2	0.729	1	0.426	0.426	0.426	0.426
3	0.426	0.426	1	0.675	0.675	0.672
4	0.426	0.426	0.675	1	0.729	0.672
5	0.426	0.426	0.675	0.729	1	0.672
6	0.426	0.426	0.672	0.672	0.672	1

$$R^4$$

	1	2	3	4	5	6
1	1	0.729	0.426	0.426	0.426	0.426
2	0.729	1	0.426	0.426	0.426	0.426
3	0.426	0.426	1	0.675	0.675	0.672
4	0.426	0.426	0.675	1	0.729	0.672
5	0.426	0.426	0.675	0.729	1	0.672
6	0.426	0.426	0.672	0.672	0.672	1

Since in the series of max-min compositions $R^3 = R^4$, the transitive closure is

$$R = R \cup R^2 \cup R^3 = R^3$$

Since R is a similitude relation, it can be decomposed into equivalence classes with respect to the degree of similarity α.

Notes

1. The degree of discrimination 'refers to the capability of a method to differentiate between alternatives the ratings of which differ only slightly from each other' (Zimmermann 1987:174).
2. By compensation in the context of aggregation operators for fuzzy sets is meant the following: 'Given that the degree of membership to the aggregated fuzzy set is $\mu Agg\ (x_k) = f(\mu A(x_k), \mu B(x_k)) = k$, f is compensatory if $\mu Agg\ (x_k) = k$ is obtainable for different $\mu A(x_k)$ by a change in $\mu B(x_k)$' (Zimmermann 1986:36).

References

Anderberg, M.R. (1973), *Cluster Analysis for Applications*, New York: Academic Press.

Archibugi, F. and Nijkamp, P. (eds) (1990), *Economy and Ecology: Towards Sustainable Development*, Dordrecht: Kluwer Academic Publishers.

Bana e Costa, C.A. (ed.)(1990), *Readings in Multiple Criteria Decision Aid*, Berlin: Springer-Verlag.

Bezdek, J.C. (1980), *Pattern Recognition with Fuzzy Objective Functions Algorithms*, New York and London: Plenum.

Costanza, R. (ed.) (1991), *Ecological Economics: The Science and Management of Sustainability*, New York: Columbia University Press.

De Swaan, A. (1973), *Coalition Theories and Cabinet Formation*, Amsterdam: North-Holland.

Gamson, W.A. (1962), 'Coalition Formation at Presidential Nominating Conventions', *American Journal of Sociology*, **68**, pp. 157–71.

Hartigan, J. (1975), *Clustering Algorithms*, New York: John Wiley.

Holler, M.J. (ed.) (1984), *Coalitions and Collective Action*, Wuerzburg, Germany: Physica-Verlag.

Leiserson, M. (1966), *Coalitions in Politics*, unpublished PhD dissertation, Yale University.

Leung, Y. (1988), *Spatial Analysis and Planning Under Imprecision*, Amsterdam: North Holland.

Miyamoto, S. (1990), *Fuzzy Sets in Information Retrieval and Cluster Analysis*, Dordrecht: Kluwer Academic Publishers.

Moulin, H. (1988), *Axioms of Cooperative Decision Making*, Econometric Society Monographs, Cambridge University Press.

Munda, G., Nijkamp, P. and Rietveld, P. (1992a), 'Comparison of Fuzzy Sets: A New Semantic Distance', submitted to *Ricerca Operativa*.

Munda, G., Nijkamp, P. and Rietveld, P. (1992b), 'Qualitative Multicriteria Methods for Fuzzy Evaluations Problems. An Illustration of Economic-Ecological Evaluation', submitted to *European Journal of Operational Research*.

Nagel, S.S. and Mills, M.K. (1991), *Systematic Analysis in Dispute Resolution*, New York: Quorum Books.

Neumann, J. and von Morgenstern, O. (1947), *Theory of Games and Economic Behaviour*, Princeton: Princeton University Press.

Nijkamp, P. (1980), *Environmental Policy Analysis*, New York: John Wiley.

Nijkamp, P., Rietveld, P. and Voogd, H. (1990), *Multicriteria Evaluation in Physical Planning*, Amsterdam: North-Holland.

Riker, W.H. (1962), *The Theory of Political Coalitions*, London: New Haven.

Roy, B. (1985), *Methodologie Multicritere d'Aide a la Decision*, Paris: Economica.

Shubik, M. (1983), *Game Theory in the Social Sciences*, Cambridge: MIT Press.

Stewart, T.J. (1991), 'Decision Analysis in Public Policy Evaluation', paper presented at *EURO XI*, Aachen, Germany.

Zadeh, L.A. (1965), '*Fuzzy Sets*', *Information and Control*, 8, pp.338–53.

Zimmermann, H.J. (1986), *Fuzzy Set Theory and its Applications*, Boston, Kluwer-Nijhoff Publishing.

Zimmermann, H.J. (1987), *Fuzzy Sets, Decision Making, and Expert Systems*, Boston: Kluwer-Nijhoff Publishing.

11. Sustainable development and project appraisal

Behrooz Morvaridi

This chapter looks at the difficulties in operationalizing sustainable development at the project level. It examines why the synergism metaphor — the cumulative interaction of development variables — cannot be easily translated into project appraisal. A case study of dams, typical of large development projects, illustrates the need for integrating the qualitative and quantitative sides of sustainable development into project design despite the theoretical and practical problems.

Human actions affect environmental change in every sector of the economy — energy, transport, industry and agriculture. It was with the emergence of 'new' environmentalism of the 1980s that an attempt at reconciling development and the environment was born. While the question of reconciling development and environment is no longer ignored, consensus has not been established on how a sustainable development process can be operationalized and achieved, or how environmental degradation can be defined and measured in the context of sustainability. Many diverse definitions of sustainable development focus on the interaction of social, economic and environmental issues, rather than the constituent parts of the development process, but empirical evidence to allow a full appreciation of the processes of these interactions is scarce.

The synergistic intercourse that distinguishes sustainability has increased our awareness of the importance of empirical links between several observable variables. However, emphasis has tended to be on identifying and quantifying the impact of proximate determinants, such as technological change, on the production and consumption of environmental resources. This analysis reflects preoccupation with the economic aspects of sustainable development, while the underlying social processes are given secondary importance. At the project level, this economics bias means that attempts at integrating social and environmental appraisal have tended to be in economic terms with social principles merely noted (Winpenny 1991).

Sustainable Development at the Level of Project: Conflicts and Limitations Practice in International Institutions

World Bank projects are typically large, capital loans with major natural resource components, such as dams, and therefore require rigorous assessment from the point of view of environmental impact. The World Bank notes that prior to the sustainability approach to development, environmental considera- tion was 'based on Environmental Impact Assessments of individual projects and an investment in programmes such as pollution abatement, afforestation, or waste management strategies' (World Bank 1991). However, whether World Bank and United Nations (UN) guidelines for environmental impact assessment (EIA) have adapted to recognize the role of intersectoral linkages in the sus- tainability of socio-economic processes is open to question.

The UN system integrates environmental aspects into the decision-making process for projects which are designated environmental projects. However, projects which are classified as non-environmental do not automatically have potential environmental impacts assessed. Most UN agencies are using an *ad hoc* approach to environmental assessment, which means that procedures are not clearly defined and regulated reflecting the fact that there are no guidelines as to what viable environmental assessment procedures need to include. Some UN agencies, such as FAO and UNIDO, are in the process of developing procedures to be built in at various stages of the programme or project: at the level of agency/government negotiations; in the process of screening projects for potential environmental impacts, both negative and positive; monitoring, evaluation and feedback in the project cycle; and at the technical and procedural level.

The World Bank's EIA begins with screening to evaluate a project or project components according to the degree and sensitivity of the environmental issues raised (World Bank 1991). This determines the type of environmental analysis to be conducted for the project — whether a full environmental assessment or no further analysis. EIA might include an economic valuation of environmen- tal effects, depending on decision-makers' preferences and data and may also indicate whether the design of a project should be changed to mitigate, prevent or compensate for any environmental damage it causes. However, the World Bank does not stipulate the criteria or methodology of environmental appraisal nor do they impose sustainability criteria on borrowers which involve analysis of the mechanisms and processes of interactions between environmental impact and socio-economic and cultural factors.

Almost every development project has a potential environmental impact of some sort and most projects could be designed to have a positive environmen- tal impact, such as environmental training. The World Bank categorizes projects as to their likely impact on the environment: projects requiring environmental assessment as their environmental impact is certain, for example water projects; projects where a more limited environmental assessment would be appropri- ate, such as measuring the effects of a factory once completed; projects where environmental assessment is not seen to be necessary, such as family-planning programmes; and, lastly, projects not requiring additional environmental assessment as they are environmental projects, for example reforestation.[1]

Even though it was the UN sponsored report *Our Common Future*, by the World Commission on Environment and Development (the Bruntland Report) (1987) that launched the concept of 'sustainable development', an operational context for the concept has made slow progress from within the major donor agencies. This can be attributed in part to difficulties in defining sustainability and the various levels at which it could be achieved.

Sustainable Development and Appraisal Criteria

The emphasis placed on the interactions between economic growth, social and cultural transformation and environmental conservation distinguishes sustainable development as a separate concept in the development discourse. However, the unevenness of the global pattern of resource depletion makes for complex analytical material from which to give sustainable development a uniform or cohesive structure. That sustainable development means different things within different intellectual paradigms, complicates the matter of translating what is a broad development concept into strategy and policy, even though it may be argued that the vagueness and hence flexibility of the concept of sustainable development becomes its strength (Redclift 1990). The theoretical literature offers a statement of intent, not an analytical framework from which a development strategy and project planning could be developed (Brookfield 1991:46). This means that analytical tools and methodologies necessary to take account of not only the economic effects but also the social and environmental consequences of development have not been refined.

What from the extensive literature on sustainable development could inform and influence decision makers and how? Key elements from the many definitions of sustainable development can be identified and it has been argued that from these appraisal criteria can be drawn to offer guidelines for policy and project planning (Markandya 1992; Pearce *et al.* 1990).

The concept of intra- and inter-generational equity is common to most definitions of sustainable development. In short, this means approaching current poverty from a position of equity, while ensuring that this does not compromise the right of future generations to have equal access to resources as the present generation. Future generations will secure compensation through the inheritance of non-declining capital stock (WCED 1987; Pearce *et al.* 1990; Markandya 1992). Pearce sees the importance of a natural resource base in terms of economic, social, welfare and cultural impacts. However, to Pearce a major problem is the trade-off between present and future generation needs and between the quality of resources and economic and social welfare (Pearce *et al.* 1990). The idea of equity between generations only has value if subsequent generations are guaranteed livelihoods. If, for example, as a result of rapid population growth inheritances are too small to provide livelihoods for the next generation (a process that has already taken place in many Third World countries and in particular in India) intergenerational equity may be hard to establish.

The concept of efficiency underlies most development concerns and is used in terms of sustainable development to refer to efficient use of natural resources (Markandya 1992:291). Efficiency alongside conservation is considered necessary to provide both equity and economic gains in the short and long term.

However, sustainable development is not just about resource use, although the idea of sustainability is identified as the antithesis to resource abuse. An important contribution of the various approaches to sustainable development is the recognition that environmental degradation, poverty and underdevelopment result in a process of 'cumulative causation' (Barbier 1987). Dealing with the problem of poverty is a goal in itself as well as a means to protecting the environment and increasing economic output. In terms of appraisal criteria, these interactions cannot be ignored. Chambers (1987:10) writes: 'Poor people in their struggle to survive are driven into doing environmental damage with long-term losses. Their herds overgraze; their shortening fallows on steep slopes and fragile soils induce erosion; their need for off-season income drives them to cut and sell firewood and to make and sell charcoal; they are forced to cultivate and degrade marginal and unstable land.' Chambers refers to the need to secure sustainable livelihoods, which means securing food and basic needs, resources and income. A minimum condition for sustainable development is that the environment is valued as an integral part of the socio-economic process.

Concepts in the sustainable development literature like 'equity' lean towards an economics bias and are not well-defined in social terms. Although sustainable development is a means to achieving resource conservation and environmental integrity, it is also a means of ensuring some accountability for social justice: 'Many resource conservation issues, for example, cannot be resolved without addressing the grinding poverty and social marginality that drive rainforest destruction, land degradation and so on' (Buttle 1992:18).

The need to involve local participation at a grass-root level is an integral part of most definitions of sustainable development, since economic and social impacts of resource use cannot be assessed in isolation from local people. Ecological knowledge is acquired by indigenous and local peoples over the generations through direct contact with the environment.

Gender relations and the division of labour impact on resource use but have tended to be neglected in the theoretical debate and reasoning of sustainable development as in most development strategies. The concept of equity between social groups and generations has not been extended to include equity between the sexes. Furthermore, women play a vital role in household production and reproduction and household decision-making on, for example, choice of household fuels and consumption patterns. Since women are usually the household members responsible for collecting firewood and drawing water for household consumption, any environmental conservation decisions which will directly affect their work should involve them.

Sustainable development has been criticized as a strategy aimed at 'greening the institutions of development finance and assistance' (Buttle 1992). By addressing the question of environment the World Bank, for example, has been criticized for moving on from 'economising ecology' to 'ecologising the economy' (Michael 1989). This is because for some, integrating the concerns of sustainability into project appraisal has fallen short of expectations. A major area of concern is problems of measurement at the different levels of project appraisal and analysis: assessing qualitative as well as quantitative impacts; evaluating the synergistic relationship between variables; understanding the proximate determinants of socio-economic processes; and establishing a hierarchy of appraisal criteria and values which represents the synergism of sustainability and can be adapted to local conditions.

Sustainability at the Project Level: Problems of Measurement

The development of new tools for macro, sectoral and project planning and appraisal is not easy. Where several sectors are included in project designs, they are often considered in isolation from each other in appraisal. The question yet to be sufficiently answered is one of either expanding traditional appraisal techniques or devising new techniques to address sustainability.

Difficulties in applying the concept of sustainable development at the project level arise from operational problems of measurement and valuation. Much of the appraisal of environmental degradation at different stages of project design and implementation is concerned with the symptoms rather than the process of degradation. Identification of symptoms, such as salinization and desertification, have been forthcoming, but there is generally little success at assigning weight to causal factors or establishing links between environmental degradation and socio-economic variables. This is particularly true with regard to explaining the relationship between degradation and productivity (Blaikie 1992).

Attempts at expanding cost-benefit or multi-criteria analysis to include sustainability tend to draw on the narrow definition of ecological or environmental sustainability (Van Pelt *et al.* 1990). Such definitions limit themselves to resource use and abuse and avoid the issue of measuring social as well as environmental change. Although the measurement of costs and benefits is useful in project appraisal, sustainability, which goes beyond assessment of indicators of environmental degradation to include the interaction of degradation with socio-economic variables, is too complex to be disaggregated into 'rules' for the purposes of cost-benefit analysis.

Pearce suggests that sustainability could be introduced to cost-benefit analysis by 'setting a constraint on the depletion and degradation of the stock of natural capital' (Pearce *et al.* 1990:58). However, he also notes that this is likely to be unfeasible at the project level but valuable at the programme level where the negative and positive environmental effects of several projects can be compensatory. He argues for including a compensating project into the analysis of a programme of projects, rather than altering discount rates which may discriminate against future generations or make the future impact of environmental projects appear insignificant (see Markandya and Pearce, Chapter 3, in this volume). The modification of traditional cost-benefit analysis to incorporate sustainability has limits in accounting for risk and uncertainty which underlie the concept of sustainability with equity. Advances have been made in giving values in monetary terms to environmental variables under valuation techniques such as contingent valuation and contingent ranking. Pearce argues that an important aspect of valuation is that monetary value is seen from the perspective of ordinary local people and not just that of outside experts. Such attempts at valuation should take account of indigenous knowledge to better understand the relationship between natural resources and local people to whom the project should be tailored.

From the perspective of sustainable development it is hard, however, to estimate the needs of future generations in monetary values to be balanced in terms of costs and benefits. A problem with intergenerational equity is that the future value of the natural resource base cannot be well predicted, for example under unknown technological conditions. Assumptions and value judgements have to be built into analysis and these involve a certain amount of guesswork.

Markandya suggests that the best way of operationalizing sustainability at the project level is to apply a set of working rules covering equity, resilience and efficiency to existing valuation techniques based on use and non-use values. The resulting estimates are then used as inputs into existing methods of project appraisal and investment analysis (Markandya 1992). This is being explored further (see, for example, the chapters by Pearce (Chapter 6) and Brown and Pearce (Chapter 7) in this volume).

A major problem in incorporating sustainability at the project level is understanding how sustainability at different levels is related. Sustainability criteria for project appraisal may be invalidated if they ignore environmental and social impacts at the regional or national level. According to Redclift (1990:87): 'Sustainable development,...., is either about meeting human needs, or maintaining economic growth or conserving natural capital, or about all three'. There is, therefore, likely to be conflict between what is sustainable at the global, national, regional or project level because what is sustainable at one level, may prove to be damaging or simply unrealistic at another. However, there has been little attempt at establishing sustainability links between different macro and micro levels, yet a project cannot be isolated from the wider socio-economic context. Can sustainability criteria be made operational at the project, household or community level without macro support? Potential problems arising from the contradictions of diverging macro and micro policies have been noted by the World Bank (1991:54):

> Although the macro approach seems better from the point of view of a country applying a national policy, the micro or project level rules may be more relevant from the point of view of a development bank that is committed to sustainable development as a criterion governing its own lending, but which is not in a position to dictate national policies at the macro level.

A growing awareness of the need for a sustainable development approach to project appraisal has been in the area of large development projects, where the catastrophic effects of ignoring the interactions between resources and human life have been clear to all. The following section examines how the environmental and socio-economic impact of development projects are interrelated in the context of large dam projects.

Large Dams, Local People and Resource Distribution

Large dam projects exemplify the core issues of the trade-off between development, the perceived essential technology for that development, and costs to the environment and local people. Technology as such cannot be considered the cause of environmental problems, but there are cases where development and technology have placed undue stress on the environment. The reasons are multiple, for example: lack of consideration of environmental impacts in project planning; lack of concern for the impact on local people; bias towards achieving engineering goals at the expense of other criteria; and engineering failure, such as the sedimentation of reservoirs.

Dams are built to convert water into electricity for industrialization and agroindustry and to provide irrigation for agriculture and drinking water. Wider objectives which are often cited as major benefits include the control of drought and flooding and the development of less developed regions characterized by poverty, overpopulation and unmechanized farming. These justifications have to be set against the negative impact of dams to which local people respond. Dams have been criticized as 'technocratic' development projects whose costs exceed initial estimates. Environmental impacts of dams which lead to reduced benefits or increased costs are both physical and social. These include the poor implementation of irrigation, waterlogging and salinization, spread of waterborne diseases, loss of historical or cultural sites and forest areas, and resettlement of people. Resettlement involves social and economic upheaval, and new sources of energy and irrigation do not necessarily benefit resettled poor people living in the dam and reservoir area. This is because large development projects which affect resources may neglect factors, such as prevailing land ownership patterns, which will influence the extent to which local people, the poor and the landless ultimately benefit. Access to resources such as land, credit and machinery is important for the social acceptability of conservation policies and sustainable development strategies.

A number of common problems are associated with large-scale dam projects and their impact on the environment. These include soil erosion, losses of agricultural land due to reservoir flooding as well as dam construction, salinization and water logging in newly irrigated areas, resettlement, health effects, and fishery effects. For example, the Tucuri Dam in Brazil has had a negative impact on subsistence farmers around the Tocantins River, who have witnessed the continuous destruction of their resource base made up mainly of fish and shrimps (Oliver-Smith 1991). After water impoundment in the Aswan High Dam reservoir in Egypt, siltation, salinization and changes in hydrobiological quality have negatively affected water quality and fish species (Abu-Zeil, 1987). Dam construction on free-flowing rivers results in changes in water temperature and velocity, which alter the balance of fish and their environment. Fish movement and breeding is affected by disturbance of river flora and fauna and disturbance of water distribution.

Several studies have shown that the bias of dam implementing institutions is optimizing the hydrological system, whereas environmental and social factors are either ignored or given a subordinate role to engineering in both project planning and post-completion assessment (Baboo 1991; Cernea 1988; Abu-Zeil 1987). In the past, the environmental analysis of some projects was conducted after the decision to construct a project had been made, or even after construction had begun. Negative impacts have often been discovered after project completion and utilization. For example, in the cases of the Tarbela Dam in Pakistan which was completed in 1976 with finance from the World Bank, a number of serious social, environmental and technical problems became apparent as soon as filling the dam began. A ten-year effort costing hundreds of millions of dollars was needed to overcome the problems of the Tarbela Dam. Total costs rose from $800 million in 1966 to $1.5 billion on completion (Dixon 1989). The Tarbela Dam provides an example of negative impacts on land quality surrounding the dam. Water seepage and continual irrigation over the years has led to a gradual upward movement of the groundwater table which has resulted in waterlogging, salinity and therefore declines in productivity for local, poor farmers.

There are different dimensions to the dam-environment trade-off. The strategic planning of a large dam project often involves the dislocation of people from the dam and reservoir site, which was previously their home, and often provided their source of livelihood. Involuntary resettlement is destructive of lives and livelihoods and can also have environmental consequences. Yet, resettlement policy is often a neglected area of project design and suffers as a result of the overriding concern with engineering rather than the social and environmental aspects of large dams. Between 1980 and 1990 the World Bank approved financing for 101 projects which would involve the resettlement of people and it is estimated that 1.6 to 1.8 million people would be adversely affected by these projects (Cernea 1991).

Resettlement, Socio-economic Change and the Environment: the Question of Land

The impact of involuntary resettlement on the structures of economic and cultural life can be disruptive for both resettlers and host populations. Patterns of socio-economic organization in receiving areas are faced with the challenge of absorbing the new settlers and adapting to new conditions which involve sharing resources.

Long-established communities are often disorganized by the building of large dams. Resettlement can mean the breaking up of kinship groups and households. In the case of the Volta Reservoir in Ghana, around 77 000 people from 55 villages and hamlets were resettled. People of different ethnic and religious groups from several villages were resettled together to build new towns. Competition over resources in the region was a result of farm sizes considered too small for adequate income (Schmidt-Kallert 1990).

Production systems are often dismantled, and markets and income-generating assets lost when people are involuntarily resettled. Unemployment and disruption of local labour markets can cause chaos for both resettlers and host populations. Since implementing agencies can rarely find 'empty lands' to place resettlers, the risks are that population density in receiving areas increases suddenly to levels above the carrying capacity of the land. Intense pressure on the area's natural resources and increasing demands for land, water and services may mean that natural resources available in receiving areas are insufficient to ensure sustainable livelihoods.

This is well-documented in the Nam Pong Water Resources Project in Thailand. After the completion of the dam many people were forced to move from the reservoir to the watershed area. The watershed area attracted many people from other regions and as a result the population almost doubled, placing huge demands on the area's resources, including soil and forests. This has been blamed for rapid deforestation which in turn has resulted in soil erosion and accelerated sedimentation of the reservoir with 'adverse effects on the reservoir fishery and reduction in the outputs and benefits from energy, irrigation, and flood damage reduction' (Hufschmidt 1990:147). In the Chittagong Hills of Bangladesh the lives of tribal peoples were disrupted by the building of the Kaptai Dam. The dam displaced 100 000 people, many of whom believed themselves to be worse off economically after being moved. The building of the dam also attracted an influx of Bengalis into the newly-irrigated lands, which had previously been inhabited mainly by tribal people of different ethnicity. The two populations clashed over limited resources resulting in an armed resistance by the hill tribes (Oliver-Smith 1991).

The livestock of resettlers has to compete with livestock of the host population for grazing lands which are often scarce. Overgrazing can damage soil structure and contribute to soil degradation. Heavily grazed lands tend to have considerably low water infiltration capacity which means that the natural moisture status of the soil is tampered with. This often means the acceleration of surface run-off and soil erosion.

Resettling rural populations is problematic because of the inflexibility of the supply of cultivatable land. The scope for land distribution and land security for resettlers and host populations depends on the prevailing land ownership pattern in the dam area. The case of the South East Anatolia Dam Project (known as GAP) in Turkey shows how the dominance of land ownership by a few families makes it difficult to implement an equitable resettlement scheme, with possible consequences for the environment (Morvaridi 1992).

Many of the social and economic problems associated with resettlement in rural areas relate to land and natural resource entitlement. Few resettlement schemes adequately compensate people for the resources and social and economic livelihoods that they lose when they are forcibly moved. Case studies show that resettlers lives often fare worse after resettlement rather than better and that they do not benefit from the dam's construction. In the Kiambere reservoir area in Kenya the average landholding of resettlers fell from 13 hectares to 6 hectares after resettlement. Yields dropped dramatically (down by 68 per cent for maize) and household income directly suffered (down by up to 82 per cent) (Cernea 1991). A major predicament in compensating resettlers for lost resources, in particular land, is that many cannot prove legal ownership. The Itaipu Dam in Brazil–Paraguay has necessitated the resettlement of 8000 families but there have been many problems ascertaining land ownership and establishing the appropriate compensation. In the case of the Sobradinho and Tucurui Dams in Brazil, expropriated land was not compensated in many cases because locals did not have land titles or deeds. 'Squatters' were given far less in compensation than those who could prove legal right to the land, and were unable to purchase equivalent land to that they lost (Monosowski 1984).

As a result of land scarcity, its value rises and many small and poor farmers are unable to purchase land. They are often pushed to marginal lands and the ratio of land to household members can decline. There is a link between limited access to crucial resources, such as land and energy, and environmental degradation. The quality of poor farmer's resources is often low as a result of continuous use without adequate capital inputs such as fertiliser and reworking the same plot of land year after year without fallow. Lack of security of tenure and land rights decreases farmers' investment for the future. In the case of Thailand, the reduction of forest damage has been attributed in part to the provision of land titles to Thai farmers (Steer 1992).

Bias towards engineering achievement means that large dam projects have tended not to make adequate provisions for achieving sustainability for local people. Land reform alone is not the answer, especially under conditions where high population growth makes land distribution unfeasible. What is needed is a wider policy-oriented approach reflected in project appraisal criteria which rates securing resources for the poor, landless and marginal farmers as important objectives. It may well be, for example, that the dam projects mentioned here all generated adequate economic returns to justify the original investment. However, concern for a genuine sustainable development requires that the sorts of costs mentioned here should both be identified at the appraisal stage and appropriate measures taken to ensure that they are either prevented or compensated. This is, of course, consistent with a compensating project approach, but such measures should be incorporated into the overall project framework rather than seen as supplementary projects.

Conclusion

Since there is no general consensus on a theoretical definition of sustainable development, it could be argued that this has led to contradictory expectations about policy and assessment procedures. The question of reconciling the trade-offs between development and environment is no longer being ignored, but there is no consensus on how a sustainable development process can be achieved.

The purpose of procedures for environmental assessment are to ensure that development projects are 'sustainable' according to the World Bank's guidelines. Although creation of a new development assistance target in 'environmental projects' is constructive, the critical area remains the effective incorporation of linkages between environmental and socio-economic dimensions into the routine programme and project decisions of governments and donor agencies aimed at socio-economic development.

EIA does not as a matter of course reflect a sustainable development approach to project design or implementation.

Appraisal of individual projects fits into a wider system of thinking which should recognize the cumulative interaction of economic, social and environmental concerns and intersectoral linkages. Sustainable development is not just about protecting the environment but how we can best make productive use of our natural resources in order to eliminate poverty and improve human welfare. The objectives of sustainable development, therefore, go beyond the project level and its achievement must rest on macro-economic strategies which incorporate the needs of the micro level and the poor.

Note

1. Although environmental assessment may not be considered necessary for projects which involve clear environmental targets, such as reforestation, the social and cultural impacts of resource conservation on local people, especially the poor, would still require appraisal under sustainability criteria. There are many case studies showing how reforestation as a conservation policy is in conflict with the interest of the local people. In 1983 the Indian government's proposal to consolidate three contiguous wildlife sanctuaries into 820 km^2 of national park in Uttar Pradesh displaced 2000 tribal Gujjar families from the entire park area in the districts of Dahra Dun, Haridwar and Pauri Garlwal, where they have lived for at least two centuries. The government constructed a resettlement scheme for the Gujjars at Pathri in 1987, but the displaced people have refused to move there because of squalid living conditions and the absence of forests nearby. The Gujjars are a nomadic tribe, splitting their time between the forest of the proposed park area and the hills in Himachal Pradesh and Uttar Pradesh where they keep buffalo during the summer. In September 1992 when they came down to the forest, there was fierce conflict when the tribe refused to go to the designated area for resettlement. The tribe was only prepared to accept rehabilitation within forest land since they did not consider themselves or their herds equipped to survive outside it. The Forest Department claims that the tribals should learn to survive without the forest, dismissing the indigenous knowledge of the tribals of how to survive in harmony with the ecosystem of the forest (India Today 1992).

References

Abu-Ziel, M. (1987), 'Environmental Impact Assessment for the Aswan High Dam, Egypt' in A.K. Biwas and V.Q. Geping (eds), *Environmental Impact Assessment for Developing Countries*, London: Tycooly International.

Baboo, B. (1991), 'State Policies and People's Response: Lessons From Hirakurd Dam', *Journal of Political and Economic Weekly of India*, October, pp. 2373–80.

Barbier, E.B. (1987), 'The Concept of Sustainable Development', *Environmental Conservation*, **14**, (2), 101–10.

Blaikie, P. (1992), 'Population Change and Environmental Management: Coping and Adaption at the Household Level', paper presented at the Conference on Population and Environment, Exeter College, Oxford, September, pp.1–20.

Brookfield, H. (1991), 'Environmental Sustainability with Development: What Prospects for a Research Agenda?', in O. Stokke (ed.), *Sustainable Development*, London: Frank Cass.

Buttle, F. (1992), 'Environmentalisation: Origin, Processes, and Implications for Rural Social Change', *Rural Sociology, ***57**, (1), 1–27.

Cernea, M. (1988), 'Involuntary Resettlement and Development', *Finance and Development*, September, pp.44–6.

Cernea, M. (1991), 'Involuntary Resettlement, Social Research, and Planning', in M. Cernea, *Putting People First,* Oxford: Oxford University Press.

Chambers. R. (1987), 'Sustainable Livelihoods, Environment and Development: Putting Poor Rural People First', *IDS Discussion Paper,* 240, December.

Dixon, J.A. (1989), *Dams and the Environment: Consideration in World Bank Projects,* Washington, DC: World Bank.

Hufschmidt, M. (1990), 'The Nam Pong Water Resources Project in Thailand', in J.A. Dixon and M. Hufschmidt (eds), *Economic Valuation Techniques for the Environment,* Baltimore: Johns Hopkins.

India Today (1992), 'Gujjars: Victims of Conservation', no. 3, 148.

Markandya, A. (1992), 'Criteria for Sustainable Agricultural Development', in A. Markandya and J. Richardson (eds), *Environmental Economics,* London: Earthscan.

Michael, C. (1989), 'The Evolution of Paradigms of Environmental Management in Development', *World Bank Working Paper,* No. WPS 5313. Washington, DC.

Monosowski, E. (1984), 'Brazil's Tucurui Dam: Development at Environmental Cost', in E. Goldsmith and H. Hildyard (eds), *The Social and Environmental Effects of Large Dams,* Vol 2: Case Studies, Wadebridge Ecological Centre.

Morvaridi B. (1992), 'Large Dams and Environment: A Case Study of the South East Anatolia Dam Project, Turkey', *Development and Project Planning Centre Discussion Paper,* No. 24, University of Bradford.

Oliver-Smith, A. (1991), 'Involuntary Resettlement, Resistance and Political Empowerment', *Journal of Refugee Studies,* 4, (2), 132–49.

Pearce, D., Barbier, E.B. and Markandya, A. (1990), *Sustainable Development: Economics and Environment in the Third World,* Aldershot: Edward Elgar.

Redclift, M. (1990), 'The Role of Agricultural Technology in Sustainable Development', in P. Low, T. Marsden, T. and S. Whatmore (eds), *Technological Change and the Rural Environment,* London: David Fulton.

Schmidt-Kallert, E. (1990), 'The Volta Reservoir in Ghana — A Review', *Geography,* April, pp.77–93.

Steer, A. (1992), 'The Environment and Projects', *Finance and Development,* June, 18–21.

van Pelt, M., Kuyvenhoven, A. and Nijkamp, P.N. (1990), 'Project Appraisal and Sustainability: Methodological Challenges', *Project Appraisal,* 5, (3), 139–58.

Winpenny, J.T. (1991), 'Environmental Values and Their Implications for Development', *Development Policy Review,* 9, pp.381–90.

World Bank (1991), *Guidelines and Procedures for Environmental Impact Assessment,* Vols 1, 2 and 3, Washington, DC: World Bank.

World Commission on Environment and Development (WCED) (1987), *Our Common Future,* Oxford: Oxford University Press.

Index

abatement actons 130, 132
  see also marginal abatement costs
accounting for multiple functions 22–3
agriculture 8–9, 90, 93, 128, 130
  shifting cultivation 111–12, 117–19
aid agencies 1, 35, 98, 186
Amazon (deforestation) 12, 80–99
Amazon Conservation Fund 6, 95
Amazonia Mineraçao (AMZA) 135
Amerindian Protection Project 141–2,
  143
AMZA 135
animal values 95–6
annual deforestation 14, 146–8
APP 141–2, 143
appraisal criteria (sustainable development) 186–8
assimilative capacities, waste 20, 21
Aswan High Dam 191
attribution to projects (global warming)
  131–2
attrition 71, 73–4

Balbina Dam 90
base level of consumption 59, 63
beef cattle ranching 87–9
'benefit optimism' 37
benefit side approach 5, 129
benign government 8, 9, 14
bequest values 103
biomass 12, 78, 85, 106–7, 113–19
  passim
biophysical assessment 20, 21
Brazil (Carajás project) 13–14, 90, 135–55
'bribes' not to develop 103
Bruntland Report (1987) 186
Bundestag 111, 115–16, 118

capital
  discount rate 10, 17, 55, 69–73, 76–7
  marginal productivity of 42

opportunity cost of 10–11, 37–9, 40,
  64
stock (natural) 7–8, 10–11
capital asset pricing model 70
Carajás iron-ore project 13–14, 90,
  135–55
Carajás Railway (EFC) 90, 136, 137–8,
  144–5
carbon
  changes 116–17, 120
  credits 102, 104–6, 120
  cycling 92–5, 98, 132
  debits 102, 104, 106–7
  dynamics 106–13
  storage 7, 12–13, 92–5, 102–20
  in subsequent land use 117–20
  tax proposal 132
carbon-dioxide emissions 31, 125–6,
  180
  greenhouse effect 92–5, 98, 132
cardinalization (qualitative information)
  163
cash flow 97
  discounted 11, 53, 57–8, 60–61, 65,
  6–71, 75
  logging projects 53
  plantation projects 69–71, 75
cattle ranching 87–9
certainty equivalence 40–41, 43
CFCs 31, 98, 125–6, 128, 132, 133
characteristic function 168–9
charcoal 14, 90, 145–7, 148, 150, 151,
  154–5
chlorofluorocarbons (CFCs) 31, 98,
  125–6, 128, 132, 133
Classic Amazonia 81–2, 88, 89
clearance option (tropical forests) 93,
  97, 102–3
closed forests 108, 114–15, 117–18, 120
cluster analysis 169–71, 176–7
'clustering criteria' 170